Working
with
people

It is in conversation, rather than in advance of it, that we discover, never alone but always together, what it means really to listen and what tone may properly be taken. In conversation we discover the many things conversation can be.

Raimond Gaita (1999, p. 106)

Working
with
people

COMMUNICATION SKILLS FOR REFLECTIVE PRACTICE

Louise Harms

OXFORD
UNIVERSITY PRESS

OXFORD
UNIVERSITY PRESS

253 Normanby Road, South Melbourne, Victoria 3205, Australia

Oxford University Press is a department of the University of Oxford.
It furthers the University's objective of excellence in research,
scholarship, and education by publishing worldwide in

Oxford New York

Auckland Cape Town Dar es Salaam Hong Kong Karachi
Kuala Lumpur Madrid Melbourne Mexico City Nairobi
New Delhi Shanghai Taipei Toronto

With offices in

Argentina Austria Brazil Chile Czech Republic France Greece
Guatemala Hungary Italy Japan Poland Portugal Singapore
South Korea Switzerland Thailand Turkey Ukraine Vietnam

OXFORD is a trademark of Oxford University Press
in the UK and in certain other countries

National Library of Australia Cataloguing-in-Publication data

Harms, Louise
   Working with people: communication skills for reflective
   practice.

   Includes index.
   ISBN 9780195558821 (pbk.).

   1. Communication in human services. 2. Interpersonal
   communication. 3. Human services personnel. I. Title.

361.32

Edited by Pete Cruttenden
Cover design by Mason Design
Text design by Patrick Cannon
Typeset by Cannon Typesetting, Melbourne
Proofread by Anne Mulvaney
Indexed by Russell Brooks
Printed by Ligare Book Printers, Australia

Contents

Contributors

Carolyn Aston is a Social Worker, Educational Consultant and Child/Adolescent Psychotherapist, in Private Practice, with a background in teaching, community health and child psychiatry. As founder of the Connect-a-Kid Mentoring Program in 2002 for at risk middle school students, she welcomes the opportunity to work innovatively with parents, teachers and colleagues to maximise the wellbeing and educational potential of vulnerable young people. A former tutor in the Bachelor of Social Work, University of Melbourne and Lecturer in Education, Deakin, she currently lectures in Counselling Techniques for the Graduate Diploma of Mental Health for Teaching Professionals, Monash University, and is a clinical supervisor in the Master of Child Psychoanalytic Psychotherapy.

Heather Carmichael has experience in the Disability Field, Quality Assurance Accreditation Consultancy and has been practising in the Alcohol and Other Drugs field for years in a range of areas including prison, withdrawal, counselling, supported accommodation. She currently co-ordinates several projects at UnitingCare Moreland Hall including the Intensive Playgroup, Student Unit, Intensive Support Program and several youth programs. Her academic background is in social work and psychology and she has a Diploma in AOD Work.

Louise Harms is a social worker, who worked for nine years in hospital and educational settings, before moving into social work teaching and research. She has worked at the School of Social Work, The University of Melbourne, since 2001 in a full time capacity, where she is Senior Lecturer and coordinator of the entry-to-practice social work programs.

Suzie Hudson has worked in the Social Work field for ten years in various Australian states and overseas. While her main passion has been clinical work with adolescents and adults in the areas of substance use, offending behaviour and group work, she has also had the opportunity to teach at both Edith Cowan and Melbourne Universities. Suzie completed her Masters in Social

Work at the University of Melbourne and she is currently completing a PhD at the University of New South Wales which is an ethnographic study of the lives of street-based sex workers who inject psycho-stimulants in Sydney's Kings Cross area.

Rebecca Parsons has a Bachelor of Arts (majoring in psychology) and a Bachelor of Social Work degree. She has just finished her social work training and has taken a position in Alice Springs. She is interested in continuing her work with children and young people.

Melissa Petrakis has worked in public mental health service provision, management and research over the last decade. Her Master of Social Work research was in applied solution-focused brief therapy for telephone counselling and referral. Her PhD on suicide relapse prevention was submitted in January 2007. Melissa has tutored and been a guest lecturer in the undergraduate program at University of Melbourne School of Social Work for the last six years.

David Rose is a social worker with over fifteen years experience in direct practice and management roles in the alcohol and drug treatment, offender support, and forensic mental health areas. He is currently in a part-time position as the Chief Social Worker, Forensicare- The Victorian Institute of Forensic Mental Health, while undertaking a PhD in the School of Social Work at The University of Melbourne.

Jane Sullivan is a senior social worker at a paediatric hospital. Her areas of practice include disability, chronic and life-shortening illness, palliative care and bereavement support. She has qualifications in adolescent and child psychology and theology and a research Masters degree in Social Work. Jane believes that developing communication skills is a life-long process!

Nicole Tokatlian is a senior social worker and team leader in a paediatric hospital. She has worked in a number of hospital units and is currently working in oncology. She has a particular interest in the impact of trauma on children, adolescents and families as well as management and leadership in social work. She has undertaken post-graduate study in Child, Adolescent and Family Mental Health and Family Therapy.

Karen White has worked for over twenty years as a social work practitioner in the areas of child and family welfare and community and mental health. Concurrently, since 1996 she has taught a range of social work subjects at the University of Melbourne. From 2004, with the support of an Australian Research Council scholarship, she has been researching children's perspectives and participation within the family welfare sector, which was submitted as a PhD thesis in 2007. Karen is an active member of the AASW with regard to ethical issues and is interested in promoting children's rights in practice and policy.

John Douglass Whyte is a social worker, who undertook his MSW at Michigan State University, US, before completing a PhD within the School of Social Work at The University of Melbourne. He has also taught sessionally within the School. He has worked for many years within community development projects in the US, and is currently working as a Research Fellow on an Australian Research Council Linkage Grant examining social work practice with Indigenous communities.

Preface

Who is this text for?

Human service work is about working with people. Government and non-government organisations provide services to enhance people's lives and the communities in which they live. These services aim to help people cope better with daily stressors and demands, as well as preventing the occurrence of these stressors and demands in the first place. The 'territory' of human service work includes work with individuals, group work, social policy, management, leadership and administration; work with families and partnerships; community work; research and evaluation; and education and training (Chenowith & McAuliffe 2005, p. 14). Human service workers are committed to making a difference at individual and structural levels.

Workers listen and respond to the unique stories of each person, family, group or community. Good communication skills are fundamental to engaging and working with others about their needs and rights. This book aims to explore the place and challenges of communication and interviewing skills within the context of human service practice.

Some key emphases within this book

This book focuses particularly on:

- *Applying a multidimensional approach*—A multidimensional approach interprets human experience as arising from inner and outer world influences. A multidimensional approach not only acknowledges all these dimensions of an individual's experience (referred to as the biopsychosocial-spiritual dimensions), but it also suggests that any responses by human service workers also need to be multidimensional, addressing both cause and consequence, for example, of human adversity and difficulty. A multidimensional approach emphasises the importance of understanding experiences of both vulnerability and resilience, and therefore understanding both risk and protective factors.
- *Drawing on practitioner experiences and the unpredictable nature of the work*—Much of what is considered to be human service work happens 'on the run' and in diverse and uncontrollable settings, and in single contacts. This book,

therefore, looks at all these dimensions as expected components of practice, rather than as the surprises that interrupt a more controlled counselling approach. Contributions from experienced practitioners in the field ensure that the examples are grounded firmly in everyday practice realities.

- *Thinking beyond the first point of contact*—Communication and interviewing skills are introduced often in relation to only the early phases of working with people. While you gain a sense of the skills to begin and (sometimes) end the work, no real sense emerges as to what the actual work might be 'in the middle'. This book identifies skills across a range of human service work encounters so that you can move beyond the first interview or the first contact point.

- *Reflecting on how you make decisions*—Many of the frequently utilised micro-skills of interpersonal communication and interviewing are introduced. Greater emphasis is placed, however, on the critical decisions we make in using these skills in any given situation. It is not just 'what' these skills are but 'why', 'how' and 'when' we use them. Working creatively, critically and consciously with other people is the focus. The book will not provide you, therefore, with a 'prescription' for practice, but will instead raise lots of possibilities for you to consider and practise throughout your career.

  In human service work, we bring together our theoretical knowledge of human beings and the social environment, of adversity and oppression, and of coping and adaptation. At the same time, we bring our practice knowledge and self-awareness to each situation. Given each situation's uniqueness, no 'right' way to communicate exists. The challenge is to develop 'communication sensitivity'. Communication sensitivity is 'the ability to identify circumstances in which communication is required, the nature of that communication, the persons or organisations that should be communicated with, and so on' (Thompson 2003a, p. 33). This involves paying attention continually to a multiplicity of factors at any one time.

- *Practising in a critical, reflective way*—You will be encouraged think about your own communication style: how it has developed over your life course, the ways in which it impacts on communication with others, and, in turn, how it influences the lives of others and the outer worlds we occupy.

An overview of each chapter

This book is divided into five major parts, each dealing with a specific part of the communication process in human service work.

Part 1: Framing the relationship

This first part of the book explores the ways in which human service workers conceptualise key practice issues.

Chapter 1 explores why human services are provided in the first place, and what key values are at the forefront in any professional client–worker relationship. In the final part of this chapter, some ways in which change is thought about are introduced—change through methods of practice, through various stages or phases and through the use of particular microskills.

Chapter 2 examines current conceptualisations of communication processes. What are the micro-processes that take place within human communication processes and how can they be used to communicate more effectively? This chapter focuses on how change occurs through communication processes, at verbal and non-verbal levels, and the individual through to collective levels. The chapter also explores subjective perceptions of good communication and why good communication matters.

Chapter 3 presents theoretical perspectives as ways of informing practice. It looks at the influence of three dominant paradigms—the positivist, constructivist and critical. Then, a multidimensional approach is introduced as a way of understanding human adaptation, as well as providing a broad perspective on intervention. The chapter looks at some theoretical approaches to practice: task-centred, crisis intervention psychodynamic, cognitive behavioural, narrative, solution-focused, feminist and critical approaches.

Part 2: Forming the relationship

The second part of the book focuses on understanding yourself in the role of worker, your context and the very specific microskills used in communication and interviewing processes. While they are described individually, they are part of an overall communication process. Therefore, the decisions we make in using these skills at different times for different purposes are vital.

Chapter 4 explores why we need to critically reflect on our own communication style and experiences. In human service work, the worker is the key 'tool' in the process. Conversation is the means by which most of the work is conducted and we need to understand our own role within that process. The focus is on understanding and building empathy. Thus, 'use of self', and identifying the purpose and context of work with individuals, families or communities, are key themes of the discussion.

Chapter 5 focuses on the essential preparatory work in relation to your self-care and professional development. This preparatory work is as much about your self-care as your skill development. Supervision, debriefing and critical self-reflection are introduced as important maintenance strategies given the ongoing challenges of human service work.

Chapter 6 examines how a good engagement and rapport with clients can be built. The focus is on preparing to meet, making initial contact and engaging with people. We also consider issues of confidentiality and your use of self-disclosure.

Part 3: Focusing the communication

The third part of the book explores how communication can be focused more specifically to explore a person's key concerns and how we might work with them to formulate an assessment of their circumstances and areas for work.

Chapter 7 presents the processes of focusing the interpersonal contact through asking questions. Chapter 8 provides an overview of paraphrasing and summarising skills. These skills are important for clarifying and challenging what is being heard, in order to establish what is important to the client. The importance of empathy will be revisited in this chapter.

The final chapters in Part 3 focus on forming an assessment of the work to be undertaken. Chapter 9 examines the skills involved in setting specific goals for the work, goals that are mutually agreeable. Chapter 10 then focuses on assessing, and responding to, particular situations of risk.

Part 4: Focusing the intervention

Part 4 looks more closely at the ways in which our practice is informed by theory.

Chapter 11 examines the skills of task-centred and crisis intervention approaches. Chapter 12 presents the skills of psychodynamic and cognitive behavioural approaches. Chapter 13 addresses narrative and solution-focused skills. Chapter 14 explores feminist and critical approaches, and their key skills.

Part 5: Finishing the work

The final part of the book explores how endings are understood. Chapter 15 focuses on the skills of finishing, including dealing with endings that are both anticipated and unanticipated, contracting for further work and referral. An emphasis is placed on evaluating practice, through evaluations with clients and other stakeholders and through critical self-reflection.

A map for your practice

This book proposes that you use the following task map to think about your practice:

Part 1—Framing the relationship:
- the purpose of human service work
- your value base
- your theoretical and factual knowledge.

Part 2—Forming the relationship:
- your use of self

- your organisational context
- your ongoing support and professional development needs
- meeting the people involved
- opening the communication
- actively listening
- listening empathically
- using self-disclosure.

Part 3—Focusing the communication:
- establishing the story
- forming an assessment
- goal setting.

Part 4—Focusing the intervention:
- drawing on theoretical perspectives
- doing the work.

Part 5—Finishing the work:
- ending well
- evaluating the work.

Acknowledgments

My deepest gratitude goes to:

- the students of the School of Social Work at the University of Melbourne who continue to teach me so much
- Melissa Petrakis, Karen White and Chris Daicos, the Communication Skills teaching team
- my colleagues and friends who have so generously contributed stories from their practice and helped to bring this book to life
- the publishing team from Oxford University Press—particularly Debra James, my publisher, and Pete Cruttenden, my editor
- my ever-supportive and loving parents, Glenys and Peter
- Jane Sullivan, who listens, lives and talks in excellent measure.

Louise Harms

How to Use This Book

Learning Goals at the start of each chapter encourage identification of the skills required to communicate effectively in any given situation or scenario.

Notes in the margins highlight key points and refer to other chapters in order to facilitate understanding of more challenging concepts.

Focus on Practice boxes throughout the book draw on practitioner experience to reveal and examine the multidimensional approach of human service work.

Reflective practice questions encourage critical reflection about many of the frequently utilised microskills of interpersonal communication and interviewing.

Establishing the Story | 7

LEARNING GOALS

- Understand the purpose of minimal encouragers.
- Describe and use a range of probing skills.
- Differentiate the types of questions and their purposes.
- Understand the skills involved in using statements and tracking responses.

The task of establishing the story

As Chapter 1 outlined, your focus will be on building a multidimensional understanding of the client and their story. This means understanding the client's story in relation to their inner and outer worlds.

Specific verbal skills are used to support and encourage the client in telling their story. We look at minimal encouragers and probing skills in this chapter.

Using minimal encouragers

In Chapter 2, we looked at the verbal and non-verbal skills that enhance or inhibit a conversation. In order to keep talking in a conversation, we need some feedback from the other person that it is all right to continue. The verbal and non-verbal cues we give to another person are often **minimal encouragers**. That is, they are minimal in the sense of not being major statements or question or reactions, but they encourage the person to continue in their talking. Minimal encouragers can be verbal or non-verbal. Verbal minimal encouragers include:

| 129

---

128 | PART 2 FORMING THE RELATIONSHIP

■ Each theoretical perspective would understand these interactions differently. These understandings of Mrs B's situation will be revisited in Chapters 11–14.

In this interaction, Nicole and Mrs B have been able to openly discuss the situation. Nicole framed the discussion in terms of supporting Mrs B. She was open to critical feedback from Mrs B about understanding why the engagement process had gone the way it had. This enabled Mrs B to talk about the difficulties both between them and in relation to the ongoing issues with which Mrs B was grappling. In this example, despite the difficulties in mutually engaging, a good engagement and rapport between Nicole and Mrs B seems to be beginning to occur, as demonstrated below.

Focus on practice

'One of the things I noticed early on that helped me and the client(s) to relax on the first session was to be very aware of the environment and how I might feel for them on their first visit. I would make sure they knew where the toilet was should they need it and offer to make them a tea/coffee or get them some water. This initial exchange enabled a type of "settling" time before anything more formal had commenced. I also find it useful to establish the amount of time you both have to avoid interruptions and, more importantly, to be able to create a safe place where there is some type of wrapping up or setting up of the next session before they hang up. This will helps to provide that safe environment for you and your client.'

These engagement difficulties illustrate that clarifying the initial reason and ongoing basis for contact is critical. In some settings, clients can be bewildered by the sudden arrival of a worker, for example. They may not know why a referral has occurred, what is known about them and what the role of the worker is all about. In other situations, as in Mrs B's case, her own assumptions, needs and expectations strongly influenced what occurred. These are all important introductory clarifications that may need revisiting throughout the length of work together.

■ Reflective practice questions

How would you respond to the following questions?

- Do you have children?
- How old are they?
- Do you have a boyfriend/girlfriend?
- Do you earn a lot of money doing this job?
- What time do you finish work today?
- Where are you off to for your holidays?

In these situations, role clarification and contracting are even more important factors in the establishment of a working relationship. Role clarification

PART 1

Framing the
Relationship

In this first part of the book, we explore ways in which the relationship between you, as the worker, and your client can be understood. We look at some of the ways in which human service work can be conceptualised, which enables you to think about the ways in which core understandings about your role, about communication processes and about practice theories influence what you will do.

Chapter 1 explores why human services are provided in the first place, and what key values are at the forefront in any professional client–worker relationship. We also look at understanding change processes.

Chapter 2 examines current conceptualisations of communication processes. We look at how change occurs through communication processes, at verbal and non-verbal levels, as well as the individual through to collective levels.

Chapter 3 presents theoretical perspectives as ways of informing practice. It looks at the influence of three dominant paradigms—the positivist, constructivist and critical. A multidimensional approach is introduced as a way of understanding human adaptation, as well as providing a broad perspective on intervention. The chapter then looks briefly at some theoretical approaches to practice.

Part 1—Framing the relationship:

- the purpose of human service work
- your value base
- your theoretical and factual knowledge.

Working Towards Change

- Consider experiences of human adversity and adaptation.
- Describe the general nature and purpose of human service work.
- Understand who is involved in human service work.
- Analyse the different value bases of human service work.
- Describe and critique key practice values.
- Describe how human service workers seek to bring about change.

Experiences of human adversity

People experience **adversity** as a result of many different circumstances. Adversity arises from experiences of poverty and depleted personal resources. Adversity arises from exhaustion, depression and despair; from experiences of hatred, abuse and life's traumas. Some adversities are short term and crisis-driven, while others present long-term concerns and difficulties. Demands arise from the social, structural and cultural contexts in which we live, as well as from our relational and inner-world experiences. Human services aim to alleviate adversity and to promote well-being and health in all of these circumstances.

Consider the following four scenarios.

Focus on practice

Scenario 1

A child protection worker is making her way to meet with a parent, against whom allegations of abuse have been made. The worker, on arrival to the family home, notices that the parent is drug affected and not happy at all about the notification to protective services.

Scenario 2

A housing worker is meeting with a group of concerned tenants to look at writing a letter of protest about the reopening of a road through a housing estate where children have been playing. The group includes many people from culturally and linguistically diverse backgrounds. Other actions may be developed after a community consultation.

Scenario 3

A duty worker on a telephone crisis line receives a call from a young distressed woman who has been assaulted by her partner. She doesn't know what to do—whether to leave or stay—and asks the worker to tell her what she should do.

Scenario 4

A worker has been involved with one family for many years, from the time when their child was diagnosed with cancer through to her death six months ago. The worker wants to invite the siblings to a support group, which will involve contact with both the parents and the siblings.

These scenarios demonstrate how different the life stressors and traumas are for people and how different the human service workers' responses need to be. In one, the worker has an established relationship, whereas another has no face-to-face relationship at all. In another, the worker receives a very hostile reaction, compared with a more sought-after and sustained relationship. In working with people across such a broad spectrum of experience, human service workers need to develop an adaptable repertoire of **skills** to engage, assess and intervene appropriately with people.

These four scenarios raise questions as to how you would respond as a worker. In particular, they raise questions about the change agenda, and who is driving that agenda. In order to begin this discussion, this chapter is structured around four core questions. First, why are human services provided as a response to these experiences? Second, how do we think about who is involved? Third, what are some of the core **values** that underpin human services? Finally, how is change thought about within the human services, from the perspective of different values, **methods** and stages?

Why do we have human services?

Underpinning the provision of human services is the belief that resources should be provided in situations of adversity to support and enhance the well-being of individuals, families and communities. The benefit of people supporting each other through times of adversity is well documented, whether through practical and instrumental support (Harms 2005, pp. 38–9; Hobfoll, Ennis & Kay 2000; Ife & Tesoriero 2006) or emotional support, through talking with someone or writing about experiences (Lepore & Smyth 2003; Pennebaker 1995; Pennebaker & O'Heeran 1984).

Studies of individual and community experiences of grief, trauma and stress have consistently identified the availability of resources, social support, secure attachment relationships and affirmation as key protective factors. A sense of control (Kobasa 1979) and a sense of coherence (Antonovsky 1987) are also vital protective factors. All of these factors can be translated into practical, instrumental and emotional interventions.

Human services are based on beliefs, therefore, about intervention at two levels. Supportive relationships are a protective factor in their own right, and are also effective vehicles for change in other circumstances—for example, providing resources such as education, skills, information and other practical resources. A relationship base, therefore, is at the core of human service work. This is reflected within the social work profession's Practice Guidelines (AASW 2003, p. 7), where the objective of practice is discussed:

> The outcome of direct social work practice is that: needs of clients are met; their potential is developed; and their control over their lives is fostered; this being achieved through mutual engagement and the application of the social worker's knowledge and skill.

To make an assessment of someone's needs and potential, and the type of engagement required, is an inherently complex process. As Banks (2006, p. 49) comments:

> Promoting someone's 'good' or welfare is … open to interpretation depending on what we think counts as human welfare (happiness, pleasure, wealth, satisfaction …) and whether we adopt our own view of what a person's welfare is or the person's own conception of their welfare.

The four scenarios earlier in this chapter raise some of these key questions about well-being. For example, how does a society decide what constitutes risk for children within the context of family life? How does a society determine access to resources such as playing grounds in housing estates? How does a society provide the necessary resources for women and children separating from family violence? How does a community respond to a family whose child has died? How do these questions get translated into relevant and effective human service policies, programs and practices?

Human services are based on notions of well-being, but these notions can become the source of both support and risk. One person's notion of well-being can lead to culturally inappropriate solutions for others and result in generations of damage and harm (Haebich 2006). The balance between human service workers being agents of social care, change, cure or control (Howe 1994) is a delicate one and is dependent upon a constant review of the values underpinning our work.

Who is involved in human service work?

Many people seek support voluntarily as a result of particular experiences of upheaval and crisis in life—experiences of poverty, unemployment and migration; of violence and abuse; of illness, disability and death; or family stress and breakdown. Other people are involuntary users of services, mandated as a result of various court orders or legal reasons relating to child protection, juvenile justice or community treatment orders, for example. They are involuntary **clients** in that they are required to have contact with workers as a result of behaviour deemed to be risky by others. In these instances, human service workers can be an unwanted intrusion into their lives. Other people are somewhere in between the experience of being a voluntary or involuntary client—they experience violence in the context of an abusive relationship or they are admitted to hospital following a fall and consequently have to access human services for support and recovery. Circumstances force many people to become human service clients rather than people choosing freely to access those services.

For the four groups of people introduced in the scenarios above, language becomes very important in influencing how they are regarded by the workers who interact with them. A parent, a group of concerned citizens, a person at the end of the telephone and a family come to be termed clients, **consumers**, customers or service users depending upon the agency with which they come into contact. From a client perspective, these labels can be experienced as negative and de-identifying. These terms raise fundamental questions about your perception of who is accessing services and how their experience is framed and understood.

The term 'client' is used by the Australian Association of Social Workers (AASW). This term is used in a broad sense to refer to 'individuals, groups, communities, organisations and societies, especially those who are neglected, vulnerable, disadvantaged or have exceptional needs' (AASW 2003, p. 6). The term 'client' will be used throughout this book, consistent with this professional base.

The term 'service user' is also reflective of many of these assumptions—that is, that they are people accessing services because of neglect, vulnerability, disadvantage or needs. This term differs, however, in that the assumption is that they are active users of a service, possibly denoting a more voluntary approach to accessing the organisation or service. In some contexts, the term 'customer' has been adopted, although this has not been widely done so in the Australian context. The underlying assumption here is that the customer has purchasing power, which may be the case in only some contexts.

In some specific contexts, such as Centres Against Sexual Assault (CASAs) where a feminist philosophy underpins all dimensions of service delivery, the term 'victim/survivor' is used in order to demonstrate the status of the person independent of an agency involvement. This emphasises both their risk and strength status.

The use of the word 'client' or 'service user' self-referentially, however, is rare. These terms tend to be used by workers to identify the people they work with, and are not necessarily used by the person themselves. One term more readily adopted by the people using the service has been that of 'consumer' (Happell, Pinikahana & Roper 2003), adopted by many within the mental health sector as a more appropriate self-referential term.

Each of these terms has particular connotations about the nature of the relationship between the service, the worker and the person accessing the service. Throughout this book, the term 'worker' will be used when talking of human service workers. Many other terms are frequently used, including 'helping professional', 'social worker', 'community worker', 'child protection worker', 'counsellor', 'practitioner' and 'therapist'. All of these terms reflect different training, emphases and values in human service work.

Values in the relationship

Values are central to human service work. As a worker, you rely on processes of personal, professional and wider cultural beliefs and values to form an assessment which will lead to interventions. According to Banks (2006, p. 6):

> … 'values' can be regarded as particular types of belief that people hold about what is regarded as worthy or valuable. In the context of professional practice, the use of the term 'belief' reflects the status that values have as stronger than mere opinions or preferences.

These strongly held beliefs about what is worthy or valuable also have other qualities, in that they are recognised as being: 'generalized, emotionally charged conceptions of what is desirable, historically created and derived from experience, and shared by a population or a group within it' (Weber in O'Hara & Weber 2006, p. 18).

This definition captures some essential components of our value bases: they can be emotionally charged and, therefore, sometimes fiercely protected; they are developed within a specific historical and experiential context, and are, therefore, not always readily transferable; and they are upheld by a group of people as a way of bringing a shared focus and understanding. Values-based practice is complex when uncertainty and unpredictability are constant factors in your work. While there are ethical guidelines for practice, even referring to these at times of a particular crisis will not always lead you to a straightforward solution or strategy. You need to constantly revisit and reflect upon your value base.

Professional value bases

Extensive and useful discussions in relation to values can be followed in texts by Payne (2006), Reamer (2001) and Banks (2006). Practice values do differ across professions and it is important to be familiar with your professional value base. Organisations such as the Australian Association of Social Workers (AASW 1999), the Australian Psychological Society, the Psychotherapy and Counselling Federation of Australia, and the Australian Medical Association all have codes of ethical conduct that highlight ways of relating to the people with whom they are working. These codes have adopted what Payne (2006, p. 85) describes as a list approach to values, in that the perceived correct ways of behaving are listed and people are held to account to these behaviours.

The fundamental values underpinning social work practice are as 'driven by a mission of **social justice** and change to balance inequities and to create a more enabling society' (Fook 2000, p. 129). Others, such as Lynn (1999), identify the values of social justice and personal care as the two core values.

Within the Australian Association of Social Workers' *Code of Ethics* (2002, pp. 8–10), five core values are outlined, relating both to views of the client and the working relationship.

Focus on values

In carrying out their professional tasks and duties, social workers strive to act in ways that give equal priority to respect for *human dignity and worth* and the pursuit of *social justice*. This commitment is demonstrated through *service to humanity*, *integrity* and *competence*, which characterise professional social work practice. Social work principles are derived from the values; together, they underpin ethical social work practice.

3.1 Value: Human dignity and worth

The social work profession holds that:

- every human being has a unique worth
- each person has a right to well-being, self-fulfilment and self-determination, consistent with the rights of others.

3.2 Value: Social justice

The social work profession holds that each society has an obligation to pursue social justice, to provide maximum benefit for all its members and to afford them protection from harm.

The profession understands social justice to encompass:

- the satisfaction of basic human needs
- the equitable distribution of resources to meet these needs
- fair access to public services and benefits to achieve human potential
- recognition of individual and community rights and duties
- equal treatment and protection under the law
- social development and environmental management in the interests of human welfare.

3.3 Value: Service to humanity

The social work profession holds service in the interests of human well-being and social justice as a primary objective. The fundamental goals of social work service are:

- to meet personal and social needs
- to enable people to develop their potential.

3.4 Value: Integrity

The social work profession values honesty, reliability and impartiality in social work practice.

3.5 Value: Competence

The social work profession values proficiency in social work practice.

Such a statement immediately determines some particular practice directions. For example, the practice frameworks cannot be just about inner-world change. They must include a focus on outer-world dimensions.

Personal value bases

While many practice standards and codes of ethical conduct highlight values that are core to a particular profession, workers within each of these professions will still vary enormously. Your view of social justice may differ from your colleagues, as a result of different experiences and expectations. While people work under the assumption of a common value base, individual workers will have their own experiences of culture, religion, gender and class that will vary. Talking about these values is important.

Balancing our personal and professional beliefs is also important. O'Hagan (2001, p. 144) describes the ways in which workers may be publicly respectful of, for example, a client's religious value base, but privately contemptuous. Thus, we can differ not only along a spectrum of professional values about a particular issue, but also along a spectrum of personal and professional consistency.

Cultural value bases

The above discussion has focused on the professional and personal location of values in practice. Our values are also historically and socially situated. These broader social and cultural attitudes influence profoundly our beliefs about well-being, for example. The political and cultural values held by a nation or a state influence which services are provided and how they are subsequently delivered.

Human service work in Australia predominantly assumes a Western frame of reference, originally based on values and practices from European and Judeo-Christian pasts (Cnaan 1999; Cox 1982). Links with a Judeo-Christian religious base and liberal democratic philosophies are implicit in many of the assumptions underpinning human service work in the Australian context (Lohrey 2006).

A major consequence of globalisation is that assumptions of a universal value base no longer hold. Different value bases are acknowledged as existing in Indigenous (Lynn 2001; Connolly 2001) and non-Western communities (Esteva & Prakash 1998). For example, Dwairy (2006, p. 61) provides an overview of how the individual is regarded from an Islamic perspective, which presents some major discontinuities with, if not contradictions to, Western values:

1   The self is not autonomous but is connected to an extended family or tribe. It directs its energy towards achieving group rather than personal goals.
2   The behaviour of the individual is more situational and contextual than dispositional. It is controlled by external factors such as roles and norms rather than internal factors such as personal attribution of behaviour.
3   Priority is given to interpersonal responsibilities rather than to justice and individual rights.
4   More other-focused emotions (for example, sympathy and shame) are experienced rather than ego-focused ones (for example, anxiety).

He argues that, contrary to Western cultures, the main source of suppression is external rather than internal forces. This can lead to major incompatibilities with many of the practice perspectives widely used in the Western context, which focus more on the individual and on liberal understandings of well-being, such as psychodynamic, cognitive behavioural and feminist.

He argues for a continuum for understanding work with Arabic or Islamic clients: a continuum from individualism to collectivism, and from liberalism to authoritarianism (Dwairy 2006, p. 5), the two main dimensions on which he argues cultures are spread.

These cross-cultural issues raise some fundamental questions for you as a worker in an Australian human service delivery context in relation to shared beliefs about well-being, the nature of relationships, expectations about communication and intervention, and who is the identified client. The following example raises some of these cultural differences.

Focus on practice

An inner-city school is experiencing difficulties with young boys who are displaying aggressive behaviour, particularly towards girls. These boys are from recently migrated families from a war-torn country. The teachers have sought assistance from a worker because they are concerned about the increase in the levels of violence and the possible trauma reactions these young boys may be expressing. In consultation with the families, however, there is not a shared concern about this behaviour.

1 What would you see as some of the important issues to be addressing in this situation?
2 What is your initial reaction to it?
3 What would you find most challenging in this situation if you were the worker called in to develop a response with the teachers and the parents?

As a worker, you will need to find a common language of rights and responsibilities that respectfully can be developed out of these diverse experiences. Discussion and dialogue are critical steps in this process (Furlong & Ata 2006; Miller, Donner & Fraser 2004).

Five core practice values

We will now consider five specific practice values. They are: respecting the human person; promoting social justice and people's right to a good life; privileging the right to self-determination, empowerment and autonomy; valuing people's strengths and resilience; and being authentic.

Respecting the human person

The value of '**respect** for persons' is regarded as central to human service work. As Dowrick (1983, p. 14) states, it is about 'assuming the intrinsic worth of individuals regardless of their attributes or achievements'. How this is actually achieved is less frequently articulated.

The philosopher Gaita (1999, pp. 17–19) reflects on how this fundamental respect for another human being was shown when he worked in a psychiatric hospital in the 1960s, where 'the patients were judged to be incurable and they appeared to have irretrievably lost everything which gives meaning to our lives' (Gaita 1999, p. 17). He relates the following experience:

Focus on practice

One day a nun came to the ward. In her middle years, only her vivacity made an impression on me until she talked to the patients. Then everything in her demeanour towards them—the way she spoke to them, her facial expressions, the inflexions of her body—contrasted with and showed up the behaviour of those noble psychiatrists. She showed that they were, despite their best efforts, condescending, as I too had been. She thereby revealed that even such patients were, as the psychiatrists and I had sincerely and generously professed, the equals of those who wanted to help them; but she also revealed that in our hearts we did not believe this.

1   What do you think were the qualities of her demeanour—the way she spoke to them, her facial expressions and the inflexions of her body—that demonstrated this respect?
2   What prevents us from demonstrating this respect for others at times?

Respect for another human being, and the importance of an authentic engagement, is described in this brief encounter. The scenario highlights that we can make all sorts of assumptions about our conduct until we witness truly respectful moments and interactions. Organisations can develop cultures around the levels of respect or types of respect shown to clients, which can become firmly entrenched over time to the point where they are no longer noticed, until something like the above situation occurs. This example highlights the ultimate importance of what is communicated in our behaviour and interactions with people, not the espoused value position.

Four important dimensions of respect can be identified (Brown 1993, p. 2565). To respect someone or something is to first '[r]egard, consider, taking into account, pay attention to'; second, 'treat or regard with deferential esteem'; third, 'prize or value'; and fourth, 'refrain from injuring, harming, insulting, interfering with or interrupting'. Other definitions of respect refer to 'active sympathy' towards another human being (Downie & Telfer 1989, 1980 cited in Banks 2006, p. 29). The essential characteristics of respect relate to how someone is regarded in an attentive, supportive way, not only in terms of the words that are spoken but also in the whole physical and emotional presence of someone in interaction with another person. Acknowledgment of equality of a shared humanity, although not necessarily in human circumstances, is fully recognised. Another way of thinking about respect is to think about the importance of a love of humanity (Morley & Ife 2002).

■ Reflective practice questions

1 When have you witnessed or experienced respectful interactions?
2 How would you define respect in these circumstances?
3 Conversely, when have you witnessed or experienced disrespectful interactions?
4 What were the features of these circumstances of disrespect?
5 What factors influenced these experiences, thinking particularly of gender, culture and class?

Demonstrating this respect for all people, 'regardless of their attributes or achievements' (Dowrick 1983, p. 14) can sometimes be challenging. It can be hard to respect a perpetrator of horrific abuse, a drug-affected driver who causes a tragic accident, or acts of terrorism. Respect comes to be shown through the understanding of the context of the person and a belief in the possibility of adaptation and change. Many programs, such as those for sex offenders (Adolescent Forensic Health Service 2007) or for perpetrators of gendered violence (Laming 2006), are based on a fundamental respect for the person and work successfully towards addressing the causes of violence. The programs are based on respecting the person, not the behaviour in which they have engaged.

One student shared her experiences of working in Juvenile Justice for her student placement and the ways in which her view of these young people changed throughout her placement. Respect for them as individuals was a critical dimension of that work.

Focus on practice

Working with involuntary clients is a challenge in itself. As social workers we are given all the tools and skills to equip ourselves in working with all sorts of people, but when clients are being forced to report to you, and refuse to engage in the process, it can seem mired with problems. I was working in an area with young men who had sexually offended, who were involuntary clients. Young male adolescents can be difficult to engage in therapy for developmental reasons, but coupled with a history of sexual offending, counselling can seem a difficult road to navigate.

However, given that adolescence is considered a transitional phase, it would follow that their behavioural patterns of offending do not necessarily reflect clients' lasting personal beliefs or attitudes. For these reasons I have learned that when

continues

working with involuntary clients it is important to separate their offending behaviour from who they are. Unfortunately many young men begin to identify themselves as being defined by their offence, and believe that others will do the same. Just by giving involuntary clients an emotionally safe space to share their side of the story, without judgment, can unlock many doors. In fact, an overemphasis on the individual and their offending can hide the fact that adolescents who have sexually offended can be both victim and perpetrator.

Using an anti-oppressive practice framework (Mullaly 2002) as a basis for practice can sometimes seem quite contradictory to being able to work in involuntary settings, where workers can be perceived to be agents of social control rather than social care or cure. As the examples above highlight, however, the value of respect can be demonstrated in the most difficult or constrained of settings.

Another way of thinking about how to demonstrate respect is to identify when it is absent and work to counteract these behaviours. In examining the features of inequality, the following discriminatory processes are often used to demonstrate inequality or disrespect of people.

■ Reflective practice questions

Table 1.1 Processes of discrimination

Form of discrimination	A brief description of the process of discrimination
Stereotyping	Filtering and simplifying complex information about people into fixed 'typifications' so that they are not seen as unique individuals in unique circumstances
Marginalisation	Pushing people 'to the margins of society' through various behaviours, attitudes and social structures
Invisibilisation	Rendering minority groups invisible 'in language and imagery' in the dominant discourse
Infantilisation	Ascribing a childlike status to an adult
Welfarism	Regarding 'certain groups as necessarily in need of welfare services by virtue of their membership of such groups'
Medicalisation	Ascribing 'the status of "ill" to someone'
Dehumanisation	Using language to treat people as things
Trivialisation	Ascribing a trivial status or no status to issues of inequality

Source: Thompson (2003b, pp. 82–92).

1   Where do you see these processes operating?
2   What strategies would you use to respond to these processes of discrimination?

Promoting social justice and people's right to a good life

In 1948, in the context of the post–Second World War international environment and the atrocities that had taken place, the Universal Declaration of Human Rights was developed. While this convention has undergone extensive critique, for both its gendered (Division for the Advancement of Women 2003) and Western (Esteva & Prakash 1998) biases, it highlights that people were striving for justice and equality of opportunity at a global and universal level. The first article of the declaration, for example, reads: 'All human beings are born free and equal in dignity and rights. They are endowed with reason and conscience and should act towards one another in a spirit of brotherhood' (United Nations General Assembly 1948).

Many other national and international treaties and conventions have similarly sought to establish ground rules or visions for basic human rights and needs in order to overcome inequalities and **oppression**. The Constitution of the World Health Organization (WHO), established by the United Nations, makes a strong statement about the principles that are 'basic to the happiness, harmonious relations and security of all peoples' (WHO 2003). These principles are fundamental to how we think about well-being and resilience both locally and globally, and highlight many of the common values underpinning efforts to build well-being and resilience across global communities.

Focus on rights

1   Health is a state of complete physical, mental and social well-being and not merely the absence of disease or infirmity.

2   The enjoyment of the highest attainable standard of health is one of the fundamental rights of every human being without distinction of race, religion, political belief, economic or social condition.

3   The health of all peoples is fundamental to the attainment of peace and security and is dependent upon the fullest co-operation of individuals and States.

4   The achievement of any State in the promotion and protection of health is of value to all.

5   Unequal development in different countries in the promotion of health and control of disease, especially communicable disease, is a common danger.

6   Healthy development of the child is of basic importance; the ability to live harmoniously in a changing total environment is essential to such development.

7   The extension to all peoples of the benefits of medical, psychological and related knowledge is essential to the fullest attainment of health.

8   Informed opinion and active co-operation on the part of the public are of the utmost importance in the improvement of the health of the people.

9   Governments have a responsibility for the health of their peoples which can be fulfilled only by the provision of adequate health and social measures.

Throughout all of this discussion is a fundamental valuing of the quality of the human experience and a desire for a better life or the good life for all people (Hart 2002; Singer 1995). If the aim of such interventions is the improvement of lives for individuals, families and communities, then what is valued in this is some view of what constitutes a good, happy or healthy way of living. Recent studies in the areas of a strengths perspective (Saleebey 1996, 1997, 2001) and positive psychology (Seligman 1992; Seligman et al. 1995), as well as drawing on Indigenous perspectives (Hart 2002), have given new emphasis to how central a value this is to practice.

Human service work often occurs at the interface of rights violations, so rights dilemmas are part of the territory. As Banks highlights, an ethical dilemma involves 'a choice between two equally unwelcome alternatives relating to human welfare' (Banks 2006, p. 8). Remember the earlier scenario, where a child protection worker is making her way to meet with a parent about abuse allegations. In this situation, removing the child from the violent parent may fulfil the child's right to safety, but violate the parent's right to parent as they wish.

Privileging self-determination, empowerment and autonomy

Self-determination and autonomy have been long-held core values in human service work. For example, some thirty-five years ago, Kadushin (1972, pp. 44–5) provided the key dimensions of the client–worker relationship, emphasising behaviour that showed a:

> … belief that the client has the right, and the capacity, to direct [their] own life; [they work] with the client in problem solving; [they] communicate confidence in the client's ability to achieve [their] own solution and actively help the client to achieve [their] own solution in [their] own way.

Valuing self-determination acknowledges people have the capacity to make real choices (Dowrick 1983) about their life, if they are given the opportunity. What makes it possible for people to influence their environments, drawing on their capacity for agency (Giddens 1991; Kondrat 2002) and motivation, is an important question for workers to address. In supporting the notion of self-determination, the usual assumption is made that this self-determination is positively oriented. Workers can only support the notion of self-determination so far as legal and ethical limits apply. In some cases, for example, people express a wish to harm themselves and/or others. At these times, you need to take steps to ensure safety over and above a client's right to be self-determining.

Similarly, other dilemmas arise in relation to views about how much a person experiencing illness should know about their diagnosis or illness. Again, different cultures regard this information exchange in different ways, with some cultures firmly of the belief that patients should be protected from such knowledge at all times (Duffy et al. 2006). Their right to be fully informed, and therefore potentially self-determining, is overridden by a stronger belief in the right for the patient to not be distressed by their health circumstances.

In other situations, the capacity to realise this value is compromised by the person's capacity to participate in decision-making processes or to give informed consent—for example, in situations where a person is living with a severe intellectual or psychiatric disability, or is too young to be able to verbalise an opinion. If your underlying value, however, is the promotion of self-determination, empowerment and autonomy, steps can always be taken to ensure that actions are most oriented in the best interests of the person concerned.

There is a tension in practice in emphasising autonomy. Some authors argue for the right to experience a transitional dependence at times, rather than a continual valuing of independence and self-determination (Trevithick 2005). An example of this is when a person is in the middle of a major crisis and, as a result, their usual coping capacity is overwhelmed. Assertive, directive outreach at this time by workers is advocated (Caplan 1990), consistent with the beliefs about the psychological state of a traumatised person. Within this, though, the emphasis is still on the client being self-determining, within the limits of their capacities at this time.

You will notice that some cross-cultural practices differ quite significantly as to whether an individual acts autonomously or always in the context of community and familial relationship and obligation. For example, recent work within Indigenous communities has highlighted that positive change is brought about by emphasising the individual's location within the context of their community. The use of shame through circle courts is one example of the important role of bringing about positive change through highlighting the ways in which a person's behaviour has been damaging, not only to themselves but also to their family and community. While Western approaches with involuntary clients have tended to advocate against the use of 'blame, punish and judge' strategies (Trotter 2006), the use of shaming in Indigenous contexts has been an age-old tradition that's been more recently revived (Spooner, Hall & Mattick 2001), although it is not without its critics (Blagg 1997).

Valuing people's strengths and resilience

If we are to have a positive impact as workers, a core belief underpinning our practice needs to be the belief that a client has strengths and a capacity and motivation towards change for the better (Brun & Rapp 2001). Saleebey (1997, p. 3) sees strengths-based practice as meaning that:

> … *everything* you do as a … worker will be predicated, in some way, on helping
> to discover and embellish, explore and exploit clients' strengths and resources

in the service of assisting them to achieve their goals, realize their dreams and shed the irons of their own inhibitions and misgivings.

A strengths perspective argues that it always possible to find 'constructive ways to meet, use or transcend the problem' (Saleebey 1997, p. 47). Other strengths-oriented beliefs include: that unlimited strengths can be found in every individual, group, family and community; that adversities can be both sources of loss and opportunity; and that collaboration works best.

Being authentic

Genuineness and **authenticity** on the part of the worker have been consistently highlighted as critical to the success of forming a client–worker relationship and being able to facilitate change (Rogers 1967). Gunzberg (1996, p. 34) describes this authenticity in a therapeutic context as arising in 'the nature of the connectedness that lies between both, within the meeting of both'. How you bring about this connectedness, however, is not easy to articulate. Authenticity, like respect, emerges in the totality of verbal and non-verbal dimensions of your relationships.

Rogers (1987, p. 38) emphasises some of the dimensions of this authenticity in reflecting on how he would prepare for an interview with a client. He asked himself: 'Can I be totally *present* to this client?' 'Can I *be* with him or her?' 'Can I be sensitive to every nuance of personal meaning and value, no matter how different it is from my own experience?' This captures the importance of an authentic engagement in the client's story and situation. In this sense, the authenticity is about openness to, empathy with, and the understanding of another's situation.

We can be authentic in many other ways when working with people. It is not necessarily about self-disclosure; an assumption that is often made when talking about authenticity. It can be about recognising and articulating the limits of our knowledge, our understanding or our skills. It can be about expressing our deep concern for someone at a particular point in time. It can be about articulating our time limits and our capacity to be present in an interaction with someone else. It is fundamentally about our willingness to share our humanness in the context of our professional integrity and our ability to act within the capacities and limitations of what we bring to an encounter.

This value raises many questions in relation to how authentic the relationship is that is established with a client. The expectations of a professional relationship are different from those of a personal relationship, yet many qualities are similar. Some people we genuinely like more than others in a professional context. Some people we genuinely fear. The way we express authenticity emerges in the boundaries we metaphorically and practically create in our work with another person.

How do human service workers influence change?

As a **human service worker**, you aim to bring about change through your use of skills at both individual and social levels (Payne 2006, p. 1). In this section, the ways in which change is thought to occur as a result of methods, phases and skills will be discussed.

Change is something that is deliberately fostered and worked towards through specific interventions in human service work. Change can occur in our inner worlds, in relation to how we feel and how we think. Change can also occur in our outer worlds, in relation to how we behave and how others behave towards us. In our outer worlds, change can occur in relation to particular circumstances or conditions such as the alleviation of poverty, violence or unemployment.

■ Reflective practice questions

Four client scenarios were presented earlier in this chapter.

1 Revisit each of these scenarios and reflect on what you see as the change agenda you would bring to each of them.
2 How similar or different do you think they would be compared with the clients' perception of the change agenda?

There are many different ways of achieving change, from doing very little to bringing about major and radical change. Change as a multidimensional concept will be described in further detail in Chapter 3.

The precipitants of change are similarly multiple. Some people change because they have to, as a result of rock-bottom experiences. One study found that change was triggered for women with drug addictions when they realised things could not possibly become worse (Blankenship 1998). Other people engage in change processes because either they are mandated to or because of some other circumstance; for example, to get their children back from out-of-home care. Many other people engage in change processes because they want to, recognising that they need to change. The motivations for seeking help with change are often unique and complex.

What influences people's attitudes to change? Change for some people is a terrifying prospect, full of uncertainties and unfamiliar territory. For other people, change is exciting and energising. Some of the variables that influence our attitude to change include the perceptions and realities of available supports and resources, the availability of role models, the internal and external encouragement received, and, sometimes, the negative motivational encouragers; for example, seeing someone experience major problems with drug and alcohol abuse and determining never to go down that path. For many people, internal change is possible and motivation can be extremely high, but social circumstances make it extremely difficult to maintain any gains. Working with a change agenda requires constantly asking the question of what change needs to occur and why. Engaging in work as an agent of change means that considerable influence is being exerted.

This chapter now considers some of the ways in which change tends to be conceptualised in human service work. The change process can be conceptualised as involving various methods, stages and skills.

Change through methods of practice

Working with individuals primarily involves interviewing and counselling skills in one-to-one (and typically face-to-face) focused conversation with individuals, couples or families. The term 'interview' is typically used to define this interaction, being 'any formal or semi-formal discussion between a worker and service user(s)' (Thompson 2002, p. 120). While in many settings the interview may not be a structured interaction, others describe the interview as 'the first one or two helping sessions because these sessions are usually for information gathering' (Okun 2002, p. 89).

A wide range of terms is used to differentiate this work—interviewing, counselling or therapy being three common ones. Some practitioners regard these terms as interchangeable, whereas others see them as distinct forms of individual practice. Sommers-Flanagan and Sommers-Flanagan (2004, p. 8) argue that the key differences between counsellors and psychotherapists is not that they engage in different behaviours but rather that they engage in the behaviours of 'listening, questioning, interpreting, explaining, advising, and so on … in different proportions'.

In all work with people, interpersonal skills are critical. The vast majority of work occurs at an individual interface—that is, between at least two people engaged in relationship and conversation (Perlman 1979). Group work, community development and research methods, however, similarly rely on gathering information through communicating with others, forming an assessment and undertaking some form of further intervention.

We will look at how different theoretical approaches influence the use of these responding skills in Chapters 11–14.

Change throughout various stages or phases

Change is often seen as occurring in stages or phases. For example, Prochaska and DiClemente's (1983) **stages of change** model is the most widely used in Western contexts. Developed from research in relation to addictions, the model proposes people move from a pre-contemplation to a contemplation stage, then to preparation and on to action. When change is achieved, a maintenance phase begins. Throughout all of these phases, relapse is possible to an earlier phase of change. People can move, therefore, in and out of these phases of commitment to change, depending upon a number of factors. The model is not implying that change occurs in a linear manner. Rather, it is a cycle. The cycle in more detail is as follows.

Focus on change

Here is a brief overview of the tasks within the stages of change model.

Pre-contemplation
The client:
- denies that there is a problem
- is unaware of any negative consequences of their behaviour
- minimises any consequences
- has 'given up the thought of changing because they are demoralized'.

Contemplation
The client:
- recognises the benefits of changing
- tends to 'overestimate the costs of changing'
- remains 'ambivalent and not quite ready to change'
- intends 'to make a change within the next 6 months'.

Preparation
The client:
- has decided to make a change in the next month or so
- has begun to 'take small steps toward that goal'.

Action
The client:
- is actively engaged in modifying their behaviours or circumstances
- is developing new, healthy skills, attitudes and behaviours.

Maintenance stage
The client:
- has 'been able to sustain change for at least 6 months'
- is 'actively striving to prevent relapse'.

Source: Levesque, Cummins, Prochaska & Prochaska (2006, p. 1373).

■ Reflective practice questions

Think about a major change you have been through or would like to make.

1 Does this stage approach to change help you understand what you went through/would go through?
2 Are some stages more challenging for you than others?
3 What habits do you fall back on in each of the various stages of change?

This model of change is useful in helping you to think about what might be the focus of work at a particular point in time. This model highlights also some of the unique challenges for workers engaging with involuntary clients. Often the assumption is made that the person is at least at the stage of 'contemplation of change'—in involuntary client situations, however, this may not be the case.

The stages of change model is a way of thinking about how a client changes. Change can also be thought about as a series of stages or phases within your work with your clients. These specific tasks include the tasks of engagement, assessment, planning, implementation, evaluation, termination and follow-up (Kirst-Ashman & Hull 2001). Different models are proposed, ranging from three-phase through to five-phase models of intervention.

A three-phase model (Hepworth, Rooney & Larsen 2002, p. 36) proposes that phase one involves the tasks of exploration, engagement, assessment and planning. Phase two involves the tasks of implementation and goal attainment, and phase three, the tasks of termination. Other three-phase practice models, such as those relating to child protection practices in New Zealand (Connolly 2004), propose slightly differently prioritised tasks: the phases of first, engagement and assessment; second, seeking solutions; and third, securing safety and belonging.

Another model with three phases or stages is that proposed by Egan (2007). In stage one, the question 'What's going on?' is asked in relation to the client's situation. In this stage, the three steps are to explore the story, identify blind spots and find leverage on the problem. The second stage is about examining the solutions that make sense for the client around the specific area of change that has been identified. The three steps involved in this stage are exploring the possibilities, establishing the change agenda and establishing a commitment to solution finding. The third and final stage relates to examining how a client gets what they need or want. Having fine-tuned the possibilities for change, in stage three, possible strategies are identified, the best-fit strategies are sought and a plan of action is put into place.

Other practitioners use a 'phases of contact approach' (Cournoyer 2004), which could be applied both within the context of one interview and in the context of the relationship over time. This approach identifies a beginning phase, during which the engagement in the relationship, the availability of the worker and the attuning to the client are established. Empathy is promoted so that an assessment can then take place as to the events, feelings, thoughts and behaviours experienced by the person. The assessment also includes an assessment of strengths, the establishment of areas of work and subsequent contracting around the specific work to be undertaken. In the middle phase or process, the work focuses on what it is that is being achieved. Some of the relationship issues that emerge are in relation to defence mechanisms and change processes, according to Cournoyer (2005). In the finishing phase, the process is about continuing empathy and assessment but with a move towards evaluation and finishing. The tasks of disengagement and finishing are required. This final phase, Cournoyer suggests, is as unpredictable as the beginning phases.

Other approaches advocate for a greater breakdown of phases in the process. Shulman (1999), for example, advocates a four-phase model, in which there is a preliminary or preparatory phase, a beginning and contracting phase, a middle or work phase and an ending or transition phase. A five-phase model is proposed by Corey and Corey (2007, pp. 157–77), with stage one involving the establishment of a working relationship; stage two identifying the client's problems, including conducting an initial assessment; stage three helping clients create goals; stage four encouraging client exploration and taking action; and stage five involving the termination of the working relationship.

While different perspectives emphasise and understand these tasks slightly differently, the common tasks are:

- establishing availability and a contract of work with the client
- engaging with the client in a working relationship
- expressing empathy
- exploring the problem or issue through an assessment
- undertaking work together to resolve or address the problem or issue
- finishing the work together, often with a process of review.

Many approaches, therefore, recognise that across human service settings these phases are important steps through which the work is conducted. Most emphasis tends to be placed on the initial phases, with less emphasis on the last phase—how to ensure safety and belonging, for example, or how to finish the work.

Below, these phases of work are summarised. The ways in which these phases will be understood throughout this book are presented in the top row: framing and forming the relationship, focusing the communication, focusing the intervention and finishing the work.

Focus on practice

Author/s	Framing and forming the relationship	Focusing the communication	Focusing the intervention	Finding solutions	Finishing
Connolly		Engagement and assessment	Seeking solutions	Securing safety and belonging	
Corey and Corey	Establishing a working relationship	Identifying client problems	Creating goals	Encouraging client exploration and taking action	Termination
Egan		Establishing what's going on	Examining solutions and possibilities	Finding best fit strategies	
Hepworth, Rooney and Larsen		Exploration, engagement, assessment and planning	Implementation and goal attainment		Termination
Shulman	Preliminary or preparatory	Beginning or contracting	Middle or work		Ending or transition

Such a table makes a complex, circular or unshaped process seem logical and linear. In some agencies, you may be able to function in this way. Most workers, however, are in much less predictable environments and relationships, and therefore find that these phases do not typically represent the ways in which the work is undertaken. They do provide a useful map, however, of the tasks involved in change-oriented work.

Change through the use of skills

As we explored earlier in the chapter, human services are provided because of the belief that change can occur when workers provide support, in all its forms. You need a skill base to be able to provide appropriate support to others.

The word 'skills' is used throughout all of human service practice, and for that reason it is important to consider its multiple meanings. Skills can mean, first, knowledge; second, 'the ability to do something well; proficiency; expertness, dexterity'; third, 'an ability to do something, acquired through practice or learning'; and fourth, 'an art, a science' (Brown 1993, p. 2882). Each of these dimensions is relevant to developing a base for human service practice.

In relation to *knowledge*, understandings of people and conditions of adversity are essential, as are understandings of human behaviour and development in context. In addition to these forms of knowledge, theoretical perspectives on practice are also important, along with the practice wisdom you will develop over the course of a career. Other forms of knowledge emerge from research understandings—for example, gaining an understanding of what works with whom in what context is crucial, and research provides a useful basis of understanding.

The second dimension refers to the *ability to do something well*; that is, it is not enough to know about the skills of active listening. To use a skill means that the barriers to good communication are removed or that a capacity to apply specific skills at a particular time is developed.

The third dimension, *an ability acquired through practice and learning*, emphasises that learning to communicate effectively in a professional capacity takes practice and application, right across a career.

The final dimension of the definition, that skills refer to both *an art and a science*, highlights another level of complexity (Connolly 2001). To contribute effectively to human service work, a sound evidence base for what works is important. But it is also an art to communicate well with others, to support others and to respond empathically and effectively to those experiencing difficulty and adversity. Connecting with other people and establishing a creative process of working together to resolve situations are skills of a high order.

These four dimensions are all critical in bringing about change. You will need the total package to be making decisions about how to act and what to say in various situations.

Later, we will focus on the **microskills** of communication that are used to direct change. The microskills that we will look at in later chapters help us to:

- establish and maintain empathy
- communicate non-verbally
- establish the context and purpose of the work
- open an interview
- actively listen
- establish the story or the nature of the problem
- ask questions
- intervene and respond appropriately.

Microskills are the building blocks of human communication. They are transferable skills (O'Hara 2006); that is, they can be used in many contexts, and adapted according to the setting in which the worker and client meet. You influence that process through theoretical perspectives. As Howard (2006, p. 8) states:

> From the most fundamental aspects of the relationship, such as how we greet a client, to the use of advanced therapeutic skills like making interpretations, our whole way of relating to and thinking about our client is driven by the theoretical model we subscribe to.

In the next chapter, we review these microskills before moving in Chapter 3 to how practitioners come to theorise and apply these skills.

Chapter summary

In this first chapter, we have explored the role of human services in responding to people's experiences of adversity and need. The ways in which your professional, personal and cultural value bases will influence your perceptions of human service work were also identified. Five core practice values were presented: (1) respecting the human person; (2) promoting social justice and people's right to a good life; (3) privileging the right to self-determination, empowerment and autonomy; (4) valuing people's strengths and resilience; and (5) being authentic.

We then looked at how change can be understood—through using different practice methods; through understanding individual change processes and understanding change in the phases of work you will undertake with your client; and through using particular communication skills.

Reflective practice questions

1   What have you learnt about:
    • the value base you bring to your practice?
    • the understandings of change you bring to your practice?
    • the methods of change human service workers use?
    • the phases of change within a client–worker relationship?
2   Going back to the earlier client scenarios, has your view of them changed since reading this chapter?
3   What would you see as the most important purposes of human service work?
4   What do you see as the most important values underpinning your practice?
5   What do you see are some of the tensions in those values?
6   How would you go about resolving some of those tensions?
7   What have been some of the major influences on the development of these values?

Key references

Banks, S. (2006). *Ethics and values in social work* (3rd edn). Basingstoke: Palgrave Macmillan.
O'Hara, A. & Weber, Z. (Eds) (2006). *Skills for human service practice: Working with individuals, groups and communities.* South Melbourne: Oxford University Press.
Thompson, N. (2003a). *Communication and language: A handbook of theory and practice.* Basingstoke: Palgrave Macmillan.

Additional resources

Australian Association of Social Workers (AASW): www.aasw.asn.au.

Australian Medical Association (AMA): www.ama.com.au.

Australian Psychological Association (APA): www.psychology.org.au.

Psychotherapy and Counselling Federation of Australia (PACFA): www.pacfa.org.au.

Social Care Institute for Excellence (SCIE): www.scie.org.uk.

Social Justice and Social Change Research Centre, University of Western Sydney: http://sites.uws.edu.au/sjsc/SJSC_Style06.htm.

United Nations: www.un.org/Overview/rights.html.

2

Understanding Communication and Change

LEARNING GOALS

- Identify the different ways of understanding communication.
- Understand some of the core verbal and non-verbal skills for human service practice.
- Consider the dimensions of individual and collective communication.
- Understand why communication is so linked with survival, healing and well-being.
- Reflect on the ways in which communication expresses power.

Understanding communication

Communication can be understood in many different ways by many different disciplines. Psychology, linguistics, sociology and anthropology have all contributed enormously to how we think about communication in practice. Here, however, we will consider communication issues thematically rather than through these discipline lenses. In relation to human service work, we can understand communication first as a process (involving **verbal** and **non-verbal** skills at individual and collective levels), and second, as a means of survival, a means of healing and therapy, or as the basis of **power**.

Recall the four scenarios from Chapter 1. Each situation would require different communication skills. You need skills to communicate with clients in altered drug-affected states of consciousness; involuntary clients; groups of people rather than individuals; face-to-face communication and telephone communication where non-verbal cues cannot be experienced; and communication over a long period of time where there is an established relationship. In this chapter, the dimensions of communication in all of these scenarios and others will be explored.

Communication is so fundamental to our **survival** and our well-being that we tend not to think about it as a complex skill that we have acquired across our life span. Communication can be defined as: 'The action of communicating heat, feeling, motion etc, the transmission or exchange of information, news etc; the science and practice of transmitting information; social context, personal intercourse' (Brown 1993, p. 455).

Based on this definition, communication seems to be a straightforward process of the exchange or transmission of information. In order to develop a capacity for 'communicative competence' (Tannen 1994), however, this process needs to be broken down into its component parts to analyse each of them in the overall communication process. This helps us to understand how the overall process occurs as a result of the smaller processes inherent within it. Like actors in rehearsal, this breaking down to the microskill level is done (Hargie 2006a, p. 554) 'to analyse the overall complex act in terms of simpler component parts, train the individual to identify and use the parts separately, and then combine the parts until the complete act is assimilated'. You can then influence communication processes by adapting these skills along the way as required.

■ Reflective practice questions

Think of the many skills you might draw on to raise, for example, a difficult relationship issue with a particular friend or partner.

1   What would you do to approach such a discussion?
2   What do you anticipate could happen during that discussion?
3   Share your response with someone else and analyse the points of similarity and difference in your reactions.

Communication as a process

In understanding communication as an interpersonal process, we focus on the basic skills of talking and listening. This involves the interaction of a sender and a recipient or receiver. Communication, particularly when face to face, is seen as having two major dimensions—verbal and non-verbal. When people are talking, verbal and non-verbal exchanges occur, with ideas being encoded by the sender of the message and decoded by the receiver and filtered through our senses. This process was first proposed by Reusch (1957 as cited by Shulman 1999, p. 41). A way of representing this process is provided in Figure 2.1.

More recent understandings of the anatomy of communication (Heath & Bryant 2000, pp. 75–84) highlight that communication is a process rather than an act of transmission, moving away from the more dyadic and linear notion represented in Figure 2.1. Heath and Bryant (2000) suggest that

Figure 2.1   The interpersonal communication process

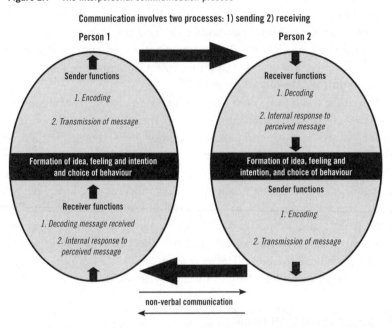

communication should be understood multidimensionally. Similar to the above model, the terms sender and receiver are still used, recognising the tasks of **encoding** and **decoding**:

> The encoder is analogous to an actor or impression manager, producing and 'sending' the behaviours to be interpreted. The decoder is analogous to an observer 'receiving' the presented behaviours and interpreting them in some fashion (Gordon, Druckman, Rozelle & Baxter 2006, p. 81).

In the moment of speaking with another person, however, it is now acknowledged that we constantly monitor the other person and adapt verbal and non-verbal responses all the time in that exchange. This focus on process is important, particularly when it is recognised that communication is a simultaneous, continuous and nuanced process.

Some expansion of what is encoded and decoded is also increasingly recognised. Acknowledged in this process is that the 'receiving system consists of the five senses, the receptors' (Kadushin 1972, p. 25). More recent understandings from both Indigenous worldviews (Lynn 2001; Hart 2002) and chaos and complexity theories (Hudson 2000) would include a sixth sense or receptor: a sense of intuition or 'knowing' at other levels of sensory awareness.

While some of the sender and receiver functions can be objectively verified—for example, through recording verbal and non-verbal exchanges—the *intent* or purpose of what is being conveyed via verbal or non-verbal means is more subjective and perhaps the most complex dimension of communication. While a person intends to be supportive, for example, their comment may be received by the other person as a criticism or as patronising. Irrespective of what is intended, the receiver receives a message that they interpret through their individual, social and cultural filters.

In processing the verbal and non-verbal messages we receive, it is as if we have an internal monologue simultaneously with the external dialogue. That is, we cognitively process the information we are receiving, and therefore process that information both through our past and our present contexts of understandings. This becomes the meaning of the message (Heath & Bryant 2000, pp. 76–9). Sometimes a shared intent can be established easily. At other times it needs to be explicitly addressed; for example, in involuntary client settings or where significant cultural or communication diversities exist.

What earlier models perhaps overlooked most was the significance of context (Heath & Bryant 2000, p. 84), with context referring both to the individual's particular biopsychosocial–spiritual context and the broader socio-cultural context. Social and cultural influences determine whether certain issues are taboo, important or valid for conversation.

Current communication models are emphasising interaction rather than transmission and reception. It is a simultaneous, reciprocal process, involving interactions between at least two people and their context. The degree of commonality of contexts becomes an important area of focus within the communication, in recognition of how profoundly the wider physical, social, structural and cultural contexts influence interactions. With these developments, the figure shown earlier might now look more like this:

■ We will explore understandings of these biological, psychological, social and spiritual dimensions further in Chapter 3.

Figure 2.2 Communication as a multidimensional process

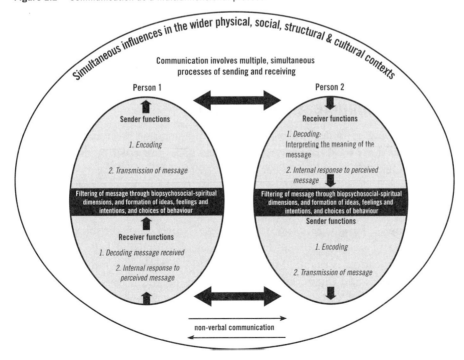

These models may seem to be stating the obvious. It is a useful reminder, however, of the depth of analysis that can be undertaken when reflecting upon interactions, particularly when they do not go so well. When we think about these skills in a professional context, the focus is on a more deliberate selection of particular skills at a particular time. For example, when we receive a message in a personal context, we might react emotionally and impulsively to it. We decode it in a particular way. When we receive a message in a professional context, we may be more acutely aware of the sender than our own self in the interaction, and we will filter the information in different ways.

In your practice, you will constantly make decisions as to how you will interact with your clients. In many situations, this will involve communicating in empathic and supportive ways. At other times, this will involve being assertive with people, setting limits, or taking decisive and directive action. On other occasions, it will involve dealing with angry, aggressive and oppressive clients and colleagues. As Hargie (2006a, p. 45) suggests: 'Effective control of emotion is a central aspect of socially skilled performance.'

What this model highlights is that communication is a continuous interaction between at least two people. Building communication skills, therefore, is not about a one-person approach (that is, what the worker should do) but about an interactive approach (in this situation, this is the right thing to do) (Koprowska 2005). The model also helps us think about different means of communication, and the strengths and limitations they present in relation to effective communication.

The model also highlights the importance of **active listening**. When we listen actively, we are both hearing what is being said, and communicating back to the other person that they are being heard. Active listening includes all the verbal and non-verbal skills that affirm another person's conversation: the verbal skills of questioning, responding, reflecting and summarising, and the non-verbal skills of physically and psychologically attending to that person.

> ■ This relates to the concept of 'use of self', which we will explore in Chapter 4.

> ■ These specific verbal skills of active listening are considered in Chapters 6–8.

Verbal communication processes

> In trying to understand how speakers use language, we must consider the context, ... speakers' conversational styles and, most crucially, the interaction of their styles with each other (Tannen 1994, p. 46).

Verbal communication processes include everything that is spoken or uttered in a conversation and refer primarily to the content or message that is exchanged. Language expressed through conversation enables the communication of needs, wants and experiences. As discussed later in this chapter, communication is essential for participating actively and influentially in daily relationships and the wider social environment, and is thus integral to human well-being and survival. In later chapters, we explore in detail how to use these verbal skills in the context of specific interviewing and interventions.

Some authors exclude paralinguistics—that is, verbal sounds or qualities of the verbal interaction such as tone, pitch and volume—from this definition (Bull 2002, p. 26), seeing them as non-verbal behaviours. For the purposes of this book, any verbal utterances will be considered verbal communication if they involve the use of voice. Changes in the quality of voice production can communicate all sorts of information relevant to an assessment. For example, when under stress, people tend to speak both faster and louder, and sometimes in a higher pitched voice (Tao, Kang & Li 2006). If you are aware of these tendencies in stressful situations, you can manage conversations differently if needed.

Verbal communication can be understood from many different perspectives. This next section highlights the ways in which people vary in their verbal communications according to the social context, to emotional expressiveness, and to meaning. The use of silence is then discussed.

Social variations

The use of language to convey experiences, emotions, needs and wants is a fundamental human capacity and skill. In this sense, language becomes the means by which people 'name and evaluate the objects, sensations, feelings and situations they experience' (Heath & Bryant 2000, p. 91). This verbal naming and availability of information enables people to survive and to establish an individual and social identity, as well as a sense of worth, role and place.

Throughout infancy and early childhood, children acquire rapidly the capacity to name their world and therefore to interact verbally with others (Harris 1995). What is increasingly recognised is that, from childhood, we learn a particular **conversational style** (or styles), in particular social groupings, with particular 'ethnic, regional, and class distinctions that have so many reverberations in society' (Tannen 2000, p. 393). In addition to the ethnic, regional and class distinctions, children also learn gender and age differences.

Some researchers have emphasised that children learn not just one overall conversational style, but multiple styles that are adapted according to specific contexts. For example, a study of dying children (Bluebond-Langner 1978) showed that children did not lack an understanding and a language about their illness and their dying, as was previously thought. Instead, these children made careful decisions as to when and with whom these issues would be discussed, often protecting parents from the knowledge that they knew about their eminent death. Similarly, immigrant children very readily adapt to the linguistic context of their peers in order to fit in with them, rather than retaining the accent of their parents (Harris 1998). Peers are the dominant influence in language acquisition rather than parents, according to Harris and others.

Emotional variation

Other variations in verbal styles relate to the degree to which individuals and families articulate their emotional experiences. The quality emphasised here is 'emotional expressiveness' (Yoo, Matsumoto & LeRoux 2006; Vogel, Wester, Heesacker, Boysen & Seeman 2006) and it has been a feature of many studies in the mental health arena; for example, where both extreme emotional expressiveness and repression have been studied.

These variations become important in client–worker relationships. A conversation that one person may perceive to be reflective, may be seen by another as deeply introspective, too emotional and, overall, inappropriate. These relative depths of experience and expression of experience become important points of congruity or incongruity in the context of conversations.

Language as signifier: language variation

The process of communication is a translation process, which often relies on assumptions—that is, we can think we know what someone means, more or less, by what they are telling us, and by their non-verbal communication (discussed later). Words carry many different meanings, however, and both individual and contextual interpretations are relied upon in practice.

In a recent research study at a major trauma hospital, social workers stepped into the role of research assistants, asking people about their perceptions of trauma and of resources when a member of their family had been admitted to the Intensive Care Unit. In their role as research assistants, the social workers were surprised by some of the information they were told when they spoke with the family members, when compared with some of the information they had received in their role as social workers. The 'research assistants' heard some new or quite different dimensions of the 'same' stories. What this example highlighted to all the research team was that the family members told different dimensions of their story to people according to what they presumed their role was at the time. Similarly, the social workers who were research assistants in this instance also found new ways of asking about issues, having stepped outside of their usual psychosocial assessment framework. Stories vary and this showed that different narratives operated in different contexts.

Many people report that one of the difficulties following trauma or grief is finding a language with which to talk about their experiences—that is, finding a way of using words that will accurately convey what has been seen, experienced and felt (Laub & Auerhahn 1993; Reiter 2000). As later chapters on narrative approaches will emphasise, finding the words to use is an important part of adaptation and recovery.

In the grief literature, great emphasis is placed on using very specific language affirming the new reality, consistent with the first task of the grief

■ This notion of narrative variation is explored in Chapter 13.

process: coming to terms with the reality of the loss (Worden 2003). In the following scenario, Jane, a senior hospital social worker, highlights how particular language can be. Words have specific meanings and loading for particular individuals and their experiences in a particular context.

Focus on practice: finding the 'right' words

Once a year our department holds an afternoon for brothers and sisters who are bereaved through the death of a sibling. As we talk with the children, we feel it is important to use *correct factual* language and not euphemisms. One year, after an introduction to an activity in which I used the terms 'dead' and 'died', a little girl who was seven years old took me to one side and whispered, 'You should say *passed away*, it's much nicer'. A little taken aback, I asked her if this is what she said. Of course it was. I asked her who else said 'passed away' and she replied 'my mother'. Her point was well made. She knew very well that her sister was dead and didn't need to have this overstated. An alternative response to the little girl may have been to ask her could she tell me *what passed away* meant, but I think we both already knew.

Language variation perhaps most fundamentally occurs across cultures. Throughout Australia's history, people have migrated from all over the world, bringing a diversity of languages. **Cross-cultural communication** not only differs linguistically, but also 'involve[s] diverse experiences, worldviews and differential social power and privilege' (Miller, Donner & Fraser 2004, p. 377).

For human service practice, you need to be culturally educated and aware. Debates about cross-cultural competence are complex, however, with some authors suggesting it is actually impossible to be a culturally competent practitioner (Dean 2001). They argue it is more important to maintain an awareness of this impossibility, which leads to far greater communication sensitivity or focus on building cultural safety.

◼ Reflective practice exercise

欢迎光临

You may or may not be able to read this word.

1 What do you notice happens if you cannot understand the word?
2 How do you go about trying to understand it?
3 What would you do if you were confronted with this word and you were required to respond, even if you do not understand it?

Working with interpreters is a vital skill in working with people from culturally and linguistically diverse (CALD) backgrounds. The Victorian Interpreting and Translating Service (VITS, 2006, pp. 19–20) proposes the following strategies.

Focus on practice: working with interpreters

- Introduce yourself and the interpreter to your client.
- Explain what the interview is about and what you hope to achieve.
- Explain to the interviewee the interpreter's role within the interview. Inform the person that the interpreter's role is to assist communication by interpreting everything that is being said, by all parties.
- Maintain control of the interview. You must ask the questions and hear the replies fully. The interpreter's task is to assist in communication, not conduct the interview.
- Position yourself in a way that permits you to speak directly with the client and allows you to have maximum eye contact with them.
- Use first person (say 'I' instead of 'Ask him/her' etc) when speaking to your client. This will encourage both you and your client to talk to each other and use eye contact and body language, which assists in effective communication.
- Keep your questions, statements and comments short and deliver them in segments, allowing the interpreter to interpret everything in stages. Take note of the interpreter's method of signalling to you that your comments or questions are too long and allow the interpreter to do the same with the client.
- Never assume that interpreting is a simple mechanical task of matching the non-English word or expression with an English equivalent.
- It is unreasonable to expect an interpreter to be a walking dictionary.
- Do not assume that because a person appears to have a basic understanding of English, they will be able to comprehend specific terms and difficult expressions or jargon, particularly when under stress.
- Do not isolate the client by engaging the interpreter in discussion. If you need to clarify or discuss something with the interpreter, request that this be explained to the client first.
- Allow the client to raise any questions or issues of concern.
- Before the end of the interview, summarise key points for the client.

The use of silence

The use of silence—that is, the *absence* of verbal communication—is an important skill. Silence can be regarded as a verbal skill in that it is a deliberate refraining from the use of words to communicate a range of different messages.

Silences can provide extremely powerful spaces in which to reflect and simply 'be' in that moment with another person. The use of silence as a form of protest has been used to bring about major change (Dalton 1993). On the other hand, silences can be agonisingly long and awkward moments. Assumptions about the appropriateness of silence and pausing are both culturally and individually based. As Tannen (2000, p. 393) notes about differing assumptions:

> The one who is waiting for a longer pause finds it harder to get a turn, because before that length of pause occurs, the other person begins to perceive an uncomfortable silence and rushes to fill it, to save the conversation.

John, a social worker who has researched differences between Indigenous and non-Indigenous communication assumptions, spoke with Margaret about the use of silence. The following is an excerpt from that interview, reprinted with permission.

Focus on practice: the use of silence

Margaret: Nah, they have to fill in every minute with talk, with words. They don't know how to just listen, to just hear silence.

John: [after a pause] How do you mean?

Margaret: It's like they can't stand it when nobody is saying nothing. Silence is important to us. But they don't get that, don't respect that … If you don't answer right away they say you're angry or not interested or something … After a while, you just say bullshit, stuff you know they want to hear.

Therefore, finding the commonalities and congruities in the content of your conversations is important. Equally important, however, is the use of non-verbal communication.

Non-verbal communication processes

The term non-verbal refers to all the cues or skills that emanate from our physical reactions and presence, including, according to Bull (2002, pp. 26–7), 'facial movement, gaze, pupil size, body movement and interpersonal distance. It can refer as well to communication through touch or smell, through various kinds of artefacts such as masks and clothes, or through formalised communications such as semaphore'.

Thus, non-verbal cues relate to both the voluntary and involuntary physical reactions and responses we have in the context of a conversation, as well as the messages we transmit physically about our social identity. We rely on these non-verbal cues to indicate that we are listening and being listened to in a conversation.

Each person has a unique repertoire of non-verbal reactions and skills. This understanding is important as many communication texts suggest that up to

85 per cent of communication is conveyed in our non-verbal language. The impact of non-verbal cues on perceptions of rapport has been particularly noted (Bull 2002, p. 38).

Understanding the context of non-verbal behaviour is vital for a number of reasons. First, non-verbal behaviour conveys information for our survival. Recent research has found that we process some information emotionally in the first instance, and then at a cognitive level as a secondary process (Schacter 1996; Schore 1994). These understandings have emerged from studying how people process traumatic situations. They contradict some earlier assumptions that a cognitive process occurred first, followed by a physiological response. At a basic survival level, we rely on non-verbal cues to read safety in situations, reacting to stress and trauma with fight or flight reactions (Selye 1987). Our non-verbal reactions, therefore, convey our immediate physiological responses to situations. In less stressful situations, it is easier to monitor and influence non-verbal reactions.

Second, given that 'negative impressions often result from differences in conversational style' (Tannen 2000, p. 394), it is important to think about what we think is being conveyed and why. Like verbal communication, non-verbal information is still 'dependent on a human observer to transcribe and, if necessary, to code the behaviour into appropriate categories' (Bull 2002, p. 25).

▣ Reflective practice questions

1 What non-verbal cues would you rely on to know that someone was:
   • agreeing with you?
   • disagreeing with you?
   • confused by you?
2 What non-verbal cues did you tend to emphasise in your interpretation?
3 Why did you emphasise these cues and not others?

Increasingly, these cues are recognised as being highly culturally and gender specific, as well as context and age specific. You can find texts that identify all sorts of cross-cultural differences in eye contact, body language and space, and verbal following skills, to name a few (Evans et al. 2004, cited in Morris 2006, p. 265). The problem in identifying differences on the basis of group membership is that the differences become overly simplified and stereotyped, and group membership is assumed, often wrongly. On the other hand, these important differences can be neglected when they are profound influences. As Clarke, Andrews and Austin (1999) note, the skill is in asking the client about what is important, and observing what is important for them. It is about listening to what these gestures or styles of communication indicate—for example, eye contact can be about respect or indifference, which are two fundamentally different messages.

The following exercise encourages you to play with some of your non-verbal comfort levels by testing out different physical proximities.

Focus on practice: your physical comfort zones

In a class or small-group situation, try to keep a conversation going while working from a number of different physical postures. For example, maintain your conversation while you are:

- sitting or standing
- back to back
- shoulder to shoulder
- three metres apart
- ten centimetres apart or toe to toe.

Then find a comfortable distance and maintain the conversation in that position for a few minutes, noticing the features of this position.

1 What changes do you make in trying to find a comfortable position in which to maintain a conversation?
2 Reflecting on the comfortable position you moved to, how similar or different is that position from your colleagues' positions?
3 What cultural factors or assumptions do you think have influenced your position?

Over many years, the acronym SOLER (Egan 2007) has been used to promote the optimal non-verbal positioning in an interviewing situation. This positioning was thought to reflect a genuine and respectful non-verbal orientation to your client. SOLER stands for sitting *s*quare on (that is, facing the client), with an *o*pen **posture** (no crossed legs or arms), *l*eaning forward towards the client to express interest, maintaining *e*ye contact and being *r*elaxed. Egan later changed the acronym to SOLAR, following feedback from a woman who had been working with blind students and found that the *a*im of eye contact, not necessarily eye contact itself in this instance, was of greatest importance (Egan 2002, p. 70). However, as a reflection of cultural changes and particularly shifts in gender relations, this acronym is now heavily critiqued. So we will think about these issues of body language more broadly under separate subheadings of facial expression, body posture and physical proximity.

Facial expression

Over past decades, a continuing effort has been made to establish whether non-verbal behaviours, particularly facial expressions, are common to all people, regardless of context. Some facial reactions are automatic responses, such as pupil dilation occurring in response to 'stimuli we find attractive' (Bull 2002, p. 28), and blushing in the aftermath of embarrassment. All humans seem to express six emotions on their face: happiness, sadness, anger, fear, disgust and surprise, and they all are 'decoded in the same way by literate and preliterate cultures' (Bull 2002, p. 29). Cultures vary enormously, however, in the so-called 'display rules' that are developed around the expression of these emotions. Major differences have been found between the extensive use of direct eye contact in Western contexts and more avoidant and hierarchical rules relating to eye contact in Asian and Indigenous contexts (Sciarra 1999).

Your understanding of cultural influences, therefore, is critical. It is difficult to develop such understandings, however, outside of a particular situation. There may be generalisations that can be drawn about specific cultural groups regarding all sorts of dimensions of communication; for example, the use of eye contact, touch, proximity and emotional expressiveness. These can also become stereotypes. On the other hand, glossing over cultural differences can mean that communication is misinterpreted because of assumptions made that do not adequately acknowledge cultural difference. This kind of 'blindness' to issues of diversity and difference leads potentially to further marginalisation and stigma because difference is no longer acknowledged (Thompson 2003b).

■ Reflective practice exercise

Watch a number of conversations taking place in different contexts—in a workplace, in public or on the television, for example. Observe how people use their non-verbal skills to communicate their message and to respond to the other person.

1 What do you see working effectively and ineffectively in these encounters?
2 What communication differences would you attribute to gender, class or cultural differences?

In previous decades of counselling training, the emphasis has been on the worker maintaining a very neutral facial reaction to a client and their story. This neutrality has been assumed so you are not reacting to the emotional experience of the client but providing a neutral sounding board for the client. Rather than working towards some artificial and neutral response, a quality of intersubjectivity is now valued instead.

One of the opportunities, therefore, throughout any skills class is to learn the skills of monitoring and/or modifying emotional reactions. Four processes of modification have been noted (Bull 2002, pp. 30–1), including: attenuation, whereby an emotional reaction is weakened in its intensity; amplification, whereby it is exaggerated; concealment, whereby it is hidden by adopting a neutral facial expression; and substitution, whereby a different expression of the emotion being experienced is reflected. For example, it is not uncommon for people to smile while they are telling you about how sad they are feeling. If you have the opportunity to record your use of these skills, you will be able to witness your own reactions to clients and their stories, even if in a role-play.

▨ This modification of your emotional responses relates to your 'use of self', which we explore in Chapter 4.

Focus on practice

If you have the opportunity, use a DVD recorder or an observer to map your non-verbal behaviour throughout a role-play interview. A DVD recording, in particular, can provide the opportunity for you to see yourself as others experience you. Often for the person on screen, there is a sense of shock in seeing oneself on video for the first time. This links our usually entirely subjectively located experience with an objective experience of ourselves.

From a British study (Cartney 2006, p. 839) of the usefulness of video recordings in developing communication skills in social work training, students had these comments to make:

> During the video you can see your practical skills and then you can analyse yourself and base this in theory and in reading from different books. So you get all parts.

> You see things that you do yourself but you never realised … you watch and re-watch and all the time you see new things.

Body posture

Many different postures have been proposed as the most suitable posture for workers, such as SOLER mentioned earlier. While the absence of clear guidelines about physical posture may seem to make the task of interpreting these cues impossible, the quality of the physical alignment does seem to be the most important factor, referring to 'the way that speakers position their heads and bodies in relation to each other, including eye gaze' (Tannen 1994, p. 86). This is echoed in the statement by Egan (2002, p. 69): 'The point is that your bodily orientation should convey the message that you are involved with the client.' This means a general orientation of your body towards the person is important, but further 'rules' may not be helpful.

In studies of gender and posture, some major differences between boys only and girls only have been identified. As Tannen (1994, p. 98) notes:

> The girls and women are more physically still, more collected into the space they inhabit and more directly aligned with each other through physical proximity, occasional touching, body posture and anchoring of eye gaze.

This finding raises questions for how we interpret the non-verbal behaviours of men and women, depending upon our own gender.

Perhaps the most important quality of any physical posture is that it conveys respect to the other person. That is, you are available to listen and respond to them, finding a sustainable posture and one free of distractions. You may need to consider how sustainable your posture is. While it may initially seem a good idea to kneel down beside a child to talk with them, for example, it can be an awkward position beyond a few moments of conversation and distracting to then shift.

Physical proximity and location

Issues of physical space and proximity are similarly important considerations. A conversation too close to another person can seem violating of private or personal space. A conversation that is conducted too remotely can seem impersonal. Individual interpretation is again influential here. At a recent cross-cultural seminar, two workers had fundamentally different reactions to a photo of two people in conversation. One worker considered them to be very awkward in their posture and disengaged, whereas another worker thought they were two people relaxed in conversation with each other. Two workers were both reading into that image two completely different possibilities. The only way to know whether it was a difficult encounter would have been by asking the participants themselves about their experience.

Another non-verbal dimension in human service work to consider is the use of physical contact with clients. This has been, and remains, a contentious area of practice. On the one hand, a rule of 'no contact' is maintained, primarily to safeguard the client from unwanted touch and intimacy. On the other hand, there are times when physical contact, such as a handshake, becomes an important marker of respect and engagement in work together (Trevithick 2005). The use of touch raises questions of personal safety, both for your client and yourself.

These non-verbal cues can become the inhibitors rather than the enhancers of good communication interactions. Rather than there being a correct way to physically interact, interactional synchrony, congruence or alignment within a conversation have been identified as core components of an effective communication. Thus, the over- or underuse of particular non-verbal skills becomes problematic, not necessarily in and of itself but when joined with other incongruities in the conversational context.

Underutilised physical cues tend to leave the talker uncertain as to how the conversation is going. If you receive no response from someone in terms of facial expression, for example, it can be difficult to continue talking. Overutilised physical cues can similarly leave the client feeling unheard in that there seems to be an overreaction. One person recounted the story of seeing a counsellor whose eyes welled up with tears every time she spoke of her parent who had died some time earlier. The person was seeking help with other matters and felt that the counsellor was overinvolved in her grief rather than the difficulties she wanted to address.

Other overbearing physical cues can emerge in relation to eye contact that is too intense or a physical presence that is too close or too overbearing, so overstepping a sense of personal space that many consider important. Fidgeting or doodling with a pen and paper can similarly indicate stress or, on other occasions, boredom and disengagement. Sometimes we are unaware of our habits—of flicking hair, clicking pens or playing with jewellery or fingernails, for example. In any of these situations, if you are distracted the client may be left feeling that they are not being attended to in the conversation.

Non-verbal cues are also presented through a bodily discourse. Our physical presence tells a story to the client. For example, how you dress and how you present in relation to confidence are interpreted by your clients. In this sense, the 'body can be inscribed with societal norms, values and mores ... and ... our actions and behaviours ... illuminate personal values and ideas' (Osmond 2005, p. 892). These worker dimensions can alienate a client or provide reassurance, depending on how congruent they are with the client's world.

Your physical proximity can sometimes be beyond your control. Human service work is done frequently in physical locations other than private rooms where people are sitting together in comfortable chairs. Many significant conversations can be in corridors standing together, over a patient's bed or in public places where someone's response to the interview may have as much to do with the overall physicality of the environment as with the immediate conversation. Your awareness of the possible impact of all of these non-verbal dimensions on your capacity to talk together is vital.

Individual and collective communication processes

So far, we have considered communication in relation to at least two people in some form of direct verbal and non-verbal communication contact with each other. Other dimensions of communication complexity are also part of this process, including thinking beyond the one-to-one context of communication and beyond a 'five senses' understanding.

Communication involving more than one person

As people are added to the conversation, so the complexity or web of the communication grows. As noted in Chapter 1, Western approaches to human services, and interviewing and counselling in particular, have been criticised for failing to recognise communication processes beyond the individual interactions. The site of intervention remains primarily the individual, even though there is acknowledgment that family, community and the broader social context are such profound influences on well-being.

This was illustrated in John's research with a non-Indigenous social worker talking about her experiences with Indigenous clients:

Focus on practice

Susan: There are two things I wish I'd been taught in school. The first about how to keep boundaries, how much to reveal—both with clients and co-workers … The second, particularly about working with [Indigenous] clients, is how hard it is to work with more than one at a time. I definitely prefer individual work. You try to work with too many of them and they get that whole group thing going.

On the one hand, pragmatic realities and limited agency resources can justify this individual focus. On the other hand, the lack of integration of recent theoretical understandings around communication and interaction into practice leads to a considerable outdatedness of practice assumptions (Whyte 2005). Seeing the client as an individual rather than as part of a family or community means that the context of the problems, and therefore often the solutions, are overlooked. This has been particularly noted by Indigenous researchers and practitioners, who emphasise that because ways of living and thinking are collective and communal (Lynn 2001), problems should be addressed in collective and communal ways.

Communication beyond the five senses

The individualised approach is privileged further within Western discourses in regarding only verbal and non-verbal interactions within the physical realms, thus acknowledging five, not six, basic human senses.

Various theorists have tried to articulate understandings of other ways of knowing. Jung (1963, p. 160) termed one dimension of this 'collective unconscious', referring to the inherited, transpersonal dimensions of communication. Dreams and intuitions are thought to be the ways in which these shared dimensions of communication are transmitted.

Indigenous cultures have always respected the reality of other levels of communication, recognising conscious and unconscious, individual and collective, physical and metaphysical, and transpersonal ways of knowing (Smith 2001).

■ Reflective practice questions

'I was in London in 2005 in the week following the terrorist attacks in the Underground. On the Thursday after the bombs, at midday, a minute's silence was held. Thousands of people across London stopped to respect this silence.

During that time, for about 30 seconds, I felt an incredible tingling sensation through my arms and neck. On talking with several other people afterwards, it seems that we had shared this experience.'

1   What is your immediate reaction to this description?
2   Have you had similar experiences?
3   What would you be thinking if a client told you this story?

The capacity for human consciousness to effect change, even when people are not physically present together, has been proven in many studies (Hudson 2000). This research is relatively new and contentious, but it highlights that there are different levels of influence in any communication process. Rogers (cited in Moore & Purton 2006, p. 11) identified this when he noted it was not so much the qualities of genuineness or empathy that influenced the process of engagement with another person, but the subsequent transcendent state of being that was experienced as a result of these qualities.

We look now at three major ways in which communication is critical in the change process. Communication influences survival, promotes healing and expresses power.

Communication for survival

Communication connects people and facilitates the formation of social bonds and attachments (Koprowska 2005), which in turn facilitate our very survival. The infant learns to cry to elicit a response from a caregiver when they are hungry. Over time, they typically acquire specific words to communicate these specific needs. Across the life span, we communicate not only our basic physical needs and wants but also our most complex intimate and psychological needs.

We rely also on non-verbal communication for our survival. For example, we experience parataxic distortions (Sullivan 1953) when we first meet someone, whereby we try to identify if this person reminds us of anyone else. We scan our memories to see if there is any corresponding cue that reminds us of this person from our experience to date. This is the typification process indicated earlier in Chapter 1 where we very quickly group people, determining, for instance, as to whether this person looks safe or threatening.

Communication impacts on our survival in other ways. In recent years, the impact of health professionals' communication styles on patients has been studied, looking at compliance with medication and rehabilitation programs, and reduction of stress and anxiety (Glintborg, Andersen & Dalhoff 2007; Yedidia 2007). Effective communication strategies enhance health outcomes.

This link is emphasised across a wide range of professional guidelines. Rider and Keefer (2006, p. 626), for example, report on the competencies that are required of doctors in the US context. They include the capacity to:

▓ Remember Thompson's definitions of the processes of discrimination in Chapter 1, and stereotyping in particular.

1 'create and sustain a therapeutic and ethically sound relationship with patients

2 use effective listening skills and elicit and provide information using effective non-verbal, explanatory, questioning and writing skills

3 work effectively with others as a member or leader of a health care team or other professional group'.

Communication generally has been found to impact profoundly on mood states and self-esteem, which, in turn, are known to impact on physical health states (Goleman 2006). Positive communications lead to positive outcomes. Thus, communication plays a key role in enhancing or inhibiting well-being.

Communication as healing or therapeutic

As a worker, you will be using communication to bring about positive change for individuals and their communities. Thus, communication is both a means and an end in itself in this regard. The telling of and listening to human stories is a well-known protective factor for well-being. The **therapeutic** quality seems to be related to both what is said and that someone has listened. Conversations can be healing, therapeutic, relieving and normalising.

Some of the therapeutic qualities that we will continue to explore are the importance of 'giving voice' to situations of adversity (Laub & Auerhahn 1993), of speaking the unspeakable following trauma, the importance of developing a coherent story, and the importance of expressing emotion. For example, Don (in Atkinson 2002, p. 198) reflects on how sharing stories is healing:

> '[M]y medicine is listening to other people too. The first time I was listening to others talking, I thought they were talking about my life". 'I am not alone' is powerful medicine for people who have felt completely isolated, unheard, unacknowledged in their pain …

A positive impact on emotional intensity and stress and distress levels of writing about personal experiences has been similarly identified (Kleinman, Das & Lock 1997; Pennebaker 1995; Pennebaker & O'Heeran 1984). The expression of emotion is seen to enhance a sense of coherence. These findings have been questioned recently (Stroebe, Schut & Stroebe 2006), however, with emotional expression perhaps only helping those with a secure attachment style. This question of who benefits from emotional expression is important, as another study (Ginzburg, Solomon & Bleich 2002) found that being an 'avoidant repressor' was more protective in the aftermath of heart attacks, a potentially counterintuitive finding.

When a person's story is not heard, however, the research conclusions are more straightforward. When a person's experience is disenfranchised (Doka

1989), minimised or ignored, the impact is negative and, in some instances, has been found to contribute more to the ongoing distress than the initial trauma itself (Holman & Silver 1996).

The orientation of human service communication, therefore, is towards the promotion of the values discussed earlier. It is intentional communication around ultimately evoking strengths, positive emotions and resilience. This can come about in many ways—through the deep listening to the story of the client, through sharing humour (Moran & Massam 1997) and through breaking down a sense of isolation and alienation.

Communication as power

Verbal and non-verbal communication are, therefore, major means of human influence. One further way of understanding and analysing communication is in relation to the power relations that are inherent in any communication process.

Power is exerted for many reasons—as a result of our unconscious motivations, our attempts to manage uncertainty or to maintain the social order. Power is exerted through the assumed ways of being, through hierarchies of interaction and through language. This plays out whether there are even words for particular experiences within a particular culture, whether recognition is granted to individual constructions of meaning, and whether knowledge bases are the privileged ones. A major contribution of postmodernist theory has been the raising of awareness of the extent to which dominant constructions of meaning support particular power relations (Fook 1999, p. 203). Written and verbal communication can stand as authoritative knowledge, maintaining power and social control over the experiences of others (Gordon 1980, p. 77; Thompson 2003a).

Power is exerted in relation to the subsequent flow of information following a conversation with clients. For example, client confidentiality is in many ways protected by privacy legislation and codes of ethical practice. At times (and for family members in particular), the power of workers to withhold this information from families, out of respect for the client and consistent with privacy laws, can lead to tensions and frustrations (Deveson 1991). Thus, not communicating information—the withholding of information from colleagues and clients, either because of legislation requirements and/or personal style—can also be an extremely powerful act. Not communicating verbally leaves people unclear, powerless and unable to ascertain limits and boundaries.

The power dynamics of any relationship, therefore, are important to attend to in the context of professional practice. Often power dynamics are talked about as if they are something that can and should be removed from a relationship. It seems paradoxical that you become a human service worker to effect change, yet would then deny there is any influence or power in that role. For example, if you are the social worker working in child protection, you have the capacity under the legislation to remove a child to safer circumstances. As a worker, you have the power to breach confidentiality in situations where there are major concerns about the safety of an individual. Another way to think about it is that power dynamics are always functioning in any relationship, along with shifting experiences of influence, interdependence, dependence and independence.

This raises all sorts of questions about the degree to which client–worker relationships are 'equal'. Some authors and practitioners emphatically state that client–worker relationships are equal or should strive to be equal—for example, 'a radical perspective always assumes equality between the professional and the person being helped' (Fook 2000, p. 143; Ife 1997). Others, just as emphatically, state that a client and a worker cannot be equal in all respects (Brink 1987). As Burstow (1987, p. 18) argues, 'the situation is unequal in that [workers] have greater authority, mobility, responsibility for other and power as regards other'. She similarly proposes that the client has power but it is necessarily less power than that of the worker. For involuntary clients, this is particularly the case.

One strategy for ensuring that this inequality is not a destructive inequality is to develop a consciousness, and an articulation of the dilemmas and decisions we encounter throughout a relationship. That is, to recognise the distinction between having power and managing this inequality respectfully and openly. There are ways of minimising the inequality and the use of power within any relationship. As Tannen (1994, p. 26) notes, hierarchical relationships can be 'seen as close and mutually, not unilaterally, empowering'.

Brink's (1987, p. 27) distinction is a useful one, even if it is in relation to thinking specifically about therapists rather than all human service workers:

> Client and therapist are equally meaning-making beings, equally human beings, of equal worth, equally capable of realizing their own unique potential; they may or may not be equal in their coping skills or in their relative comfort in the world.

■ Remember the five core practice values, including respect, that were explored in Chapter 1.

This discussion highlights the valuing of a common humanity and the respecting of the worth and dignity of each person in the encounter.

This chapter ends with an example, provided by John, of some Indigenous clients talking about their non-Indigenous social worker. It draws together some of the themes that have run through this chapter—the use of verbal and non-verbal skills, the degree to which conversations are therapeutic or not, and the degree to which power is exerted or not in client–worker interactions:

Focus on practice

Lee: We'd meet at the hall and she'd have us sitting in a row and she would sit facing us ... We'd just sit there and she would talk ...

Rita: Yeah, she'd tell us what we were there to talk about and stuff. But it's like she wasn't really listening, she just kept on talking even when we didn't answer ...

Lee: Yeah, and then she'd talk even more. Once, after [several such meetings] we just sat there, didn't say a word. After a few minutes she just got up and left ...

Rita: We broke up laughing, damn near rolled on the floor!

1 What is your reaction to this interaction?
2 Identify the dimensions that you think were problematic in the client–worker relationship.

Chapter summary

In this chapter, we have explored some of the key dimensions of communication, to highlight the many microskills involved. While communication is regarded as a verbal process, the critical role of non-verbal communication in conveying the emotional and physical components of messages has also been emphasised. We looked at the dimensions of verbal and non-verbal communication processes that enhance or inhibit effective communication.

As a human service worker, you will bring to communication with clients a particular understanding of the significance of that communication. We have looked at the impact of communication on health and well-being, the role of communication in healing, and understanding communication as sustaining, reinforcing or changing power dynamics in individual and social relationships.

Reflective practice questions

1 What have you learnt about:
   • the verbal skills of communication?
   • the non-verbal skills of communication?
   • the ways in which communication is integral to culture, survival, health and power?
   • the communication challenges within a client–worker relationship?
2 What have you learnt about your own communication style from reading this chapter—in relation to both your verbal and non-verbal skills?
3 What are some of the strengths and challenges you experience in your communication style with other people?

Key references

Heath, R. & Bryant, J. (2000). *Human communication theory and research: Concepts, contexts and challenges*. New Jersey: Lawrence Erlbaum.

Koprowska, J. (2005). *Communication and interpersonal skills in social work*. Exeter: Learning Matters.

Pennebaker, J. (Ed.) (1995). *Emotion, disclosure and health*. Washington: American Psychological Association.

Trevithick, P. (2005). *Social work skills: A practice handbook* (2nd edn). Maidenhead: Open University Press.

Additional resources

Talking Cure: www.talkingcure.com.

VITS LanguageLink: www.vits.com.au.

Theorising Communication and Change

3

LEARNING GOALS

- Analyse the influences on our listening.
- Consider the paradigms that influence listening.
- Describe the influence of theory on listening.
- Understand how different practice perspectives influence our practice.
- Apply a multidimensional approach to listening.

The influences on our listening

In Chapter 2, we looked at the communication process in some detail, breaking it down into the verbal and non-verbal skills that influence a conversation. As Thompson notes (2002, p. xviii), 'skill development does not occur in a vacuum—there are also knowledge and values to be taken into consideration'. This chapter focuses on how we can bring together these skills with a theoretical understanding of the client, their particular circumstances, and the event or conditions that require change.

Developing an understanding of the knowledge bases we bring to our practice is critical. Two knowledge bases, in particular, inform human service work—an evidence-based perspective and a reflective practice perspective (Chui & Wilson 2006, p. 2; Lewis 2002). That is, our practice is based on the use of knowledge and theory, as well as on the use of an understanding of ourselves as workers.

We can think about knowledge, theories and skills in a number of different ways. These differences often lead to confusion because a sharp distinction is not made between the level or type of **theory** or knowledge that is being presented (Walsh 2006). In this chapter, **paradigms** (or worldviews), theoretical knowledge and factual knowledge—including consumer perspectives and practice wisdom—are described. The chapter concludes with a presentation of a multidimensional approach, an overarching framework used within this book.

To focus the discussion, Jacinta's story will be used to show the different ways we might go about thinking about our work.

Focus on practice

Jacinta has rung your organisation and spoken with the duty worker about her concerns that she's going to harm her four children. She's exhausted and depressed following the birth of her baby seven weeks ago. The other three children are all under six years of age, and over the school holidays she's found it increasingly difficult to manage with them at home every day. Her partner is working part-time in the local car factory, but it has been threatened with closure. The financial stress is the worst it has ever been, with the rent in arrears and the bills piling up. If he loses his job, she does not know what they will do.

This morning, her eldest son dropped his breakfast all over the floor. His stepfather hit him and he has bruises on his face. He has been withdrawn in his room all morning and she is now feeling so angry and frustrated with him, she thinks she may lash out at him as well. She realises this and picked up the phone, calling your family service instead. She realises she needs help before things are really out of control.

1   What is your reaction to this situation and why?
2   Who would you view as your client/s in this situation and why?
3   What would you see as your main purposes in working with this situation and whoever you have identified as the client/s?
4   How would you go about that purpose? That is, what would you want to do in this situation?
5   Why do you think this situation has arisen?

Jacinta's story raises a lot of questions for your practice: where would you begin in your response to Jacinta and the others in her family? What would be the purpose of your involvement and intervention, along with the other questions raised in the shaded box above? One starting point is to think about the broad paradigms or worldviews that inform your practice.

Paradigms and worldviews

As meaning-making beings, humans 'need to find things out, build and test theories, and take action based on that knowledge-generating activity'

(Morris 2006, p. xvii). This broad view of the world and how it operates is referred to as a worldview or paradigm. These 'structures of meaning' help us to establish our own personal and social identities, and maintain some sense of predictability, coherence and control in our daily lives (Antonovsky 1987; Marris 1993, 1996). We develop these paradigms or broad understandings from our experiences across our life span as we come to form views of the nature of social reality and of people.

Worldviews are often described as differing along continua of beliefs about the nature of human and social realities. Questions about objective versus subjective truths lie at the heart of different paradigms (Neuman 1999; Trainor 2002). For example, some people understand the world in relation to an individual identity, whereas others maintain more collective notions of identity; equally, identities can be understood as stable and fixed or fluid and non-linear. Some people maintain liberal views of the world and of expectations of other people's behaviour, whereas others maintain conservative views. Some people see the inner world as the cause of human problems and suffering, whereas others attribute these experiences to outer-world causes. Each one of these dimensions is part of a different worldview, or overarching way of thinking about the human experience. In different historical eras and social contexts, different worldviews dominate.

We bring these worldviews to bear on our understanding of practice. To identify these dominant worldviews that we hold in our minds is an important step towards developing reflective practice. Worldviews need to be critically appraised for their underpinning assumptions. As Holloway (2006, p. 17) highlights, 'paradigms, scientific, religious, cultural or political, are all power systems, and the thing you ask about a power system is, "Who are the victims here?"'

Three major paradigms have been identified in social research (Neuman 1999), which are of direct relevance to practice. They are positivism, constructivism or social constructivism, and critical paradigms. General assumptions of these paradigms have been identified by different authors and some of these are summarised below, although they are by no means neat concepts and categories. The rationale for providing a brief overview about each of these three is that they link with the practice theories and related skills we look at in later chapters.

Positivism

A **positivist perspective** understands social reality as based on 'stable, pre-existing patterns' (Neuman 2006, p. 105). Thus, experiences can be objectively observed and measured, as Morris (2006, p. 3) emphasises: 'The positivist worldview assumes that an objective reality exists outside of personal experience that has demonstrable and immutable laws and mechanisms.'

A positivist paradigm is based, therefore, on assumptions of cause and effect (Morris 2006, p. 3), whereby it is possible, through the identification of various factors, to identify the cause of problems or difficulties, and intervene to alter them. In understanding Jacinta's situation, some of the emphasis might be on understanding the cause and effect issues—the impact of poverty, of depression or of abuse on individuals and families.

Constructivism

Many human service workers have embraced a constructivist or social constructionist paradigm (Ife 1997). This paradigm, in contrast to the positivist paradigm, does not consider that there is one objective truth or reality, but subjective positions only. The construction of the individual, or the family or community, is what shapes and informs 'reality'. At the extreme end of the **constructivist perspective** is the view that there is no such thing as 'reality' outside of these subjective perceptions. Thus, Jacinta's circumstances would need to be understood from her point of view as much as the multiple points of views of the other people involved in her situation. From a practice perspective, the constructionist view does present workers with some challenges—for example, Gambrill (1999, p. 343) strongly criticises this approach, given that social work in particular is committed to addressing issues of social inequality. The relativism of constructionist approach diminishes the capacity for 'truths' about, for example, economic and political power, or violence and abuse, to be collectively articulated and addressed.

Critical social science

The third paradigm, a critical social science paradigm, has a very different agenda from those described above. In many ways, it enables workers to explicitly address the above criticisms of a constructivist approach. A **critical perspective** is based on an explicit ideological or value base and has change located centrally in its agenda. It is critical of the status quo, seeing power, conflict and oppression as dominant concerns to be addressed. Jacinta's circumstances would be understood very differently from this point of view. A worker within a critical paradigm would interpret Jacinta's situation in far more structural or outer-world terms, looking at the ways in which gender roles and poverty disempower individuals. An agenda would be set with Jacinta, within the context of an equal client–worker relationship (Bishop 2002). The focus would be on both consciousness raising and social action throughout the contact (Blankenship 1998; Freire 1996; Ife 1997).

Table 3.1 is a summary of the key dimensions of each paradigm in relation to some central themes (Neuman 2006). While these dimensions have been articulated in relation to research, they are of direct relevance to practice.

Paradigms, in providing overarching worldviews, provide the basis for theories that may be directly used in practice (Healy 2005).

Table 3.1 Three dominant paradigms

	Positivism	Interpretive or social constructivist	Critical
Reason for research	To discover natural laws so people can predict and control events	To understand and describe meaningful social action	To smash myths and empower people to change society radically
Nature of social reality	Stable pre-existing patterns or order that can be discovered	Fluid definitions of a situation created by human interaction	Conflict-filled and governed by hidden underlying structures
Nature of human beings	Self-interested and rational individuals who are shaped by external forces	Social beings who create meaning and who constantly make sense of their worlds	Creative, adaptive people with unrealised potential, trapped by illusion and exploitation
Role of common sense	Clearly distinct from and less valid than science	Powerful everyday theories used by ordinary people	False beliefs that hide power and objective conditions
Theory looks like	A logical, deductive system of interconnected definitions, axioms and laws	A description of how a group's meaning system is generated and sustained	A critique that reveals true conditions and helps people see the way to a better world
An explanation that is true	Is logically connected to laws and based on facts	Resonates or feels right to those who are being studied	Supplies people with tools needed to change the world
Good evidence	Is based on precise observations that others can repeat	Is embedded in the context of fluid social interactions	Is informed by a theory that unveils illusions
Place for values	Science is value-free, and values have no place except when choosing a topic	Values are an integral part of social life; no groups' values are wrong, only different	All science must begin with a value position: some positions are right, some are wrong

Source: Neuman (2006, p. 105).

Theoretical knowledge

While we may be able to agree on what is verbally stated in a conversation and demonstrated at a non-verbal level, many interpretations can be made of what the meaning or intention may be of that communication. Theoretical perspectives provide a language and a structure for interpreting information. Theoretical perspectives inform what we ask about in the first interview (Sommers–Flanagan & Sommers–Flanagan 2004, p. 9), what we talk about with the client, how we interpret what we hear, and how we respond.

■ **Remember that in Chapter 2 we looked at how meaning and intent is a major filter on what we hear in a conversation.**

In order to be a theory or provide a conceptual framework for more therapeutic work, four main dimensions must be present (Nelson-Jones 2006, p. 6):

1 a statement of the basic … assumptions underlying the theory
2 an explanation of the acquisition of helpful and unhelpful behaviour
3 an explanation of the maintenance of helpful and unhelpful behaviour
4 an explanation of how to help clients change their behaviour and consolidate their gains

The paradigms described earlier provide a grand theory or a grand narrative. This type of perspective provides an overarching theory or explanation for human experience. Theories provide more specific explanations for why things occur and in many instances provide broad prescriptions or bases for interventions. To illustrate this point, one theory of human experience is that we need to find meaning or a sense of coherence in order to maintain well-being and function optimally. This is based on the understanding that, as individuals, from birth we develop a cognitive and emotional set of internal working models or assumptive worlds. That is, from infancy, we develop ways of making sense of what goes on in our own worlds and increasingly the worlds of others. A sense of coherence and predictability emerges for most people, through the development of a story of how the world works and how we are placed within it, which is integral to our mental health, and our capacity to relate to other people and function effectively in our daily lives. We develop a sense of meaning, order and security through these stories.

In this paragraph, a theory of behaviour and experience has been outlined, drawn from attachment and narrative theories. That is, an explanation of a phenomenon is provided—our need for theory—that has come about following the *observation* of the phenomenon by numerous authors. From that brief *description*, an *explanation* can be given as to how human beings might go about building an assumptive world, and a worker can consider how *predictions* and even *interventions* in a situation with a particular client can be undertaken. These five dimensions are identified by Howe (2002) as ways in which a theory is useful for practice.

If we are working with Jacinta as our client, we need to move from the general issues discussed above to very specific questions such as: Why have these problems occured? What can be done about them? How should change be brought about and with whom? We will need to make sense of particular dimensions or priorities in her family situation. Theoretical frameworks can provide the map for the priorities in practice and the directions of any intervention.

Theories clearly have different strengths and limitations. They vary, for example, in the degree to which they focus on change in the inner worlds of individuals and families through to focusing on change in the outer worlds that individuals and families occupy. To illustrate, the 'conservation of resources' theory (Hobfoll, Ennis & Kay 2000) is increasingly contributing to understandings of grief, stress and trauma experiences. This theory proposes that there are four domains of resources—condition, energy, personal and time—and experiences of grief, stress and trauma emerge when one or more of these resource domains is affected negatively. That is, resource losses could explain Jacinta's distress reaction. This theory provides a strong and useful explanation for why people may be experiencing stress, grief or trauma. It provides no explanation, however, of the possible trajectories of reactions experienced by an individual. No theory of intervention at an interpersonal level emerges from this, other than resourcing being the critical need.

One of the challenges students face when they turn from theories of change to actual practice is that theories of change do not necessarily lead to the detail of theories of intervention, or in particular the microskills needed to work in such a way. For example, while anti-oppressive approaches focus on change beyond the individual, they do not have theories for practice at the micro-level of interaction with another person. The focus for change is not at the interpersonal level, but the problem is that the interpersonal level is where much of the work actually begins, and indeed is often done. Theories of relationship and the focus of communication from a structural perspective do not have a theory of practice for practice at this micro-level. Similarly, theories relating to intrapsychic work do not have theories for practice in relation to the interaction with the social and structural dimensions.

Another challenge of theory is that it is often presented as if in practice we function in a 'pure' way, adhering strictly to all the fundamentals of a particular theoretical perspective. In practice, we tend to work eclectically, relying upon a range of knowledge bases at any one time and integrating these into our practice.

Another challenge is the extent to which there is consistency between what is espoused as the theoretical perspective and what is practised by each worker. That is, someone may declare that they are a feminist or a cognitive behavioural practitioner, but how would they know that their practice is actually consistent with that perspective? Banks (2006, p. 121) observes this kind of gap between theory and practice when she highlights that 'the focus in social work generally is on the individual service user or family and therefore inevitably the stress is on personal change, even if the broader societal context is acknowledged'.

One final challenge in relation to the use of theories is that they can also be contextually inappropriate or wrong. The practice of removing Australian Aboriginal children from their families, for example, was based on theories of well-being at the time. These theories are now understood as racist theories that failed to take into account Indigenous ways of living, and the importance of attachment in understanding child and family well-being. Dominant, colonising theories have been imposed on many other Indigenous populations around the world, with similarly devastating impacts on well-being (Smith 2001).

These are some of the limitations of theory. Theories play an important role, however, in guiding our practice. We now consider the ways in which a number of theoretical perspectives explain some key dimensions of human behaviour and experience, to illustrate points of compatibility and points of difference. The theoretical perspectives are examined in greater detail, and applied in practice, in later chapters in this book. The key elements for comparison are:

- What dimensions of the human person are considered core?
- What is the focus of change?
- What is the reason for the human service intervention?
- What are the major or dominant skills that are used?
- What are the core beliefs about the helping relationship?
- What are the assumptions about the length of relationship?

These approaches have been chosen as examples of each of the major paradigms discussed earlier and as examples of common practice theories emphasised in different agencies. They include task-centred and crisis-intervention, psychodynamic, cognitive behavioural, narrative and solution-focused, feminist and critical theories.

Task-centred and crisis-intervention theories

In contrast to the five theoretical perspectives considered in the following pages, the **task-centred** and crisis-intervention approaches do not fit so easily into one dominant paradigm and cannot be described as 'pure' theories. They are, however, important practice approaches and therefore are included here as a way of demonstrating more practitioner-led and practitioner-developed theoretical frameworks currently in use.

Crisis-intervention theories arose from work with people during the immediate crisis time of particular critical incidents. Lindemann's (1944) study of grief, for example, identified that there was typically a four- to six-week period, following major losses or stressors, when people's usual functioning was significantly reduced, requiring different supports throughout this change in functioning, both emotional and practical. One of the major emphases of crisis intervention, explored later in Chapter 11, is on assisting people to manage their initial extreme emotional responses, and to return to a more balanced cognitive and emotional state (Caplan 1990; Granot 1996). Crisis-intervention approaches, therefore, initially are often about quite directive and/or assertive outreach, supporting people to make decisions and to vent emotion, while over time these reactions resolve.

A study of family members of a patient in the Intensive Care Unit at the Alfred Hospital, for example, showed that family members were experiencing very high levels of posttraumatic stress symptoms (Harms, Rowe & Suss 2006). The implications of this finding are profound for the family's capacity to process the information they are receiving and to make decisions on behalf of the patient. One of the major approaches of social work in this setting is to ground people back into tasks, shifting back into cognitive and practical approaches to help mediate or settle some of the emotional response. Emotional containment and support are also key considerations. As Trevithick (2005) notes, the only social work theory developed by practitioners is the task-centred approach (Marsh & Doel 2005), where the approach is more about the doing than theorising behaviour in particular ways.

These two approaches rely on the rapid establishment of empathy and trust with clients during typically a short-term period of intervention (Healy 2005, p. 126). They are focused on interventions in both the inner and outer worlds, but view the restoration or the introduction of resources in the outer world as major facilitators of change and adaptation. They are also based on strengths perspectives.

In Jacinta's situation, responding to the immediate emotional crisis and the practical resource crisis she faces would be a major focus of interventions. Intervention would also need to be focused on the rights of the children to safety, and the legislation relating to child protection practices would influence what a worker would do in this situation. Specific interventions within these approaches tend to integrate dimensions of the various theoretical perspectives discussed in the following sections (Walsh 2006).

Psychodynamic theories

Of all the theoretical dimensions, **psychodynamic theories** place the most emphasis on the client–worker relationship and on the processes of the communication within that relationship.

Psychodynamic theories are primarily concerned with the inner worlds of individuals, and how difficulties arise in functioning because of these past and present inner-world preoccupations. Thus, psychodynamic theories are concerned with human drives or motivations in relation to pleasure, power, conflict and anxiety. These experiences are thought to develop across the life span, through various psychosocial or psychosexual phases. One of the major arguments within psychodynamic theories is that 'psychopathology arises from early childhood experiences' (Sommers-Flanagan & Sommers-Flanagan 2004, p. 41). Relating this to Jacinta's situation, a worker with a psychodynamic understanding would want to know about the conscious and unconscious experiences, Jacinta's own past patterns of being parented and how these are now being replayed in this adult context, and the fantasies and drives that motivate Jacinta's behaviour or relationship difficulties.

Psychodynamic theories are very focused on verbal and non-verbal communications: the conscious and unconscious messages directed to the worker—these processes of the telling of the story are all to be interpreted as much as the story's content. The client's relationship with the worker is seen as an opportunity to work through and experience a 'corrective emotional' relationship or the 'training ground' (Shulman 1999, p. 217) with the worker that may repair or address some of the difficulties experienced in previous relationships, primarily those with parents. Underlying this is an argument that the relationship enables the opportunity for the establishment or re-establishment of a secure attachment. That is, the secure base of this relationship provides a sense of meaning and coherence in other contexts. Transference and countertransference (Gibney 2003) become an essential focus of the work together. Thus, the experience of connection with the worker, or the therapeutic alliance, is one of the major change agents (Trevithick 2005).

> ■ These psychodynamic concepts of transference and countertransference are explored in Chapter 12.

Cognitive behavioural theories

Cognitive and **cognitive behavioural theories** are located more within a positivist paradigm. The early theorists (Ellis 1995; Beck, Freeman & Davis 2004) proposed that a person's difficulties emerged in relation to three domains—the way the person thought, the way the person felt or reacted emotionally, and the way the person acted. Cognitive behavioural therapy (CBT) is based on this understanding: create change in any of these domains and change in the other domains will follow necessarily. This relationship of reciprocal change is represented in Figure 3.1.

Figure 3.1   The reciprocal links between thoughts, feelings and behaviours

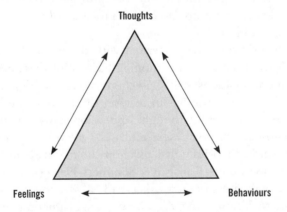

These dimensions remain very evident in other current interviewing models, such as Egan's problem-management and opportunity-development

model (Egan 2007). He presents these three dimensions as the focus of what the client talks about and that are important to understand. They talk about:

> 'their experiences—that is, what happens to them'

> 'their behaviour—that is, what they do or refrain from doing'

> 'their affect—that is, the feelings, emotions and moods that arise from or are associated with their experiences and both internal and external behavior' (Egan 2007, p. 81).

Others refer to this as the 'Think-Feel-Do' framework (Thompson 2002, p. xvii). One of the major criticisms of this approach is that many people's difficulties occur within the outer world—for example, Jacinta's poverty or the issues of men's violence towards women—but the approach does not address change at this level. Change in this model is theorised at the individual level of thinking, feeling and behaviour (Egan 2007, pp. 7–8).

CBT has tended not to focus on the client–worker relationship to the same extent as psychotherapeutic approaches, other than for it to be a collaboration that focuses on critically reflecting on a person's thinking, feeling and doing.

Narrative and solution-focused theories

As an example of the constructivist paradigm, **narrative theories** place a major emphasis on the way in which an individual constructs and relates the stories, and particularly the problem stories, of their life. This approach is grounded in the belief that meaning-making, through the formulation of narrative, is integral to well-being because it leads to an integrated inner state: '[T]he establishment of some stability for meaning is an essential foundation to any claim for a meaningful sense of felt subjectivity' (Sharp 2006, p. 66).

A particular emphasis on solution-focused or strengths-based narratives is often made, so that the focus is on developing a sense of insight, and control over the narrative. When people experience major adversity, reconstructing a sense of self that is able to influence the environment again is an important process. Thus, unlike psychodynamic and cognitive behavioural perspectives, the self or subjective experience is understood to be a more fluid state of being, rather than constructed across the life span through various developmental phases.

Narrative approaches have had wide appeal across a variety of settings and populations. Indigenous communities have used narrative extensively to retell stories of colonisation and culture (Smith 2001; Tamasese 2000; Wingard 2001), while Holocaust survivors have used narrative to recount and validate experiences of horrific trauma and torture (Laub & Auerharn 1993; Reiter 2000). Bearing witness to people's experiences of adversity and suffering has been recognised throughout the trauma and grief literature as a critical process in recovery. It also means that the telling of stories has the power to bring about change at other levels, such as at program or policy levels.

In Jacinta's situation, narrative work would focus on the ways in which she tells her story, and the ways in which it can be co-created to focus more on her strengths and to externalise rather than internalise the problem. The worker is a key influence in developing alternative narratives that empower Jacinta and her coping capacities.

Feminist theories

Feminism is a theory that can be located within the context of a critical paradigm. That is, the agenda of feminism is to create structural change as a result of the continuing oppression of women within male-dominated power structures. Feminism locates the focus of its attention beyond the inner world of an individual, to argue that these inner worlds are influenced profoundly by the wider social and political context (Dominelli 2002; Trevithick 1998).

Like psychodynamic theory, there is no one singular **feminist theory** as such, with theories polarised in views along a radical to liberal feminism (Tong 1998). Within feminism, one of the major variations in these perspectives relates to the extent to which they argue for separatist positionings of women and men.

Feminist approaches focus on empowering individuals facing adversity to change their circumstances externally, rather than internalising them as private problems.

Critical theory has many similarities with feminist theory, in that it locates oppression and disempowerment within the wider social environment as the major causes of individual difficulty (Ife 1997; Maidment & Egan 2004; Pease & Fook 1999). It does not only adopt gender and power, however, as its focus. Rather, it identifies and seeks to challenge multiple sources of oppression— gender, economic, cultural and sexual, for example. The primary focus of change is, therefore, the wider social, structural and cultural context, rather than the individual. Practice methods range from therapeutic counselling to social action and advocacy strategies.

Thus, Jacinta's depression might be understood in the context of her structural and social disempowerment (Stoppard 2000), and its resolution would be seen as occurring with appropriate social supports and recognition. Similarly, the stressors in parenting might be understood as arising from the privatisation of mothering and the unrealistic expectations that are placed on women in providing care with little social support and acknowledgment.

These theoretical perspectives are summarised in Table 3.2. The major skills associated with these theoretical approaches will be discussed in greater detail in Chapters 11–14.

Table 3.2 Paradigms and theoretical perspectives informing practice

	PARADIGM				
	Positivist	Positivist	Difficult to locate	Critical	Social Constructivist
	THEORETICAL PERSPECTIVE				
	Psychodynamic	Cognitive behavioural	Task-centred and crisis intervention	Feminist and critical	Narrative and solution-focused
Dimension of human person considered core for change	Bringing unconscious thoughts, behaviours into conscious thought and control	Primarily thought patterns, although also feelings and behaviours	Feeling state; restoration of functioning	Personal functioning and sociopolitical context	Stories we live by, particularly stories that disempower and oppress
Focus of change	Thoughts, desires, impulses: unconscious to conscious	Thoughts	The immediate tasks associated with the problem as well as the emotional response	Gender and power relations; patriarchal social structures that oppress women and other minority groups	Stories that are empowering and strengths based, often externalising the problem
Goal of intervention	Interpretation on behalf of therapist and self-reflection and insight on behalf of client; anxiety reduction	Behavioural and cognitive change	Return to functioning to be able to begin to cope emotionally and practically with crisis	Externalising of gender and power problems rather than internalising	Narratable stories of self and circumstances that lead to healthy, strengths-based ways of living
Dominant skills	Listening, interpreting relationship	Focusing on the way in which the client's thoughts, feelings and behaviours are connected Challenging patterns of thinking and behaving	Education; resourcing; emotional release	Listening to the story; empowering; externalising the issue as a political rather than personal issue; advocacy and social change	Acknowledging problem stories; externalising the problem; deconstructing negative stories; reconstructing positive ones; living out the new stories
Beliefs about helping relationship	Previously saw as 'blank screen'; now intersubjective	Listening for faulty, unhelpful beliefs; not much emphasis on relationship as a process in and of itself	Initially directive and assertive shifting after initial crisis	Equal, empowering relationship; explicit focus on gender relations and power in client–worker relationship	Helps in constructing a story and in listening to gaps/silences

Factual knowledge

To work with Jacinta we will need further information that will help us understand her circumstances. This helps us to understand what it is she is dealing with, and therefore how we might respond. Jacinta and her family are coping with many contemporary psychosocial issues. You might identify postnatal depression, emotional stress and distress, poverty and financial stress, employment uncertainty, rental arrears or the consequences of poor public housing options for low income earners, parenting difficulties or challenging children, physical and emotional abuse of at least one of these children, and extreme social disadvantage and disempowerment.

Your knowledge of these experiences from a broader research perspective is critical. For example, you could draw on recent research into the aetiology (cause) of postnatal depression (Pope 2000). An intervention will vary depending on whether you understand postnatal depression to be a mental illness—in which case you might encourage contact with a general practitioner as a first step—or an outcome of the stress, exhaustion and loneliness of becoming a mother (in Jacinta's case) for the fourth time. In this case, you might link her with a mother's group for peer support. Or you might understand her depression to be related to her extreme financial stress, and link her with a financial counsellor and emergency relief resources.

This information is in many forms—in the form of statistical data, of an evaluation or of stories provided by individuals or families. You need a foundational base of factual knowledge about the phenomena to which you are responding. Issues of child abuse and neglect, disability and chronic illness, poverty, mental and physical illness, and substance use and abuse are all issues with which workers need to be familiar. This helps you understand the context in which the lived experience of one person is taking place and the possible effects of such conditions or experiences.

Some disciplines refer to this as a 'social epidemiological' approach, whereby the medical terminology of epidemiology is adapted to understanding social issues. Epidemiology refers to 'the study of how often and for what reasons a health problem occurs in specific groups of people' (Butchart & Kahane 2006, p. 17). In an epidemiological approach, issues of aetiology (causation), incidence and prevalence, and the effects and/or outcomes (both on the individuals directly and indirectly affected) are taken into account.

Another important dimension of any work with Jacinta relates to consideration of the broader legal context of practice (Swain 2002), which influences the decisions we make in practice. These facts include the legislative and political contexts in which you will function—for example, the child protection legislation in Victoria has recently undergone a radical review, meaning that the practice context for working with Jacinta has similarly changed radically.

■ Refer to the resources at the end of this chapter for links to the Cochrane and Campbell Collaboration sites and others.

Factual knowledge is also required about interventions. Many outcome studies are available that have looked at what works and what does not work in therapeutic settings (Fonagy 1999; Hubble, Duncan & Miller 1999; Roth & Fonagy 2005). Online resources such as the Cochrane Collaboration, the Campbell Collaboration and others provide data about the known efficacy of various interventions.

Relying on randomised controlled trials has some place in human service work, but they cannot be the only ways in which human behaviour, rights and needs can be understood. Many people argue strongly that, in human service work, it is in fact not possible or desirable to apply the rigour of evidence-based practice, in that each circumstance is unique and it is not possible to research the outcomes of each unique intervention (see Duncan & Miller 2005). In the absence of evidence bases for a lot of human service work, therefore, others have called for use of the best available evidence (Kessler, Gira & Poertner 2005, p. 247) or others refer to evidence-informed practice (Evans & Benefield 2001).

You will face all kinds of contradictions, tensions and complexities in your daily practice. On the one hand, never before within the literature, research and organisations has there been such a push to have practice that adheres to certain standards, given the current risk management environment (Webb 2006). The emphasis is on workers having a strong, established evidence base to the work undertaken, and clear, accountable boundaries around time and practice with people. That is, a paradigm of positivism governs much of what is done. On the other hand, never before has there been such an 'evidence base' for the importance and influence of critical reflective practice; an emphasis on practice wisdom; an appreciation for the uniqueness of individual experience and the importance of cultural sensitivity and spirituality; and an emphasis on an authentic, open relationship between client and worker. That is, constructivism also governs much of what is done.

Jacinta's circumstances, and the possible courses of action in working with her and her family, highlight how complex human service work is. You are being called upon to mediate the unique circumstances of each person, family or community and your knowledge and skill as a worker.

> ■ See Chapter 1 for the AASW, APS and AMA websites, where practice standards are available.

Consumer perspectives

The question as to what works with whom and why in human service work is only one part of the issue. Increasingly, client perspectives are being incorporated into answering this question. What would Jacinta want from any human service worker and intervention? It is striking that this perspective is often ignored by both researchers and organisations.

A research base is emerging in relation to what clients perceive to be of most benefit to them. These studies suggest that the most important factors in interventions are the client–worker relationship or alliance (Hubble, Duncan & Miller 1999; Lambert 2005) rather than specific techniques or theories. This is referred to as the 'common factors approach' (Hubble, Duncan & Miller 1999, p. 31), which recognised that for clients in psychotherapy, change could be attributed as stemming from the following:

- 40 per cent of change arose from extra-therapeutic change
- 30 per cent arose from the therapeutic relationship

- 15 per cent arose from expectancy (placebo effects)
- 15 per cent arose from the techniques used.

As workers, we need to keep in mind the research that suggests lay interventions are just as effective as professional ones or therapeutic ones.

Clients have identified other factors in the relationship in mandated situations (Ribner & Knei-Paz 2002):

- feelings of closeness
- a working style that creates an enabling atmosphere and an equal stance
- working together on issues
- flexibility in contact—accessibility
- keeping in touch.

Another small-scale study in the field of child welfare (de Boer & Coady 2007, p. 35) focused on matched client and worker perspectives and identified similar qualities. These qualities came under two major themes of (1) a soft, mindful and judicious use of power; and (2) a humanistic attitude and style that stretches traditional professional ways of being.

Focus on practice: child welfare workers' attitudes and actions that build good relationships with clients

A soft, mindful and judicious use of power:

- being aware of one's power and the normalcy of client fear, defensiveness and anger
- responding to client negativity with understanding and support instead of counter-hostility and coercion
- conveying a respectful and non-judgmental attitude
- providing clear and honest explanations about reasons for involvement
- addressing fears of child apprehension and allaying unrealistic fears
- not prejudging the veracity of intake, referral or file information
- listening to and empathising with the client's story
- pointing out strengths and conveying respect
- constantly clarifying information to ensure mutual understanding
- exploring and discussing concerns before jumping to conclusions
- responding in a supportive manner to new disclosures, relapses and new problems
- following through on one's responsibilities and promises.

A humanistic attitude and style that stretches traditional professional ways of being:

- using a person-to-person, down-to-earth manner (versus donning the professional mask)

- engaging in small talk to establish comfort and rapport; getting to know the client as a whole person—in social and life-history contexts
- seeing and relating to the client as an ordinary person with understandable problems
- recognising and valuing the client's strengths and successes in coping
- being realistic about goals and patient about progress
- having a genuinely hopeful and optimistic outlook on possibilities for change
- using judicious self-disclosure towards developing personal connection
- being real in terms of feeling the client's pain and displaying emotions
- going the extra mile in fulfilling mandated responsibilities, and stretching professional mandates and boundaries.

Practice knowledge or wisdom

A further source of knowledge for practice is the uniquely individual store of subjective experience that is developed from experience as a worker. Over time, and through various encounters, we come to understand situations through the lens of experience as well. We can draw upon that experience to think about what we did then and what happened as a result, and change our current behaviour as a consequence. This knowledge is referred to as '**practice wisdom**' (Scott 1990). As Kessler, Gira and Poertner (2005, p. 245) highlight: 'Practitioners are expected to be pragmatic, self-reflective, and learn from their work with clients. The result is practice wisdom, or experientially and inductively derived knowledge.'

Practice wisdom has been defined as 'the accumulation of information, assumptions, ideologies and judgements that have seemed practically useful in fulfilling the expectations of the job (De Roos 1990, cited in Osmond 2005, p. 891). An understanding of practice wisdom is critical because of the widespread recognition that workers draw more explicitly on their practice wisdom, as well as values and legal parameters, than on theory or research (Chui & Wilson 2006, p. 3). Gambrill (1999, p. 348), however, cautions against the assumption that practice wisdom is necessarily a good thing: 'Experience does not necessarily result in improved performance. In fact, it may have the opposite effect. Experience does not offer systematic data about what works with what clients and what problems.'

The crucial distinction is in relation to practice wisdom, as distinct from practice experience. One of the challenges in beginning practice is, of course, that there is often little practice base from which to draw. Every encounter is a major learning experience.

■ The development of practice wisdom is explored further in Chapter 4.

How do we bring together these various knowledge bases and integrate them into a perspective or approach for practice? One of the ways is to think about a multidimensional approach (Harms 2005; Hutchison 2003), which has emerged from an ecological or ecosystemic perspective (Germain & Bloom 1999).

A multidimensional approach

Each of the knowledge sources described so far provides a useful guide for practice. The challenge is to hold all of them together in a coherent way to be able to practice with clients. The difficulty with many of the more overarching practice approaches is that they position the problem management entirely with the individual. Human service workers are often working at the interface of individual problem management and the environmental origins or contributors to these problems. Social work and the human services, therefore, take one step further to listen to, assess and effect change within the outer-world issues, not just the inner-world dimensions. For this reason, human service work, and social work in particular, has drawn on ecological (Bronfenbrenner 1979; Germain 1991) or multidimensional understandings of the person in their environment.

A multidimensional approach incorporates an understanding of the inner- and outer-world dimensions of a person (Harms 2005; Hutchison 2003). Some key themes of a multidimensional approach are now described (Harms 2005).

Focus on practice: a multidimensional approach

Theme 1: an individual's inner world is multidimensional

Each person can be thought of as having unique inner-world dimensions. Broadly speaking, these dimensions are biological, psychological and spiritual in nature.

Theme 2: the outer world or context in which individuals live is multidimensional

Each of these inner-world dimensions of a person in turn influences, and is influenced by, the dimensions of the outer world—the physical, social, structural and cultural contexts that shape daily experience.

Theme 3: time is multidimensional

Five key dimensions of time—biological, biographical, historical/social, cyclical and future time—influence human behaviour and experience.

Theme 4: human experience is multidimensional

Human experience is a combination of an individual's unique developmental trajectory and unique life events. An understanding of both the more normative tasks of development and the non-normative tasks provides a more holistic understanding of a person's adaptive capacities and resources.

Theme 5: adaptation is multidimensional

Just as the causes of adversity are multidimensional, so, too, are the consequences—an understanding of the consequences of adversity for individuals, families and communities needs to incorporate the possibilities of adaptation and maladaptation. This involves understanding notions of risk and protective factors, and notions of vulnerability and resilience. It also involves acknowledging who is making the assessment of adaptation.

Theme 6: attempts to theorise human development and adaptation should be multidimensional

Human experience, behaviour and adaptation can all be understood from multiple theoretical dimensions—theories of the inner world, theories of the outer world and those that attempt to bridge the two. Rather than this seeming as if human service professionals do not have a firm theoretical base from which to work, to the contrary, a multidimensional approach acknowledges that there are many ways of understanding human experience. The task is to discern how we come to reach certain understandings and to work towards as good a fit between the identified issues and the possible human service responses.

Theme 7: human service responses must be multidimensional

Responses by human service professionals must be multidimensional, including practices, programs and policies that incorporate prevention, intervention and postvention strategies.

The relationships between these various dimensions are illustrated in Figure 3.2, showing the reciprocal nature of the interactions between the various dimensions. By focusing on the relationships between all these dimensions, both the intangible (relationship-centred interactions) and the tangible (entity-centred person and environment targets such as experiences of poverty or violence) can be addressed (Harms 2005; Ramsay 2003).

The dimensions that are critical in the assessment and listening process are, first, the inner-world dimensions—the biological, psychological (thoughts and feelings) and spiritual dimensions. In Jacinta's situation, this could mean asking the following questions:

1 What biological dimensions are influencing the current situation?
2 What psychological dimensions are important—feelings, thoughts, other?
3 What role does a spiritual dimension play in this person's life?

Each one of us has a subjective experience of this inner-world dimension. That is, we are the only one who knows what it is like to be us, to feel and

Figure 3.2 A multidimensional approach

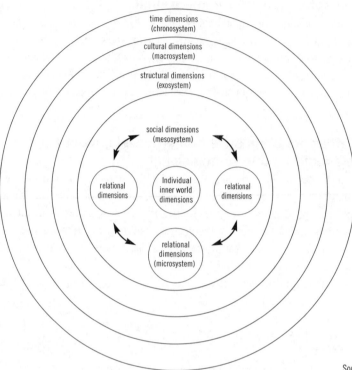

Source: Harms (2005, p. 9).

experience our world. This unique identity that each one of us forms is comprised of our experience both past and present and our contexts, including past, present and future. Our social and cultural identity is as important in determining this as our psychological identity.

Second, the outer-world dimensions—the relational, social, structural and cultural dimensions—require consideration. In Jacinta's situation, this could mean asking:

1 What relationships is the person involved in and what is the influence of these relationships?
2 How do these relationships interact as a social network, if at all?
3 What are the wider structural influences on a person's experience?
4 What are the cultural influences?

There are very strong links here with what Thompson (2003b) and others (Mullaly 2002) term the PCS model, which takes into account the personal, cultural and structural dimensions of any given situation. One of the limitations with the PCS model is the tendency to underemphasise the relational and social dimensions of any given situation. Giving unique shape to all Jacinta's experiences, for example, are individual, family and group issues of identity (Miller, Donner & Fraser 2004). That is, the unique influences of gender, class, culture and sexual orientation are understood to influence identity, and to influence the experience of problems of social identity.

This multidimensional assessment and intervention process is mirrored in the Australian Association of Social Work's *Practice Standards* (2003, p. 9), under Standard 1.4, reproduced in the box below.

The other dimension that has more recently been included in understanding a client's situation is the dimension of the worker themselves. This is in

Focus on practice: assessment and intervention

The social work assessment and the intervention taken is appropriate to the client's situation, in keeping with ethical and legislative requirements and directed towards appropriate outcomes reached in agreement with the client wherever possible.

Indicators

- Relevant information is gathered regarding the client situation.
- The client situation is assessed including identification of relevant:
  - physical factors such as health and well-being, addiction
  - social factors including family, significant relationships, social contacts and supports, experience of discrimination and oppression and community involvement
  - psychological factors, including developmental and life span factors, significant life events, grief and loss, exposure to violence, abuse or neglect
  - environmental factors, including education, employment, finances, accommodation and other services with which the client is in contact
  - legal, education, health, employment and social security systems which impact on or with which the client is involved
  - personal and other resources that might be drawn on in the situation.
- The nature and level of risk for the client, the social worker and others is assessed, and appropriate intervention is taken in relation to the level of risk.
- The client's understanding of the situation and their strengths to deal with it are assessed.
- The social worker acknowledges and respects the strengths and capacities of the client in the mutual development of the assessment and plan.
- Appropriate social work knowledge and theory is identified as a basis for offering a social work service.
- Likely or possible outcomes of the service/s offered are identified, discussed with the client and agreed to as far as possible.
- Legislative and organisational requirements and considerations are identified and explained to the client.
- As appropriate, relevant others are involved in, or advised of, the proposed plan.

recognition that the client's story is constructed in the context of what the worker brings to the relationship, too. When you tell a story, the audience influences how you tell it, what you tell and what you emphasise or omit in that co-creation. Thus, your inner- and outer-world dimensions are important considerations in any client–worker interaction.

Chapter summary

In this chapter, we have explored the ways in which paradigms, theories, factual knowledge and practice wisdom integrate to form a coherent practice base. We looked at three broad paradigms before looking at the various forms of theoretical and factual knowledge required for practice. We then considered a multidimensional approach as one way in which these many aspects of your client's world and your own could be more comprehensively understood.

Reflective practice questions

1 What have you learnt about:
   • the importance of understanding paradigms or worldviews that inform practice?
   • the knowledge bases of practice?
   • the importance of practice wisdom?
   • the strengths and limitations of the theoretical approaches that were presented?
2 Which paradigm would you locate yourself within as a practitioner?
3 What is it about this paradigm that attracts you to it?
4 Which of the five theoretical approaches appeals to you most and why?

Key references

Fook, J. (2002). *Social work: Critical theory and practice*. Thousand Oaks: Sage.
Germain, C. & Bloom, M. (1999). *Human behavior in the social environment: An ecological view*. New York: Columbia University Press.
Harms, L. (2005). *Understanding human development: A multidimensional approach*. South Melbourne: Oxford University Press.
Healy, K. (2005). *Social work theories in context: Creating frameworks for practice*. Basingstoke: Palgrave Macmillan.

Additional resources

Australian Bureau of Statistics: www.abs.gov.au.
Australian Institute of Family Studies: www.aifs.gov.au.
Australian Institute of Health and Welfare: www.aihw.gov.au.
Campbell Collaboration: www.campbellcollaboration.org.
Cochrane Collaboration: The Australasian Centre: www.cochrane.org.au.
National Health and Medical Research Council: www.nhmrc.gov.au.
Social Care Institute for Excellence: www.scie.org.uk.

PART 2

Basic
Skills:
Forming the Relationship

In this second part of the book, we focus on understanding yourself in the role of worker, your context and the very specific microskills used in communication and interviewing processes.

Chapter 4 explores why we need to critically reflect on our own communication style and experiences. In human service work, the worker is the key 'tool' in the process. Thus, your 'use of self', and identifying the purpose and context of work with individuals, families or communities, are key themes of the discussion.

Chapter 5 focuses on the essential preparatory work in relation to your self-care and professional development. Supervision, debriefing and critical self-reflection are introduced as important maintenance strategies given the ongoing challenges of human service work. We explore this as part of thinking about *forming* the relationship, rather than considering it in later sections of the book. This is because your own self-care is such a vital part of your practice that it needs to be an early part of your skill development, not an afterthought.

Chapter 6 moves into the beginning stage of directly forming a relationship with your clients. It examines how a good engagement and rapport with clients can be built.

continues

We also consider issues of confidentiality and your use of self-disclosure as important influences in this formation stage.

Part 1—Framing the relationship:

- the purpose of human service work
- your value base
- your theoretical and factual knowledge.

Part 2—Forming the relationship:

- your use of self
- your organisational context
- your ongoing support and professional development needs
- meeting the people involved
- opening the communication
- actively listening
- listening empathically
- using self-disclosure.

Preparing for Practice

- Understand why the 'use of self' is an important concept.
- Understand the concept of empathy.
- Review the dimensions of your workplace that influence practice.
- Analyse how your practice links with your organisational context.

Why the 'use of self' is an important concept for workers

In earlier chapters, we have looked at values, and theoretical and factual knowledge bases as key determinants of your practice. This chapter focuses on another critical factor: you. This is an essential difference compared with many other jobs where the worker may be one important part of the matrix, but other technical or mechanical interventions are also involved. The ways you apply yourself in your practice will fundamentally affect what happens.

A discriminating use of self is central to all relationships. Think of how you interact differently with each of your friends. Most people have a wide range of friends, with very diverse backgrounds and qualities. Compare how you interact with your friends as distinct from someone you have just met. You might be wary and self-censoring with the unfamiliar person until you have established a stronger connection. This is your use of self in action. Another way of thinking about this 'use of self' is how you apply your

social intelligence and **emotional intelligence** in relationships with others (Goleman 2005, 2006). We will also expand this to think about your spiritual and physical use of self.

Given that good relationships are core to effective practice, we need to think about what social rules come into play. Social rules exist in all communication interactions, varying according to the context in which we are functioning. As Adams, Dominelli and Payne (2005, p. 15) highlight, the assumption underpinning much of the discussion about practice is that social workers and other human service workers:

> … must form good relationships with service users for productive work to be done. This is fine as long as we recognize that the most productive social work relationship may not have much in common with other relationships such as those with work colleagues, friends and family. In these, the priority may be to maintain good relationships, and, perhaps, intimacy.

In a professional relationship, your **purpose**, boundaries and behaviour can be very different from your personal relationships. This shift to a sense of a professional use of self is challenging. It is a contentious issue within the human service field. For many students, it feels like giving up important personal traits to become someone else. This is not the aim of adopting a professional use of self at all. As Shulman (1999, p. 26) notes:

> … when workers or students ask me, 'Should I be professional or should I be myself?', I reply that the dualism implied in the question does not exist. They must be themselves if they are going to be professional.

Integrating your personal and professional skills is what becoming a worker is about. Decisions on a daily basis emerge, however, as to how you will interact. As Shulman notes, some presentations of the ideal worker are as 'an objective, clinical, detached and knowledgeable professional' (1999, p. 161), while others emphasise the qualities of closeness, flexibility and keeping in touch (Ribner & Knei-Paz 2002). Others see the ideal worker as fitting along a continuum of qualities, depending upon the circumstances (Green, Gregory & Mason 2006).

This notion of the 'use of self' emphasises that decisions are made—choices about conduct, about priorities and about responses. The term 'use of self' can therefore refer to the direct use of our own personal 'material' in terms of feelings, views and experiences, as the content in the conversation. Or it can refer to our more global understanding of how we are central in the client–worker conversation and can make conscious decisions as to how to act in each context. The 'use of self' concept acknowledges that the worker is a critical influence in both the process and content of any interaction. We make choices about how we will be in this particular interaction with this particular person at this particular time. We make the shifts in our interactions and communication skills as a result.

Focus on practice: an example of learning to use 'self' differently

In the early weeks of communication skills classes, students often express feeling overwhelmed by the client's story. How do you listen to it and remember all the details? What do you do to make some sense of it?

What they also find is that they have often 'solved' the situation they are hearing about in a role-play situation within about three to five minutes of discussion. They are engaging with the person in a role-play to 'solve' the situation rather than engaging with the person to listen to their story. The classes provide an opportunity to move towards becoming a listener rather than a solver. Finding solutions together is part of that collaborative work.

How you relate with someone varies. Like everyday relationships, we have expectations and experiences of interactions. Relationships are, however, not static or passive encounters. Your use of self changes over time. It may be about getting to know a person and moving into a more established, trusting way of relating. As a relationship develops, different strategies are used to continue the work of change and support.

Some authors emphasise the use of self as more important in the later phases of work than earlier on. For example, Hepworth, Rooney and Larsen (2002, p. 43) state: 'As helping relationships become strong during the implementation and goal attainment phase, social workers increasingly use themselves as tools to facilitate growth and accomplishment.' Good engagement, however, in an initial encounter, relies also on a conscious and active use of self as much as in later interactions.

What we are doing here, therefore, is not only thinking about the client's world from a multidimensional perspective. Your use of self can be thought about as a biopsychosocial-spiritual process. In this sense, you reflect on your practice taking into account all these dimensions—how you use yourself psychologically or emotionally, socially, spiritually and physically in an encounter. You apply yourself differently, according to the purpose of the communication. Each of these dimensions is now briefly considered.

> ▣ In Chapter 12, we explore the skills of challenging. In these instances, your engagement needs to be high so that you can present other ways of thinking or behaving within the context of a supportive relationship.

> ▣ In the next chapter, we will look at the notion of purpose in detail.

Your emotional use of self

What are the differences between the client's and the worker's emotional reactions to the circumstances and what should be the differences? How does your emotional self engage in the work you are doing? Consider the following practice example.

Focus on practice

In one of my hospital student placement experiences, another student on placement and her supervisor witnessed the horrific physical wounds of a patient's very recent surgery. The student screamed when she saw the wounds, not having witnessed anything like it before. It was her natural reaction to what she saw.

In many ways, this initial reaction was an authentic human reaction to the patient's injury. The injury, however, was not the focus of the intervention. The client was the focus of the intervention and the reaction was certainly not helpful to them in this situation. It reinforced, instead, their own horror and distress over their physical predicament.

In a sense, this is an extreme example. It highlights the dilemma, though, as to how we emotionally respond in interactions, particularly when we have an overwhelmingly strong response. While Hepworth, Rooney and Larsen (2002, p. 43) state that 'relating spontaneously and appropriately disclosing one's feelings, views, and experiences provide for clients an encounter with an open and authentic human being', where the boundaries lie, in practice, around an appropriately authentic response is not always clear. Learning to manage any immediate responses, and remain client-focused, is a critical component in your professional development. This is not about being distant or inauthentic; it is about remaining focused on the client's experience of their world rather than our own.

Emotional engagement is a key dimension of rapport building. A client and a worker, Christine Simpson and John Merrick respectively, shared their story in a newspaper's *Two of Us* column (Stansfield 2006, p. 16). In that story, Christine, whose daughter had been murdered, said of her work with grief counsellor John: 'I know there are all these theories about professionals not getting emotionally involved with their clients, but I ask how can you truly help if you're not emotionally connected?' She then said: 'He never tried to push me in any particular direction; he just walked with me wherever I was going, for as long as I needed him. His support is one of the reasons I am still here today.'

The notion of 'walking with' that Christine refers to captures the purpose of **empathy**. Empathy refers to the 'power of mentally identifying oneself with (and so fully comprehending) a person or object of contemplation' (Brown 1993, p. 808). Empathy is an active skill, and is about 'entering imaginatively into the inner life of someone else' (Kadushin 1972, p. 52). This imaginative engagement is not about a psychological process only. As Kadushin (1972, p. 52) continues, empathic 'responses have an "I am with you" quality, fitting in with the client's meaning and mood'.

A grieving mother, from a consumer perspective (Wolterstorff 1987, cited in Elkhuizen, Kelleher, Gibson & Attoe 2006, pp. 281–2), talks about what kind of understanding she wants from those around her:

What I need to hear from you is that you recognize how painful it is. I need to hear from you that you are with me in my desperation. To comfort me, you have to come close. Come sit beside me on my mourning bench.

Empathy has many dimensions. It can be seen as a skill, a value or even an outcome of an encounter. It is considered by many to be the 'glue' of client–worker relationships; the quality that enables advanced insight and work in hearing the story behind the story and the social empathy.

The capacity for empathy is a skill of affect regulation (Schore 1994) in that we mirror a positive attunement to the emotional experience of the client (Koprowska 2005) and a trait associated with a secure attachment style (Bowlby 1984). The argument is that if we have a capacity to monitor our own emotional reactions, and to be secure in our sense of who we are, we are more able to see others where they are at and appreciate their position (Schore 2005; Bandura, Caprara, Barbaranelli, Gerbino & Pastorelli 2003). This is seen to be a process of 'goal corrected empathic attunement' (Koprowska 2005, p. 48).

Empathy can be seen, therefore, as an outcome of the genuineness, warmth and unconditional positive regard a worker experiences with their client (Koprowska 2005). More than this, empathy is the totality of connection within a relationship, rather than being about mere reflecting of feeling: '"Reflection of feeling" can be taught as a cognitive skill … Genuine sensitive empathy, with all its intensity and personal involvement, cannot be so taught' (Rogers 1987, p. 39). Brink (1987, p. 33) interprets Rogers' concepts of empathy as a:

> … complex cluster of *abilities* (keen awareness and sensitivity), *attitudes* (non-judgemental, open, respectful, flexible, confident, subtle, gentle, caring, willing to articulate the not-yet-spoken, and to be wrong) as well as *skill* in communicating.

Another way of thinking about being empathic is to see it as responding to 'what it meant for a human being to have fallen into that condition rather than to what it felt like' (Gaita 1999, p. xix). This emphasises that empathy is about recognition of the worth and dignity of a human being in a particular predicament.

■ Remember the discussion of respect and authenticity in Chapter 2.

Empathy can be conveyed through an attentive presence and attunement with the client. The client needs to hear that you have heard their situation—that is, empathy must be conveyed verbally as well as non-verbally. This is what Egan (2007, p. 102) refers to as **empathic highlights**. The 'formula' for this active response is:

■ This use of paraphrasing to convey empathy is discussed further in Chapter 8.

You feel … *[insert emotion]* because … *[insert event, behaviour or condition]*

Using the formula, an example of an empathic statement is:

You feel confused because what you thought was going on actually turned out to be quite different.

A lot of 'bad press' for workers comes from the formulaic use of these statements. We rarely use such formulaic statements in practice. What the formula helps us to do is to think differently from how we do in a 'chat' with friends. Whereas with friends, we are likely to agree with them, or join with them in some way, this formula keeps us focused on a different way of listening and responding to the client. A different purpose is maintained in listening for the thoughts, feelings and behaviours, and the connections between these three and the structural and cultural environment. Advanced empathy (Egan 2007) refers to the skill of being able to hear and convey the underlying or unspoken meanings of a client's story.

Karen highlights an example from one of her classes, in which the issue of empathy became a focus.

Focus on practice: what does the client want you to hear?

An interesting opportunity arises in teaching counselling skills when student participants are required to present and re-present 'real but not current' issues for discussion in a practical classroom, to enable to development of counselling skills. The opportunity afforded by the 'client' experiencing these different directions in questioning and giving feedback subsequently can be very informative, as the following demonstrates.

One such matter raised by a student involved having been witness to an injured, possibly stabbed, person while awaiting public transport. Her description of the situation encompassed a range of elements and strong emotions:

- shock at the unexpected and traumatic event
- fear in not knowing what had happened, and of the possible whereabouts of a perpetrator
- anger and frustration about the lack of consideration by the many bystanders
- guilt herself at not being able to help the injured person
- worry that her being immobilised by the event would happen in an even more serious situation at some other time.

A number of the student counsellors concentrated on the traumatic event and became engrossed in the detail of the event; however, the one whose impact was greatest was the one who made a point of listening to the meaning of the issue for the 'client' and recognising her sense of helplessness and guilt at her role in the situation. Furthermore, by exploring this in detail, they were able to challenge the client's view (a blind spot) that she had been ineffectual by drawing out her actions, which, indeed, had involved calling an ambulance and staying with the injured person to reassure them until help arrived, in effect being extremely helpful. Subsequent feedback from the student revealed frustration at the efforts by some to explore the sensational details, and how valuable it had been when the worker listened to the bit that mattered most to her.

Empathy is about striking the right balance of focus between the worker and client. As the above example shows, focusing too much on the detail in this instance led to the client not feeling as if their experience had been understood. Similarly, focusing too sympathetically can create distance.

Sympathy is often contrasted with empathy. Egan (2007, p. 118) states: 'Sympathy denotes agreement, whereas empathy denotes understanding.' It is seen as more of a joining with or colluding with the client as distinct from being able to understand their world and feelings. Thus, Egan (2007, p. 118) suggests: 'An expression of sympathy has much more in common with pity, compassion, commiseration, and condolence than with empathic understanding. Although these are fully human traits, they are not particularly useful in counseling.' Two arguments for not using sympathy are that, first, your response could be wrong and therefore unhelpful. For example:

Client: I've just left my partner of five years.

Worker: I'm so sorry to hear that.

Client: Oh, no, no, it's such a good thing. It's not that I'm worried about …

In this instance, the sympathetic response has not helped in any particular way, primarily because an assumption was made about the experience rather than an exploration of it. Second, if you agree and support a particular emotion and affirm this, you may find this is something you want to be challenging at some point later in the process, rather than agreeing with how they are. Again, this highlights some of the **differential use of self**—what you might say to family and friends may be different from your response with your clients, because your role has a different purpose.

This negative view of sympathy is questioned, however. Trevithick and others call for recognition of the importance of sympathy, particularly early on in the relationship during the early phases of engagement.

■ Reflective practice exercise

1   Reflect on a conversation or encounter with another person, not necessarily in the context of a formal interview situation, where you have experienced what you would regard to be empathic communication.
2   What were the essential qualities, attitudes and skills that you would see as critical in this experience?

Empathy is predominantly perceived to be a positive skill. A word of caution is raised, however, in relation to working with involuntary clients. Trotter (2006, p. 26) cites a 1979 study, which found that the use of empathy with incarcerated clients was not always beneficial. Empathy in these instances was found to be counterproductive, as these supportive reflections of feeling gave 'some kind of subtle permission or sanction for continuing that behaviour with the result that further offending occurred' (Andrews, Keissling, Russell & Grant 1979, cited in Trotter 2006, p. 26). This highlights that the usefulness of even one of the most consistently identified positive skills in communication still depends upon the context in which it is used.

Empathy, as distinct from intimacy or sympathy, is about understanding and supporting someone emotionally, but not being immersed in the same feelings and reactions personally. Rogers (1980, p. 137) infamously defined empathy as being about:

> ... entering the private perceptual world of the other and becoming thoroughly at home in it. It involves being sensitive, moment by moment, to the changing felt meanings which flow in this other person ... It means temporarily living in the other's life, moving about in it delicately without making judgments.

Being immersed in similar feelings can often happen, and this is where self-awareness and self-reflection are useful skills. For example, when talking with someone who is depressed, you can find that you, too, can become more sombre in your tone and physical presence. You can begin to mirror their use of self, rather than remain aware of what the client needs in the interaction. In a community health centre context, Karen identifies how she came to manage that in her work with Mark.

Focus on practice: dealing with the unbearable

Sometimes a person's pain is so extreme that one must be affected. A man in his 30s with suicidal concerns attended a first interview. His story related to the recent traumatic event of watching as his small daughter ran across the road, was hit by a car and dragged a long distance. She had suffered multiple injuries including some brain damage, and he was wracked with guilt as well as the trauma of witnessing the terrible event. He had left his family and the state feeling bereft and hopeless.

The telling of his story, in all its graphic detail, together with his projection of his own feelings, was a moving and deeply sad experience, and my way of coping was to ask myself: 'What does Mark need from me in telling me this today?' At such a time, what he needed from me was to be able to bear to hear his pain, in all its detail, without providing either blame or reassurance. By asking myself the question I was able to contain my own feelings, not without a tear, but to the extent that he could feel allowed to move away from believing that he had no other choice than suicide.

1 What is your immediate reaction to this story and why?
2 What do you think could emerge as issues for you personally in working with someone in Mark's situation?

Your social and practical use of self

Workers also vary in the degree to which they are practically involved in situations—with and for clients. Sometimes attending to the practical needs, either directly or indirectly, can make an enormous difference—for example, making phone calls on behalf of someone or providing transport. These actions can bring about sheer relief when these basic human needs are not being met otherwise. Maslow's hierarchy of needs is a useful reminder of the importance of meeting basic human survival needs before other growth needs such as self-actualisation and self-transcendence can be realised.

Focus on practice: an adapted version of Maslow's hierarchy of needs

Motivational need	A person at this level
Self-transcendence	Seeks to further a cause beyond the self
Self-actualisation	Seeks fulfilment of personal potential
Esteem needs	Seeks esteem through achievement
Belongingness and love needs	Seeks group affiliation
Safety needs	Seeks security through law and order
Physiological (survival) needs	Seeks the basic necessities of life

Source: Koltko-Rivera (2006, p. 303).

Social support, whether it is emotional, instrumental or practical, is consistently identified as a key protective factor (Harms 2005). Sometimes, as a worker, the direct provision of this social support is vital. At other times, it is more important to link someone in with other social support networks for these needs to be met.

Your response as a worker will be determined in part by your views of empowerment and the place of independence, interdependence and dependence. Some workers view these opportunities to provide support as critical at times when a client may not have the resources, either practically or emotionally, to attend to such issues. Others view these as the vehicle by which some of the other more expressive or therapeutic processes and tasks can be undertaken. Others see these practical tasks as being as essential in the change process as the emotional tasks; indeed, possibly more important if the external environment is seen to be the cause of issues, not the inner world of the client. Trotter (2006, p. 8) reflects on his experience in two different organisations and the rationales given for responding differently. In one organisation:

... the culture was to see clients as soon as possible even if they arrived without an appointment. This was viewed as respectful. In another organisation the culture was to expect clients to make an appointment for another time. This was viewed as helping clients to be responsible.

Some authors have been highly critical in recent years of the move away from some of the earlier core supportive task agendas of social work (Specht & Courteney 1994; Ife 2001). Ife (2001), for example, urges social workers to redefine their role as rights workers rather than that of needs assessors. He maintains that a much clearer basis for action emerges when human rights form the basis of action, not needs.

Your spiritual use of self

The spiritual dimension is less frequently discussed as a way in which the worker interacts with their clients, in part because of the diverse ways in which it is both experienced and defined. Increasingly, however, clients are identifying this as an important yet neglected dimension of human service practice (Canda & Furman 1999; Lindsay 2002). What would your response be to the following situation, for example, and how would you answer the questions?

Focus on practice: considering the spiritual dimension

A client is telling you about their strong connection with spirituality, and the ways in which they know this connection has helped them overcome so many difficulties. As a way of tapping into your beliefs about the spiritual dimension in practice:

1 What is your reaction to this very brief scenario?
2 What do you think you would want to know more about?
3 Do you think you would ask more questions?
4 In what ways do you think your reaction would influence your client's experience?

■ A psychodynamic approach looks at this use of self through the terms intersubjectivity and other notions such as countertransference (see Chapter 12). A narrative approach views the worker as a co-creator of the story (see Chapter 13).

These questions about the **biopsychosocial–spiritual dimensions** of your use of self are raised to encourage you to think about your responses and interactions with clients. The purpose is not to create inauthentic responses, but conscious, helpful, deliberate and client-focused responses. These qualities play out in all relationships; they are not particular to a helping relationship. They need to be used quite discerningly, however, in different communication, counselling and interviewing contexts.

It is important to reflect on why your use of self varies across these contexts. The skills and qualities that clients have identified as being beneficial are also important to remember as part of this reflection, as discussed in Chapter 3.

■ Reflective practice questions

Two key questions may help you to focus on your use of self at a particular time:

1   What am I saying, doing and feeling in this encounter and how should I respond?
2   What is the most empowering response for the client at this point in time, given the circumstances?

Your physical use of self

Many dimensions of your non-verbal skills, and therefore your physical use of self, were explored in Chapter 2. This discussion raises two further issues—touch and availability.

Ethical guidelines across all professions prohibit sexual contact with clients, given the inherent inequalities in power and control within client–worker relationships. In this respect, professional standards have never been as articulated as they currently are in relation to physical boundaries. Yet a challenge emerges in that, theoretically, the emphasis on authentic human intersubjectivity has never been as strongly proposed, which leaves a worker wondering about some of the more subtle forms of physical interaction that commonly typify human relationships. For example, physical contact occurs at points of greeting or separation, through handshakes or hugs. Workers find themselves in situations where someone may spontaneously embrace them. To reject this embrace could be personally and culturally inappropriate.

■ As discussed in Chapter 2, the question of whether touch should ever be used in practice, is a complex one.

Your physical use of self also relates to your physical presence and availability. Punctuality and availability have been identified by clients in many studies as important issues of respect and relationship. If it is not possible to be punctual and available because of other work demands, conveying this to the client is a way of relating respectfully and genuinely.

Your use of self in context

The agency in which you work will set the agenda for much of the work you do. Agencies reflect the wider policy context in which they are established, and the subsequent resources that are provided for service delivery. Agencies make decisions about service delivery models. They develop a workplace culture, based on its employees and the work that is undertaken. These are all dimensions of your **organisational context**.

At an everyday level, the physical and the service system environmental dimensions of an agency will influence the experience for both you and your clients. These dimensions give strong messages about the underlying values of the work and of the client–worker relationship.

An agency may have unique safety issues, relating to health, violence or location. For example, in Hong Kong, at the time of writing this book, all hospital workers, irrespective of profession, were required to dress in surgical 'scrubs' and not wear any civilian clothing because of the ongoing threat of SARS and bird flu epidemics, both to hospital workers and the wider community. In this context, clients cannot even recognise their worker when they are gowned and masked in the intensive care environment. In organisations providing refuge from domestic violence, threats of violence can be common, requiring different levels of security and confidentiality. International services in zones of war or disaster clearly face unique physical and interpersonal risks. These environments will influence the precautions you need to take in your practice.

The geographical location of the organisation, whether rural, remote or urban, can present other challenges in the provision of accessible services for clients. Not only is transport accessibility an issue, but accessibility also can be influenced because of the visibility of individuals accessing a service. For example, the stigma associated with being seen to access an HIV/AIDS or domestic violence service can become a serious block to service use. In rural communities, these difficulties can be amplified because of the denser networks and reduced opportunity for anonymity (Green 2003; Taylor 2004). Many people in these instances do not access services. Workers in these agencies give careful consideration to how services can be provided sensitively and anonymously (Bramwell 2005). Another newer form of service delivery is the internet, for the provision of information and online support through group and individual connections that do not then involve the same levels of stigma.

Therefore, the actual interview or work setting (Kadushin & Kadushin 1997; Weeks 2004) is important to consider. You may work in a structured setting, with interviews taking place in interview rooms, where privacy and comfort can be assured. Or you may be talking in corridors, at the bedside, outdoors, or in people's homes or their community. In all of these situations, being mindful of who else can and should hear what is going on is important.

Agencies vary in the resources they have to provide adequate talking spaces. Some agencies are more like comfortable homes where family and community centred work can take place. Others are more formal and even sterile environments, where clients can be left feeling disempowered and alienated. We can become quickly immune to the nature of the physical environment of the organisation and no longer see how it may impact upon the client experience.

Service delivery issues are also major influences on the client–worker relationship. Some considerations are whether services are offered on a short-term or long-term basis, whether there are limitations on the number and nature of contacts with people, and whether services are focused on crisis intervention or longer-term treatment. Some other considerations that will influence your relationship and client work are:

- What client group does your agency aim to reach?
- How does the agency, as well as specific workers, understand its clients'

issues—for example, are they seen to be family issues, psychological issues or issues arising from the structural context?

- What is the workplace culture? That is, what are the written and unwritten rules in relation to worker practice?
- How culturally diverse and/or sensitive are the agency and its workers?
- Does the agency primarily work with individuals, or with families or communities?
- What staffing levels are available within the agency to meet the demands?
- What are the expectations of client caseloads for each worker?
- What budgetary restrictions influence the work you can do (Ribner & Knei-Paz 2002, p. 386)?
- Are clients voluntary or involuntary users of the agency's services?
- How does a client access or connect with your service—through a referral, a drop-in duty system or a waiting list process?
- How available are you as a worker?
- How structured is your time with clients?
- How private and uninterrupted is your work with clients?

Using the questions above, think how differently you would work if you were located in each of the following three settings.

Focus on practice: the impact of agency context

Using the questions above, think about the impact of each of these three agency contexts on your practice:

1 Remote mental health centre
You work in a remote area mental health service. While you are part of a state-wide health service, you work with a small multidisciplinary team to deliver assessment and treatment services to people in their own communities. This involves extensive travel across your state, often for weeks at a time.

2 Rural CASA
You work in a rural Centre Against Sexual Assault. Your agency offers emergency or crisis care, counselling and support for victim/survivors of sexual assault. You are also involved in research projects, resource development and community education and training. You work with a small team of counsellor/advocates who are committed to feminist understandings of violence and recovery.

3 Aged care and hospital
You work in a large, outer-suburban public hospital that provides specialist assessment, rehabilitation, advisory and psychiatric services to older and disabled people. You are involved in assessments and discharge planning, as well as individual patient and family support throughout the time of an admission. You work within a large multidisciplinary team.

In the following two vignettes, Jane provides an insight into how many of the agency issues described above influence work in a hospital parent bereavement group. The group Jane describes is a co-led group, enabling the two workers to support the many tasks and processes involved in such a program. Clients and workers alike can be quite unprotected from some of the agency activities and disruptions, outlined above. For example, Jane recounts the impact of workplace interruptions on her work with one particular mother.

Focus on practice: coping with interruptions

Despite the best preparations and intentions in our agency, the phone can interrupt times with parents. Some may say don't answer it. Yet long ringing can be very disruptive, ignoring a call could give the message we don't respond to calls here and answering even very briefly can imply someone else is more important than you! In any response the worker makes, they have to preserve confidentiality. Additionally, if a call comes through, there is always the possibility (as has happened) that there is an emergency in the worker's own family.

During an interview with a mother who was grieving for her baby daughter, her only child who died within days of her birth, the phone rang and rang. I apologised to the parent, and took the call. I asked our administration worker if she could take a message, saying, 'I'm with someone, a client' [not a term I usually say], then, looking directly at her, I said, 'I'm with a mother'. From the look on the mother's face these words were probably the most meaningful in the appointment. Our choice of language is so important yet so loaded.

To resume a conversation after such a discussion is difficult; it is helpful to try to hold the last words in mind and then to do a brief summary of what had been said so far:

'You were telling me about ...'
'You were saying that ...'

Sometimes this can be hard, especially if the call brings its own issues or tasks to be done, to acknowledge this:

'Sorry, it can be difficult to get back to where we were after being interrupted like that. Where should we pick up/continue?' can restart the conversation.

1 What do you think you would do and say under similar circumstances?

Client interactions impact on the work as well the organisational issues. Jane talks about some of the challenges of beginning on time a session of a bereavement group, given the diversity of arrival times and the continuing organisational interruptions:

Focus on practice: managing interruptions

It is supportive to begin on time, especially as some parents may have come early and may find it excruciating to wait for such a group to start. Before the formal commencement of the group, as refreshments are offered, we give a brief description of the group (some of this recaps what has been sent in the letter). We would also foreshadow who is already in the room and then do a round of introductions.

Sometimes parents may arrive half an hour into the group when the discussion, presentation or experiential process is well under way. This may include those coming for the first time who may feel very unfamiliar with the group. A quick welcoming and accepting response is called for; one that does not distract too much from the group or draw undue attention to them or make them feel awkward. We stand up, move to them and quietly do introductions, write out name tags and ensure there are seats in the circle. We say what has been happening or, if it hasn't been long, 'We've just begun', or 'We haven't been talking for long'. The presenter may also recap what has been going on; however, this cannot be assumed.

Interruptions have come from security opening the door and looking in at us (occasionally then locking us in, giving new meaning to the expression 'closed group'!), and rowdy staff or students in adjoining rooms or someone turning off the lights in the corridor. These are the realities of the situation. Parents have dealt with much more difficult matters, yet these situations can been distracting; once more a brief reference to this can be helpful, sometimes even gentle humour. Sometimes such *outside world* distractions can symbolise what's being or has been said in the group:

'What were we saying about others not seeing you or your grief …'

'Well, that's how others can be …'

'OK we're on our own now …'

'That's what they think …'

'As impossible as it seems, the outside world keeps going on …'

1   What do you think you would do and say in similar circumstances?

The purpose of your agency

Many communication skills texts focus on skills for work that is primarily 'social care' oriented. Your use of self in these instances can be spelt out relatively specifically, in that the primary aims of your work are therapeutic. You may also be engaged in work that is focused on social control or social cure outcomes (Trevithick 2005). This type of work demands that you use different influencing skills. The overarching purpose of your agency and the work you undertake within it is important to articulate and critically review.

The purpose of your work can be thought about at even more micro levels; that is, within the context of individual conversations and interviews. Is the purpose to give bad news, to change difficult behaviour or is it to challenge the breach of an order with a parent? Kadushin (1972) identified three primary purposes influencing the structure and the conducting of interviews, including informational or social study purposes; diagnostic or decision-making purposes; and therapeutic purposes. All three elements can be operating in the one conversational context.

You will draw on different skills depending upon the different purposes of your relationship and the specific communication situation you are working in at any one time. For example, within the medical interview literature, the tasks are mapped out in relation to the doctor's role in the interview, from being patient-centred at the beginning and shifting to a doctor-centredness by the conclusion whereby the assessment and information phase is guided more by the doctor than the patient (Smith et al. 2000). The purpose here is to move towards diagnosis and treatment. In an educational or welfare setting, a student may need support and information about coping strategies, so there may be movement from a supportive listening role towards more of a psycho-educational role within the communication. These examples highlight quite different purposes in a client–worker interaction, and therefore quite different uses of self.

Chapter summary

In this chapter, we have looked at some of the core ways in which you make use of yourself in your practice. We have explored both the ways in which you consciously learn to use this self in practice in different ways—including all your biopsychosocial-spiritual dimensions, depending upon the circumstances. Agency contexts have been identified as crucial influences on this 'use of self', both at the macro level of determining the nature of the work that is undertaken within a particular setting, and at a micro level of the daily structure of interactions with people.

Reflective practice questions

1 What have you learnt from this chapter about:
   • your differential use of self?
   • the importance and potential impact of agency context?
   • defining the purpose of your work?
2 What are some of the unique tensions and questions for you in relation to these issues?

Key references

Goleman, D. (2005). *Emotional intelligence.* New York: Bantam Books.

Goleman, D. (2006). *Social intelligence: The new science of human relationships.* London: Hutchinson.

Green, R., Gregory, R. & Mason, R. (2006). Professional distance and social work: Stretching the elastic? *Australian Social Work, 59*(4), 449–61.

Rogers, C. (1987). Comments on the issue of equality in psychotherapy. *Journal of Humanistic Psychology, 27*(1), 38–9.

Additional resources

The Conflict Resolution Network: www.crnhq.org/twelveskills.html. Empathy skills are overviewed within a twelve-skill conflict strategy.

Daniel Goleman's website (Social and emotional intelligence): www.danielgoleman.info.

5 Sustaining Your Self in Practice

LEARNING GOALS

- Learn about your self-care and professional development strategies.
- Understand the nature of critical reflective practice.
- Review the purposes and tasks of supervision.
- Describe the processes of debriefing and when it is useful.

Self-care and professional development

In human service work, you are working with people who are coping with life's difficulties, challenges and opportunities. The impact will be significant— both across the accumulation of experiences and through single, complex incidents that confront who we are and what we are doing. This chapter explores some of the ways in which you can prepare and sustain yourself for this personally confronting and rewarding work. These issues are dealt with early in this discussion, given how fundamental they are to preparing yourself as a practitioner and sustaining yourself in the longer term.

Focus on practice: 'Protectors need protecting too'

Maria McNamara described her experiences of working within the child protection system:

> Given the unique difficulties of the job, it is possible there is widespread undiag-
> nosed and untreated PTSD [posttraumatic stress disorder] among current and
> former child protection workers. Researchers have theorised that when protective

workers deal with violent families, they are not immune from the violence. Not only are they vulnerable to assaults and abuse, but they can also experience secondary trauma from witnessing the violence and abuse to which children are subjected.

I was abused countless times over the phone and in person, and I was assaulted once during an after-hours call-out. This happened one summer evening while I was questioning a woman about her young children, who were on a protective court order.

Source: McNamara (2006, p. 9).

Good **self-care** skills are essential, right throughout your career. You need to be aware of the risk and protective factors in your work and your workplace. The risk factors or the 'costs' of caring have been understood in a number of ways.

Human service work can lead to what is termed compassion stress (or compassion fatigue) or burnout (Jenaro, Flores & Arias 2007). Burnout arises in relation to chronic workplace stress. It is characterised by 'negative attitudes and feelings toward co-workers and one's job role, as well as feelings of emotional exhaustion' (Jenaro, Flores & Arias 2007, p. 80). These experiences can lead to a pervasive cynicism or a lack of enthusiasm and motivation that can be harmful to both yourself and your clients.

Compassion fatigue (a term that can be used interchangeably with secondary traumatic stress) refers to the experience of 'a sense of helplessness and confusion, and a sense of isolation from supporters' (Figley 1995, p. 12). Unlike burnout, however, compassion fatigue can happen following a single incident. A useful checklist has been developed by Figley (1995) for you to screen for your own levels of compassion fatigue and burnout.

Focus on practice: compassion fatigue self-test

Rate yourself on each of the following questions, using the 1–5 rating scale, where:

1 = rarely/never   4 = often
2 = at times   5 = very often
3 = not sure

	Question	Score
1	I force myself to avoid certain thoughts or feelings that remind me of a frightening experience.	
2	I find myself avoiding certain activities or situations because they remind me of a frightening experience.	
3	I have gaps in my memory about frightening events.	

continues

4	I feel estranged from others.	
5	I have difficulty falling or staying asleep.	
6	I have outbursts of anger or irritability with little provocation.	
7	I startle easily.	
8	While working with a victim, I thought about violence against the perpetrator.	
9	I am a sensitive person.	
10	I have had flashbacks connected to my clients.	
11	I have had first-hand experience with traumatic events in my adult life.	
12	I have had first-hand experience with traumatic events in my childhood.	
13	I have thought that I need to 'work through' a traumatic experience in my life.	
14	I have thought that I need more close friends.	
15	I have thought that there is no one to talk with about highly stressful experiences.	
16	I have concluded that I work too hard for my own good.	
17	I am frightened of things a client has said or done to me.	
18	I experience troubling dreams similar to those of a client of mine.	
19	I have experienced intrusive thoughts of sessions with especially difficult clients.	
20	I have suddenly and involuntarily recalled a frightening experience while working with a client.	
21	I am preoccupied with more than one client.	
22	I am losing sleep over a client's traumatic experiences.	
23	I have thought that I might have been 'infected' by the traumatic stress of my clients.	
24	I remind myself to be less concerned about the well-being of my clients.	
25	I have felt trapped by my work as a social worker.	
26	I have felt a sense of hopelessness associated with working with clients.	
27	I have felt 'on edge' about various things and I attribute this to working with certain clients.	
28	I have wished that I could avoid working with some clients.	
29	I have been in danger working with clients.	
30	I have felt that my clients dislike me personally.	
31	I have felt weak, tired and run down as a result of my work as a social worker.	
32	I have felt depressed as a result of my work as a social worker.	
33	I am unsuccessful at separating work from personal life.	
34	I feel little compassion towards most of my co-workers.	
35	I feel I am working more for the money than for personal fulfilment.	

36	I find it difficult separating my personal life from my work life.	
37	I have a sense of worthlessness/disillusionment/resentment associated with my work.	
38	I have thoughts that I am a 'failure' as a social worker.	
39	I have thoughts that I am not succeeding at achieving my life goals.	
40	I have to deal with bureaucratic, unimportant tasks in my work life.	

When you have completed the survey, you can work out your score by circling these 23 questions: 1–8, 10–13, 17–26 and 29. You then add up the numbers you wrote next to the items for a total compassion fatigue risk score, which is rated as follows:

- You are at extremely low risk if your total score is 26 or less.
- You are at moderate risk if your total score is 31–35.
- You are at high risk with a total score of 36–40 and extremely high risk with a total score of 41 or more.

You then add up the numbers you wrote next to the items not circled to estimate your risk of burnout.

- You are at extremely low risk if your total score is 17–36 or less.
- You are at low risk with a total score of 37–50.
- You are at high risk with a total score of 51–75 and extremely high risk with a score of 76–85.

Other impacts of the work emerge from more acute experiences of distress and trauma, as distinct from the accumulation of stress over time. Certain events in the workplace can lead to experiences of secondary victimisation, **vicarious traumatisation** (Pearlman & Macian 1995) or secondary traumatic stress disorder. As Pearlman and Saakvitne (1995, p. 31) describe:

> … vicarious traumatization refers to the cumulative transformative effect upon the trauma therapist of working with survivors of traumatic life events … it is a process through which the therapist's inner experience is negatively transformed through empathic engagement with clients' trauma material.

The negative transformations include disruptions to your personal frame of reference about self and others in the world; your sense of safety, dependency and trust; your sense of power, esteem and independence; and your capacity for intimacy (Figley 1995; White 2004). Other trauma reactions include 'feelings of emptiness, desolation and despair', or as White (2004, p. 47) describes, it is about becoming 'overwhelmed by a sense of hopelessness and paralysis, and [believing] that there's nothing whatsoever they can do to affect the shape of their life or the shape of events around them'.

Janoff-Bulman (1992) describes this as the shattering of our assumptions—that is, the assumptions we hold that the world is benevolent, the world is meaningful and that the self is worthy.

For workers and clients alike, the goals of trauma work are often summarised as including three tasks: re-establishing safety, experiencing processes of remembrance and mourning, and achieving an eventual reconnection with ordinary life (Herman 1992). Strategies to support these processes are critical. So your self-care skills and strategies are usually about maintenance and prevention functions, but sometimes about intervention; in particular, instances of stress and trauma.

Maintenance functions relate to the ongoing development of knowledge and skills, as well as care of yourself as a person engaged in demanding, interpersonal work. This enables you to continue to develop as a worker and be well supported in that work. Some key strategies workers adopt in relation to this include:

- supervision, which will be discussed extensively in the following section
- formal peer support strategies, which include journal clubs, ongoing practice discussion groups and professional development activities
- informal peer support strategies, such as social clubs and activities
- personal maintenance strategies, such as humour, fitness, sleep, diet, maintaining a good psychological sense of well-being and maintaining a good network of friends outside of the workplace.

Intervention functions relate to the more immediate strategies used at key times of stress or crisis; that is, when something in particular has happened. Some key strategies adopted at these times include supervision and debriefing.

This support as a worker is most typically provided by the agency in which you work. Other support strategies are part of your own personal lifestyle. Self-care strategies are relatively straightforward and typically relate to a biopsychosocial-spiritual balance within a worker's daily life. Making them happen regularly in a preventive way is typically more of the challenge. Getting caught up in the busyness of your work can erode your commitment to these strategies.

One of the ways in which we can bring about an understanding of these issues is to think through in critically reflective or reflexive processes.

Critical self-reflection

Reflecting on your practice is an important skill. Numerous terms are used for this activity—reflection, reflectivity and **reflexivity or critical reflection**, to name a few. Reflectivity can be defined as (Fook 1999, p. 199):

> … the ability to locate oneself in a situation through the recognition of how actions and interpretations, social and cultural background and personal

history, emotional aspects of experience, and personally held assumptions and values influence the situation.

Another term often used in discussions of critical reflection is reflexivity, meaning more of 'a bending back onto a self, [which] can encompass many diverse processes, depending on what manner of connection, or relationship, is accomplishing the bending back' (Steier 1995, p. 63).

Kondrat (1999) provides a useful distinction between three conceptualisations of the self in self-awareness. The first is a simple consciousness, which makes our experience and memory possible. The second is a reflective awareness, which relies on a sense of self who has the experience. The third is a reflexive awareness, which is not about standing back, objectively, but knowing because 'I am on more or less familiar terms with the self' (Kondrat 1999, p. 468). Through a process of reflexive awareness, one of the questions we begin to ask is: 'What do I (we) do in the agency on a day-to-day basis that might contribute to the structuring of unequal outcomes?' (Kondrat 1999, p. 468).

Reflection on and in all dimensions of our practice has a number of key functions. First and foremost, ongoing critical reflection is one way of ensuring good outcomes for clients. As Kondrat (1999, p. 468) states in relation to social workers: 'As individuals and as professionals, social workers' daily interactions with clients and others have consequences for maintaining or altering society's structures.'

Ongoing awareness of these interactions is an essential part of transforming the lived experiences of clients. Second, it enables the impact of the work to be addressed. Human service work often provokes strong physical and emotional responses such as intense sadness and distress, or anger and frustration. Some experiences can be overwhelming and evoke a sense of helplessness or powerlessness.

▓ If we do not maintain an awareness of this possibility, we can perpetuate the very oppressions we are looking to eradicate. Chapter 14 looks at these issues in greater detail.

This work can bring you into contact with violence or extreme poverty, for example, for the first time in your life. For others, it brings up reminders of past and present experiences. This type of work will inevitably have an impact upon you. Its positive impact is the accumulation of practice experience and practice wisdom. Its negative impact can lead to distress, stress, burnout or cynicism.

Critical reflection provides an opportunity to reflect upon these experiences, to integrate them in some way and to develop assessments and interventions that lead to further change. Reflective practice builds the bridge between theory and practice (Payne 2006), but also maintains a focus on change. Schon (1987) highlighted the importance of reflecting not only on what had occurred but learning to reflect *in* the midst of practice to influence the process there and then. A reflective worker can be defined (Thompson 2002, p. 235) as someone:

… who is able to use experience, knowledge and theoretical perspectives to guide and inform practice. However, this does not mean applying ideas in a blanket form, unthinkingly and uncritically, regardless of the circumstances. Reflective practice involves cutting the cloth to suit the specific circumstances, rather than looking for ready-made solutions.

Reflection alone can be an introspective process that may influence our own practice but not influence the outer world in any substantial way. That is, problems in the outer world that lead to inner- and outer-world distress or difficulty for others remain unaltered. Critical self-reflection takes this reflective process one step further:

> Processes of dialogue and self-reflection are important in providing critical understandings of how internalised discourses (particularly those we have internalised ourselves) have created the situation. Processes of dialogue are crucial in reformulating and changing discourses that are relevant across different interest groups (Fook 2000, pp. 131–2).

A number of strategies can be adopted to practice reflection and critical reflexive practice. The first strategy is to complete a social awareness exercise, such as the one proposed by Fook.

Focus on practice: social self-awareness exercise

A multidimensional approach suggests that all dimensions of our experience interact to form a personal and social identity. Reviewing the dimensions of our own experience through a social, structural and cultural analysis can help us understand how various dimensions have shaped our life and our life choices.

Reflect on the impact on your life and ways of being of the following dimensions of your life. Fook (2002) has identified the following dimensions and you might add others:

- relationship status
- occupation
- social class (past and present)
- education
- family type and background
- ethnicity
- nationality
- religion

- membership of groups or subcultures
- gender
- sexual orientation
- health
- age
- particular historical period (past and/or present)
- particular ideologies.

Source: adapted from Fook (2002, pp. 156–7).

This exercise raises crucial questions about what experiences influence us. A further step with this exercise is to ask yourself how we influence more broadly each of these dimensions of our social identity, so that their means of expression and understanding are perpetuated or changed in our wider contexts. This is important in relation to what happens for the individual client, as Sharp (2006, p. 67) notes: 'In other words, if we are not focused on the factors that influence the "what" of who we think we are, we may find ourselves unwittingly imposing that same sense of being on the client.'

This is the essential component of reflexive practice and it raises more questions again about how we then respond. A study that explored working with couples in interfaith relationships, specifically Muslim and Christian relationships (Furlong & Ata 2006, p. 259), highlighted these dilemmas. Workers were aware of the importance of cultural awareness and awareness of difference generally, but also the study highlighted that verbalising it may not be enough:

> As practitioners, we are never neutral and we do not wish to be. Yet, it is naïve to believe that the simple declaration of one's position will always be received as courteous and engaging. Nor is it always the case that such declarations will facilitate the outcome that is desired.

Thus, the first step is about recognising your position, but as Furlong and Ata highlight, other steps are involved. Changing existing power relationships not only happens through becoming aware of the language that is used or declaring a position—it is about developing a change agenda.

Another possibility is to work with these identities very explicitly in a role-play situation, to begin to actively address such meanings and intentions.

Focus on practice: working in triads

Use the earlier social awareness exercise to identify an issue for role-play. For example, it may be about how gender has impacted upon your choice of work or study.

In a role-play situation, one person is assigned the role of interviewer, one the role of client and one the role of observer (coach, advisor).

The observer can participate in a number of ways:

1   They can watch the interview and provide comment at the end as to what they saw happening. This can lead to a critical discussion of what happened, what was intended to happen from both worker and client perspectives, and a way of discussing the implications of the direction of the interview. For example, how was the problem constructed by both the client and the worker? Were there ways in which the interview perpetuated the social discourses for the client and reinforced their oppression rather than redressing it?
2   They can choose to intervene at points in the interview where they think the interviewer could have directed the interview differently. This actively interrupts habits of thinking for the interviewer and can provide useful new insights. It encourages a process of thinking together in action by 'freeze framing' certain choices the interviewer has made and enabling discussion to take place.
3   The interviewer can call on the observer when they feel they are stuck or heading in an unhelpful direction. This relies on the worker recognising those moments and reflecting on new possibilities for action.

continues

The aim of externalising the role of the observer is to develop an awareness of thinking outside your practice. Ultimately, the goal is to internalise this process so that you can have this 'dialogue' with yourself in your future practice. This skill is referred to as being a participant–observer in your practice—you are simultaneously both participating and observing the conversation.

Another strategy for developing critical self-reflective practice is to undertake a process record. A process record is a systematic, written analysis of an interview, typically in terms of both its content and process. It is usually written in columns, so that the simultaneous moments of a conversation can be illustrated. It usually includes the transcribed (or approximated) content of the conversation, from both the interviewer and the client, and then varying degrees of comment or critique. For example, many process records include a column looking at what the interviewer was thinking or feeling, or what they could have done differently, as well as a column documenting the perceived reactions of the client. Others will include a column in which comments are made about why something was said or not said from a theoretical perspective, in an attempt to bridge both theory and practice. The opportunity for critical reflective practice emerges with another column in which the client–worker relationship can be analysed as to whether it is reflecting, perpetuating or challenging broader structural issues.

■ Reflective practice exercise

Content	What did you think was happening?	What would you do differently?
Worker: 'So you need to find somewhere else to stay tonight? Have you got someone to stay with?'	I thought the client was really needing the housing crisis fixed, and that they didn't want to talk about anything else but this task.	I asked two questions without waiting to hear the answer to the first question. The second question might have seemed a bit accusative.
Client: 'Nah. Nowhere to go tonight. Nowhere to go after what I did last night. Nobody will have me.'	I think the client is more depressed than I'd originally thought. My questions seemed to have reinforced the lack of solutions rather than giving them a chance to talk further about what had happened last night.	Now I felt I needed to understand what had happened last night rather than move too quickly to the solution of housing for tonight.
Worker: 'Can you tell me a bit more about what happened last night?'	I invited the client to talk more about the original issue.	This was where I should have stayed with the story from the start rather than rushing to 'fix' the housing problems with him.
Client: [tells more of their story]		

A process record gives a good insight into the interactions at the direct interface of a conversation, and, in particular, where change is identified as occurring.

A more extensive analysis of a conversation or a particular incident can be done using a **critical incident** analysis framework (Cleak & Wilson 2004, pp. 73–5). The reflective practice exercise below shows how a formal analysis, done in writing or in conversation, can assist with this process of reflection.

■ Reflective practice exercise: completing a critical incident analysis

Consider a critical incident that occurred in your practice and reflect on why it happened and why it was critical:

1 What images do you recall?
2 What sounds, smells and tactile sensations do you recall?
3 Which people, comments or practice stand out in your mind?

Next consider the affective domain—reflect on how you felt:

4 What was the high or low spot of the incident?
5 Were you surprised, angered, elated, curious, confused or depressed by anything in the experience? Describe your mood and feelings.
6 What do you think others were feeling?

Now interpret the events:

7 What have you learnt from this incident?
8 From this experience, what can you conclude about your understanding of and skills in assessment or analysis?
9 What was your key insight or learning?
10 How does this relate to your framework for practice?

Finally consider your decisions:

11 What skills and areas of understanding do you need to develop further as a result of your reflection?
12 What would this require?
13 What methods does this experience reinforce as valuable for future practice?

Source: Cleak & Wilson (2004, p. 79).

Overall, processes of reflection and reflexivity are highly valued by workers as they enhance learning and insight, and personal and professional development; build theoretical knowledge bases; and, most importantly, should lead to better client outcomes (Crawford 2006, p. 139).

One of the practice arenas where critical self-reflection most commonly occurs is within the context of supervision.

Supervision and other supports

One of the major supports typically available to you in your workplace is **supervision**. Supervision in different professions has different meanings. For human service workers, a supervisor is someone who takes responsibility, typically within the context of your agency, for you, your learning and your practice. A supervisor assists you in developing your practice and practice wisdom through direct modelling, support and intervention as an experienced worker.

Historically, three key functions of supervision have been identified: administration, education and support. In relation to administration, supervisors provide accountability to the organisation and to clients through monitoring caseload issues and worker issues. The educational focus is on providing opportunities for learning and discussion, as well as exploring professional development needs. The support function relates to providing staff care, through the provision of an opportunity to reflect critically on practice and receive support and encouragement (Kadushin 1972). Thompson (2000, p. 146) has added a fourth dimension: mediation.

Carroll (1996, p. 53) has expanded these three tasks of supervision to seven specific tasks:

1 to set up or create a learning relationship
2 to teach
3 to educate
4 to monitor professional ethical issues
5 to counsel
6 to consult
7 to monitor administrative aspects.

Thus, supervision has preventive and supportive functions, which is important for the worker *and* the agency, and therefore ultimately to the benefit of clients. Many people have noted, however, the very limited research evidence base for supervision (Holloway & Neufeldt 1995; Carroll 1996; Carroll & Gilbert 2006).

At its best, supervision can provide a safe learning environment; a place to test out new ideas and integrate them into practice. It can provide a place to integrate theory and practice, and the personal and the professional. Supervisees can deal with both the ongoing accumulation of work issues, as well as gain support around particular crises.

Supervision varies according to the agency, to the theoretical and personal orientation and skill set of the supervisor, and to the expectations and skills of the supervisee. In many agencies, supervision and support are offered regularly in a structured format and are valued dimensions of the agency's functioning (Renzenbrink 2005). In other agencies, supervision tends to be overlooked or undervalued. Some agencies structure individual supervision relationships according to management hierarchies within the organisation. A senior worker provides support and mentoring to a junior one. Others run with peer models and/or group supervision models.

Heather works in a drug and alcohol treatment service, where a group model of supervision operates. She describes her experience.

Focus on practice

I was having a conversation in our supervision group with several clinicians about the difficulty of establishing a good rapport with a client who has been reluctant to engage due to past trust issues. This can increase the difficulty when the clinician is in a situation where they are mandated to notify protective services about this client. This can amplify the conflict that this scenario can place a clinician in. Often the clinician is wishing to retain the hard-fought therapeutic alliance with the client, but is also well aware of risk issues requiring notification. We highlighted the importance of consultation and debriefing when facing these dilemmas especially in long-term therapeutic work.

1   What do you think Heather gained from this group supervision?
2   What do you think would be different in individual supervision?

The usefulness of the supervisory experience depends upon the agenda and the combined skill set of the supervisor and supervisee. As in any relationship, unrealistic or unclear expectations can inhibit a supervisory relationship (Bucknell 2006, p. 45; Reid & Westergaard 2006), as can major differences in opinions about how practice should take place, or what are the important skills to demonstrate, for example. Some other challenges or barriers have been identified as personality or value clashes, issues of hierarchy and management, and issues of trust given the inherent risks of disclosure, both personal and professional (Carroll 1996). Supervision relies on a high level of trust for it to be successful (Dyregrov 1997). Sometimes, the expectations of both the supervisor and the supervisee can be unreasonable. Supervisors can be busy and stressed, working under similar agency demands as the supervisee, and often with higher management responsibilities. All of these dimensions can influence the availability, quality and effectiveness of the relationship.

Like other professional relationships, having an initial discussion about the mutual expectations of supervision is important. Difficulties in the supervisory relationship occur when these expectations differ or needs cannot be met within the context of the relationship. It is important to make an assessment as to whether supervision can be an effective learning space or not. Sometimes a change of supervisor is both possible and necessary. In other circumstances, an assessment as to what can be gained from supervision and what cannot, and what part each person plays in that situation, is needed.

> ### ■ Reflective practice questions: establishing a supervisory relationship
>
> Here are some questions that workers have found useful to discuss with a prospective supervisor.
>
> #### Questions relating to the structure of supervision
>
> 1 When and where will you meet (including time, day and length of time)?
> 2 What should happen in relation to phone calls, pagers and other interruptions?
> 3 Will a record of supervision be kept? If so, who will document it?
>
> #### Questions relating to the process and function of supervision
>
> 1 What will be the expectations and goals of you both in supervision? For example:
>   - How will the agenda be set and revised?
>   - What should the supervisee 'bring' to supervision (for example, case material, workplace/team issues and personal issues)?
> 2 What are your learning and communication styles?
> 3 Are there possible incompatibilities in the ways in which you both work?
> 4 How should conflict or disagreement be managed?
> 5 What review processes will be in place?

Other possibilities for ongoing professional development include using supervision that is external to the agency. A major benefit of this arrangement is the ability to step outside the politics of the workplace and have someone as a more objective sounding board and independent support for you and your work. The loss is the ability to bring about change within the organisation through direct consultation and negotiation with your work-based supervisor.

Outside of the forum of supervision, learning, reflection and self-care can take place through numerous strategies:

- recording yourself in an interview (either audio or audiovisually, and with the consent of the client) for review and critique
- undertaking joint work with a colleague, which provides the opportunity for critical feedback and discussion
- undertaking a process recording
- maintaining a personal journal, in which you critically reflect on your work
- maintaining reading of professional journals and texts.

Debriefing

Critical Incident Stress Management (CISM) has been increasingly recognised as an important dimension of workplace support, in the aftermath of specific events or critical incidents. Recognition of critical incidents came from emergency services work, and in this context was defined as: '[A]ny situation faced by emergency services personnel that causes them to experience unusually strong emotional reactions which have the potential to interfere with their ability to function either at the scene or later' (Mitchell 1983, p. 36).

This definition has also been applied to incidents involving a wider range of work contexts. It does raise the question as to whether it is the worker, or the organisation or wider community, who identifies the risk situation, an issue to which we will return later.

The tasks of CISM, as identified by Poindexter (1997, p. 125), include:

- offering an immediate response
- giving support
- providing focused problem solving
- aiding in the enhancement of self-image
- setting limited and specific goals
- identifying and getting access to resources
- initiating new modes of thinking, feeling and coping.

A formal **debriefing** is one process that can be used to address these factors. The aim is to reduce distress, to educate and provide support around reactions, and, in many instances, to review workforce strategies.

Debriefing provides an opportunity to emotionally ventilate and psychologically process what has occurred. It can occur in dyads or in larger groups, and usually occurs between the first twenty-four hours following an incident, up until three days afterwards. It is used in many different practice contexts, such as schools, hospitals and the community, particularly in the aftermath of distressing or traumatic incidents. In the context of human service practice, this could include a wide range of events such as natural disasters, deaths, accidents and violent incidents.

Since its implementation, extensive debate has continued as to the effectiveness of debriefing and additional support interventions that make up CISM (Deahl, Srinivasan, Jones, Neblett & Jolly 2001; Dyregrov 1997; McNally, Bryant & Ehlers 2003; Mitchell 1983). The Mitchell Model, the debriefing model developed for fire-fighters in the USA, follows a facilitated six-stage group structure, moving from the incident details to issues of personal reactions and education around self-care strategies (Everly, Flannery & Mitchell 2000; Mitchell 1983, 2004).

The introductory phase includes introductions of everyone in the group, an introduction of the purpose of the meeting and the establishment of group rules, particularly in relation to confidentiality. The fact phase invites participants to give their account of what occurred, including their roles and responsibilities. This account includes 'where they were [and] what they heard, saw, smelled and did as they worked in and around the incident' (Mitchell 1983, p. 38). The intention is to re-create the incident with as many perspectives as possible.

The feeling phase involves asking questions relating to emotional reactions, such as:

- 'How did you feel when that happened?
- How are you feeling now?
- Have you ever felt anything like that in your life before?' (Mitchell 1983, p. 38).

The emphasis is on hearing all emotional reactions and privileging none over the other. The symptom phase focuses on questions of reactions through asking such questions as:

- 'What unusual things did you experience at the time of the incident?
- What unusual things are you experiencing now?
- Has your life changed in any way since the incident?' (Mitchell 1983, p. 38).

This phase focuses on possible disruptions to functioning as a result of stress reactions. The teaching phase provides an opportunity for the facilitator to discuss normal stress and/or trauma reactions with the group and to educate around possible future reactions. The final phase of the debriefing session, the re-entry phase, draws the session to a close through review and through careful planning about next steps, including what people might do immediately after the group, both individually and as a work group.

A follow-up debriefing is often included as a seventh stage. This provides an opportunity to review how people are coping and to implement other coping strategies as required.

Some research has found that this intervention can effectively assist 'emergency service workers return to work, reduce sick leave and aid in trauma recovery' (Robinson 2003). Supporters of debriefing argue that a stress response is normal and usually follows a regular pattern among the majority of individuals and it is this pattern that debriefing addresses. The major criticism of debriefing efforts is that they are not effective in reducing the longer-term posttraumatic stress impacts of traumatic events. The studies that critique such debriefings suggest that positive results attributed to debriefing interventions may have in fact occurred spontaneously anyway, particularly when emergency workers typically informally debrief among colleagues in the workplace (Gordon 1995a). They also maintain that debriefing alone does not necessarily assist in the prevention of traumatic stress, a finding supported by a number of studies (Deahl et al. 2001; Gordon 1995a). Others have gone so far as to argue that debriefings may be harmful processes in that they interfere with an individual's usual coping processes in the early phases after exposure to a traumatic event (Gist & Woodall 1999; Arendt & Elklit 2001; Campfield & Hills 2001).

After years of debriefings being offered, a more cautious approach is now being recommended. For example, Rose, Bisson and Wessely (2003) recommend that it is sensible to restrict 'across the board' immediate psychological debriefings, but important to ensure early practical support and note those with possible acute stress disorder, an important predictor of PTSD. Mitchell's work, however controversial, has radically altered people's thinking about psychological first-aid responses, and enabled a far greater awareness to develop around the immediate and potentially devastating effects of critical incidents.

A significant issue influencing the efficacy of any CISM effort is the overall work environment. For example, if tensions or low levels of trust exist among work colleagues, the literature indicates that debriefings may not be beneficial; indeed, they may be counterproductive (Dyregrov 1997). In negotiating complex workplace dynamics, adequate training of those who are to conduct a debriefing is essential. The status of the debriefer as either an insider or an outsider is an important consideration (Dyregrov 1997). These dimensions are overviewed in Figure 5.1 and provide a useful checklist to think about as to whether a debriefing process is appropriate or whether a smaller-scale strategy is warranted. The question of who decides whether an incident has had a significant impact and whether debriefing is required is important, as raised earlier in this discussion.

Focus on practice: workplace conditions for a debriefing to occur

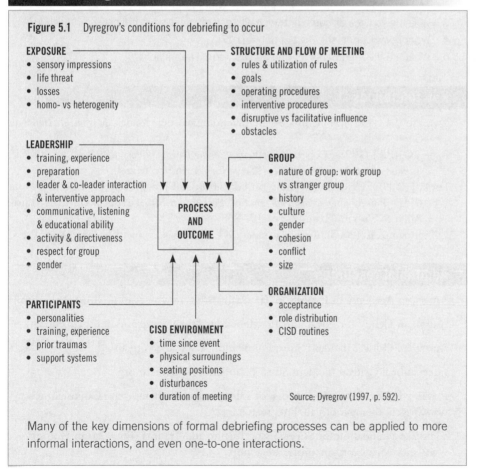

Figure 5.1   Dyregrov's conditions for debriefing to occur

EXPOSURE
- sensory impressions
- life threat
- losses
- homo- vs heterogenity

LEADERSHIP
- training, experience
- preparation
- leader & co-leader interaction & interventive approach
- communicative, listening & educational ability
- activity & directiveness
- respect for group
- gender

PARTICIPANTS
- personalities
- training, experience
- prior traumas
- support systems

CISD ENVIRONMENT
- time since event
- physical surroundings
- seating positions
- disturbances
- duration of meeting

STRUCTURE AND FLOW OF MEETING
- rules & utilization of rules
- goals
- operating procedures
- interventive procedures
- disruptive vs facilitative influence
- obstacles

PROCESS AND OUTCOME

GROUP
- nature of group: work group vs stranger group
- history
- culture
- gender
- cohesion
- conflict
- size

ORGANIZATION
- acceptance
- role distribution
- CISD routines

Source: Dyregrov (1997, p. 592).

Many of the key dimensions of formal debriefing processes can be applied to more informal interactions, and even one-to-one interactions.

Chapter summary

In this chapter, we have explored some key questions in relation to your ongoing learning and support needs. These have been dealt with at this point in the text to highlight that they are core skills to acquire preventively for your practice. Using supervision preventively, and debriefing when required, serves to minimise the impacts of stressful and traumatic events, often preventing vicarious traumatisation and burnout. We also explored the processes of critical self-reflection, supervision and debriefing as three ways in which you can be sustained in your practice.

Reflective practice questions

1 In thinking about your readiness for practice, what do you have in place in relation to:
   • self-care strategies, both personal and professional?
   • critical self-reflection processes?
   In particular, what support networks do you have and when do you use them?
2 What have been your experiences of supervision or mentoring in other contexts, and how do you think they will influence your current expectations?
3 What do you see as some of the challenges of engaging in critical self-reflection?
4 What is your understanding of debriefing?
5 What are the arguments for and against formal debriefings?

Key references

Dyregrov, A. (1997). The process in psychological debriefings. *Journal of Traumatic Stress, 10*(4), 589–605.
Figley, C. (Ed.) (1995). *Compassion fatigue: Coping with secondary traumatic stress disorder in those who treat the traumatized.* New York: Brunner/Mazel.
Fook, J. (1999). Critical reflectivity in education and practice. In B. Pease & J. Fook (Eds), *Transforming social work practice: Postmodern critical perspectives.* St Leonards: Allen & Unwin (chap. 13, pp. 195–208).
O'Donoghue, K. (2003). *Restorying social work supervision.* Annandale: Federation Press.

Additional resources

American Academy of Experts in Traumatic Stress: www.crisisinfo.org/articles.htm.

Australian Centre for Posttraumatic Mental Health: www.acpmh.unimelb.edu.au.

Australian Critical Incident Stress Foundation: www.acisa.org.au.

International Critical Incident Stress Foundation: www.icisf.org.

Psychoz Publications—Resources for Effective Psychotherapy and Counselling: www.psychotherapy.com.au/link_search.asp.

Victorian Foundation for Survivors of Torture and Trauma (Foundation House): www.survivorsvic.org.au/professional.php.

Victorian Government Department of Human Services—Emergency Management: www.dhs.vic.gov.au/emergency.

Establishing a Good Working Relationship

6

LEARNING GOALS

- Describe what you need to think about before meeting with someone.
- Know how to open the communication process.
- Understand the processes involved in engaging with and actively listening to your client and their story.
- Analyse the concept of confidentiality.
- Critique the notion of self-disclosure, understanding why it is such a controversial skill.

Preparing to meet

Chapter 4 outlined many of the questions you could consider prior to your contact with any client in your organisation, including questions of the physical environment and of the type of service delivery. This discussion focuses more specifically on preparing for an initial contact with someone, and highlights three particular issues.

The first relates to who it is that you will be seeing. The initial engagement process needs to be thought through. For example, in working with Indigenous clients, thinking about who you will meet with, and whether Elders need to be approached before contact can be initiated, are important considerations (Clarke, Andrews & Austin 1999; Rigney & Cooper 2004). Working with family members may be more appropriate. For survivors of torture and trauma, working with a support person present may be more

■ Remember Carl Rogers's statement (1987, p. 38) about the importance of being psychologically available to someone: 'Can I be totally present to this client?' 'Can I be with him or her?' 'Can I be sensitive to every nuance of personal meaning and value, no matter how different it is from my own experience?'

appropriate (VFST 2004). Working with children may require parental consent or the accompaniment of independent adult support.

The second issue is whether you are able to psychologically attend to this person or people. An attitudinal readiness is vital. Many factors will impact on this attitudinal readiness. For example, your contact with someone will be influenced by what has immediately preceded it, and what you might be anticipating afterwards. Being fully present in a conversation with another person is difficult if we are distracted by other issues in our day. Meeting people involves a biopsychosocial-spiritual attentiveness and, if for some reason it is not possible to be attentive, discussing the options with your supervisor is an important step.

The third issue relates to what you already know of this person, if anything. Someone in your organisation may have already been working with this client and an extensive case note history may be available to you. Or this person may never have had contact with a worker or an agency before in their life. This history, or lack thereof, is important for you to be aware of prior to any contact. The history can convey important details, such as prior risks to be aware of, that may impact on your new involvement with the person. For example, if someone has a history with the organisation of being aggressive if they perceive their needs to be unmet, you may want to consider where you meet with this person, and indeed whether you meet alone or with a co-worker. On the other hand, a case history can serve to maintain a particular story about a person that is never verified in any way and lead to the perpetuation of incorrect labels being imposed on the person. Equally important in this interaction will be what the other person knows about you and what they bring in terms of expectations and attitudes, drawn from knowledge of you or other workers.

Making initial contact

Whether in an involuntary client setting or a voluntary one, welcoming skills are used to ensure that 'the welcome people receive is warm and respectful' (Trevithick 2005, p. 150). Introductions and welcomes aim to help people feel at ease and to start to break down some of the initial anxiety or **anomie** that is often experienced in unfamiliar relationship contexts. Typically, people approach new relationships with some tentativeness, until trust and familiarity are established. Common questions clients have in mind are, according to Shulman (1999, p. 94):

What is this going to be all about?
What kind of worker is this going to be?

The initial phase of work together should enable these two questions to be somewhat addressed. These two questions influence the possibility of

engagement, as a major choice the client makes early on is 'whether or not [they] will engage with the worker in a meaningful way and begin to develop what has been called "the therapeutic alliance"' (Shulman 1999, p. 95). Equally, again, this question is important for the worker to acknowledge in their initial reaction to the client and their story. We make choices about the information we will reveal about ourselves early on in relationships with others, depending on what we read into the other person, and whether we feel they are safe, interested, neutral or non-judgmental, for example. The establishment of a client–worker relationship is similarly influenced by these factors. Creating a mutually safe environment is a priority in the initial contact.

Below, Suzie, a worker in a drug and alcohol treatment service, describes some of the other steps she takes to create such an environment for her clients.

Focus on practice

'One of the things I noticed early on that helped me and the client(s) to relax on the first session was to be very aware of the environment and how it might feel for them on their first visit. I would make sure they knew where the toilet was should they need it and offer to make them a tea/coffee or get them some water. This initial exchange enabled a type of "settling" time before anything more formal had commenced. I also find it useful to establish the amount of time you both have to avoid interruptions and, more importantly, to be able to create a safe place where there is some type of wrapping up or setting up of the next session before the time runs out. This all helps to provide that safe environment for you and your client.'

The 'settling in' process may vary according to where the conversation is taking place. In some instances, this will not be in an organisation but in the client's home or community. Respecting the practices and space of another's world is critical. Suzie highlights the importance of a 'settling' time before any formal work has commenced, as well as the importance of being clear about the boundaries of the contact. These are important steps in engaging with another person.

Another decision point relates to the role of 'small' talk in engaging with people—even the term is curious in that it implies that there is 'big' talk (the important talk) and trivial talk. The beauty of small talk is that it puts us all at ease—and sometimes this is the most important process in engaging with someone in a working relationship. It connects again with how we regard our role and what kind of relationship we want to establish with people.

Introductions are part of this process. Anecdotally, we typically need to hear a new person's name up to three times to connect it into our memory. It is an important dimension of a person to remember. If we are not named properly, we can feel misunderstood or isolated. Getting to the end of an interview with someone and realising that we cannot remember their name can be embarrassing. It is better to spend time at the start of any contact ensuring that names are remembered by both client and worker, and that other introductory issues are attended to, such as our role and reason for contact.

Whoever is present should be engaged directly in the conversation, as individuals. In many family meetings in hospitals, for example, the person who is the patient can be referred to as 'he' or 'she', as if they are somehow not present in the room and not part of any decision-making process. This immediately disempowers and silences people, as their basic right to recognition as a human being is being denied in this way.

A key moment or question may not be needed to shift the focus of the discussion onto the issues at hand. If someone is presenting for structured counselling at a set time in an agency, however, there will typically be a moment of transition into a session. Some ways of getting started are outlined below:

■ **Ways of opening an interview are considered in more depth in Chapter 7.**

Focus on practice: getting started

Some ways of opening an interview include:

What's been happening?
What would you like to talk about?
How can I help you?
What is the problem?
Tell me about what's been going on …

1   What do you see as the risks and benefits of each of these different questions or invitations?
2   How would you open a conversation with a person you have just met?

Engaging

Engagement refers to the process of entering into and establishing a positive working relationship or alliance with people. As argued earlier in Chapter 1, the client–worker engagement or alliance is seen as fundamental to good work being able to occur together. While it is seen as fundamental, in relation to engagement in a therapeutic context, Gibney (2003, p. 81) questions the prevailing assumption that all clients 'engage in the process with a full and genuine intensity'.

Engagement varies in its intensity and also in how it can be negotiated between the worker and the client as a result of external factors. Below, Jane talks about some of these dimensions in the parent bereavement support group discussed earlier in Chapter 4.

Focus on practice: initial engagement

Unexpected processes also happen when we hold our evening support group for parents who are bereaved. As it is an open group and no reply about attending is asked for, it is difficult to know how many people are coming. The room in which the group is held is located deep within a non-clinical area of the hospital, and lost visitors or parents or staff looking for other groups or meetings does happen from time to time.

From the outset it is critical to establish in a welcoming, respectful way that those coming are for the appropriate group. Signs along the way and on the door of the room are no guarantee of this, as we have found. Returning to the hospital and/or coming to the group for the first time may confront or overwhelm parents with powerful memories, images or emotions. If couples are coming, one may have agreed to come for the sake of the other and bring their own reluctance. Some may find it hard to speak.

Jane then describes some of the ways in which she goes about the actual introduction and engagement processes with group members.

Focus on practice

Our greeting and the process of engaging takes place outside the door. 'Hello, are you here for/looking for the parents' group? I'm Jane. Welcome.'

We extend our hand for a handshake—there may be some instances when this is not appropriate, perhaps with some members of certain faith and cultural communities, and again a quick decision may need to be made, assumptions about CALD [culturally and linguistically diverse] citizens may be incorrect, despite the context a small smile may add to the sense of welcome, sensitivity is needed.

Parents mostly volunteer their names, and the name of their child who has died. If, however, they are too distressed, it may be impossible for them in that moment to speak and we need to acknowledge this—a gentle nod and some brief words may help: 'It can be very hard coming to the group for the first time.' 'Many parents who have come to the group have found it difficult, too.' We may add, 'See how you go tonight'.

Depending on how the parent responds, it may be sensitive to ask the name of their child (if not already given) and how long it's been since they died. There have been times when a parent is coming for the first time, several years after their child's death. At such times we would ask 'What brought you tonight?' or 'Is there something about tonight's topic?' A fine line has to be trodden between introductions and moving too far into their story. Sometimes it may be appropriate to say 'Perhaps we'll be hearing more about [their child's name] or just more through the night'. We then encourage the parents to write out a name tag and their name and their child's in the book (placed just inside the room) and offer refreshments and gesture to the seats.

The assumptions we make about who a person is, based on momentary contact with them and 'first impressions', profoundly influences the initial engagement. Studies have demonstrated that information about another person's gender, sex, ethnicity and age is processed within seconds of encountering someone. From a survival perspective, this makes sense. This enables us to make quick decisions as to whether this new person is 'safe', based on our 'typing' of them according to previous encounters with others like them. In psychodynamic terms, this process is referred to as a 'parataxic distortion' (Stack Sullivan 1953), where we draw on our past knowledge of people from the same (*para*) group (*taxis*) to make sense of the present person. The danger of this process is that this typing becomes stereotyping, and prohibits us from seeing individuals as individuals, outside of 'labels' (Thompson 2003b, 2006).

Engaging or bonding with another person can happen very quickly under some conditions. Working intensively as a small group over a weekend, for example, can build a very strong sense of cohesion, particularly if contact with others outside of that group is discouraged and intense time is spent together talking about emotional issues. Some groups rely on this process to form rapid and seemingly strong bonds. The phenomenon of 'speed dating' is based on this process of quick assessment and engagement with another person. Within a matter of minutes, people have decided whether they wish to continue to engage with a person.

These decisions are complex processes, and different theoretical perspectives understand why this is so in very different ways.

Focus on practice: finding commonalities

In a small group, form pairs and talk for one minute with that person before moving around to talk for one minute with other group members. Find as many points of commonality as possible.

1 How did you gather the information from the other person? For example, did you ask questions or did you talk with each other in a non-questioning way?
2 When did you realise there were points of commonality or not?

Gibney (2003) proposes four levels of engagement occur in a therapeutic context. Level one refers to the negotiation around whether therapy 'is required, wanted or needed or is even appropriate at this time, in this place, between these people in attendance' (Gibney 2003, pp. 81–2). Level two refers to a form of problem-solving or solution-focused therapy: '[T]hey perceive something is wrong that they want fixed, and they have no particular wish for understanding or insight' (Gibney 2003, p. 83). Level three refers to engagement when the therapeutic relationship is seen as the 'nexus of change' by both the therapist and client. Level four refers to a deep engagement in the relationship that is regarded as transformative, and the therapist is 'an implicated witness' (Gibney 2003, p. 86). While specific to psychotherapy, what this typology does highlight is that even in the most mandated of client–worker relationships, it may be possible to achieve level three or four engagement, returning to the arguments of Chapter 1 that the client–worker relationship can be positively influential in and of itself.

Nicole, another social worker at a children's hospital, wrote about her experience of engagement with Mrs B, a client whose story has been de-identified.

Focus on practice: initial engagement with Mrs B

Mrs B is the mother of an eight-year-old son diagnosed with a treatable but life-threatening condition. I was allocated to the family at the point of her son's diagnosis and Mrs B spent two formal sessions with me discussing the impact of the diagnosis on her, her son and their family. Mrs B did not attend a subsequent appointment, but was informed by me that she could have ongoing sessions with me and that I would also make contact with her during her son's subsequent outpatient appointments.

In the introduction, notice the process of establishing a relationship. Nicole was allocated to the family as their worker. This often occurs through weekly team meetings or daily intake reviews of clients. It raises important questions about the goodness of fit or the compatibility between the worker and the client. Nicole describes what happened next.

Focus on practice: working with the difficulties in engaging

After two months of no contact from Mrs B, and little contact in outpatients due to me feeling that Mrs B did not want to further engage with me, I heard via a colleague that Mrs B was not happy because I had not spent enough time with her. I organised a session with Mrs B to discuss her support needs. I began by inquiring about Mrs B and her family's current situation. I then stated that I would like to discuss openly the concerns that Mrs B discussed with her colleague. I said that the purpose of the discussion was to ensure that Mrs B and her family received the support that was needed. I had discussed this strategy with my supervisor and attempted to ensure that I was not defensive of my actions during my sessions with Mrs B.

Mrs B stated she felt that other parents saw their social workers on a more regular basis and that she would like another social worker who could spend more time with her. I said that it was very important that Mrs B had access to the level of support that she felt was necessary. I commented that Mrs B had given me the impression that she was not comfortable receiving support from social work and that she seemed reluctant to engage in anything more than discussion about practical issues. Mrs B disclosed that she did find it difficult to trust people and that she felt that some of the material discussed with me in the first two sessions was 'more than I've discussed with most people'.

■ Each theoretical perspective would understand these interactions differently. These understandings of Mrs B's situation will be revisited in Chapters 11–14.

In this interaction, Nicole and Mrs B have been able to openly discuss the situation. Nicole framed the discussion in terms of supporting Mrs B. She was open to critical feedback from Mrs B about understanding why the engagement process had gone the way it had. This enabled Mrs B to talk about the difficulties both between them and in relation to the ongoing issues with which Mrs B was grappling. In this example, despite the difficulties in initially engaging, a good engagement and rapport between Nicole and Mrs B seems to be beginning to occur, as demonstrated below.

Focus on practice: moving on with the work together

Mrs B stated that she knew that she had given me the impression that she didn't want to speak to me but was angry that I did not persevere. Mrs B and I spent a session discussing the difficulty Mrs B was experiencing with a number of intense and sometimes conflicting emotions and how difficult it was for Mrs B to access help. Mrs B disclosed that she was concerned that she may have said something to me that may have changed the way that I perceived her. Mrs B decided that she wanted to continue seeing me for assistance and that it was helpful that I was able to 'take the criticism without getting angry at me'.

1   What level of engagement would you see Mrs B and Nicole engaging in?
2   What would you have done in Nicole's situation?

These engagement difficulties illustrate that clarifying the initial reason and ongoing basis for contact is critical. In some settings, clients can be bewildered by the sudden arrival of a worker, for example. They may not know why a referral has occurred, what is known about them and what the role of the worker is all about. In other situations, as in Mrs B's case, her own assumptions, needs and expectations strongly influenced what occurred. These are all important introductory clarifications that may need revisiting throughout the length of work together.

The discussion of engagement so far has focused on working with clients who choose to engage in the process. Some clients, however, will not want to talk with you at all, and the process of engagement becomes more challenging. Trotter (2006, p. 1) identifies some of these questions:

How do you help someone who has no interest in being helped? … How do you counsel someone who does not even recognize they have a problem? How do you work with someone who has a totally different set of values from yourself?

In these situations, role clarification and contracting are even more important factors in the establishment of a working relationship. Role clarification refers to the process of establishing clear understandings of purpose. That is, to answer as clearly as possible why it is you are meeting together. In some instances, this will involve explicitly addressing the lack of interest or free will in the contact; for example: 'I doubt you want to be here, talking about what's happened. What if we agree on talking for ten minutes about some things the magistrate is going to need to know to make their decision?' It also involves talking very explicitly about the purpose of the contact and what the outcome or next step may be:

Hi, my name is Jo. I'm a social worker with the Department of Human Services. I'm here because concerns were raised about some bruising on your daughter's arms and legs and we need to understand what's going on. Given that a notification's been made, we will need to assess whether there are ongoing concerns about your daughter's safety.

Other issues that may need to be addressed in the initial contracting phase include:

- the length of time in this contact and ongoing contact
- the purpose of the conversation
- what will happen with the information discussed—that is, what are the limits of confidentiality?

This initial conversation is about establishing the when, where, why and how of the work. A respectful and empowering strategy is an explicit discussion of the anticipated contact (Trotter 2006). Sometimes this is more possible than others. However, an assumption that our mandate as a worker—our theoretical orientation or the limitations of confidentiality, for example—are immediately understood by a client can be very wrong. This may need to be outlined in detail so that the client is empowered to make decisions within that conversation.

One central tenet of the process of engagement is to start where the client is wanting to start. As Marsh and Doel (2005, p. 13) propose: 'From the very start of the work, the expressed views and preferences of people are central. Finding ways to help people express them as clearly as possible is a prime practitioner task.'

Starting 'where the client is at' is illustrated in Karen's work with Myrtle and the setting of the priorities for their work together. An initial priority may seem to be the grief issues, but another priority emerges.

> This section explores the initial contracting of the relationship. In Chapter 9, we will look at the processes involved in contracting around specific goals once an initial assessment has been done.

Focus on practice: engagement is about starting where the client is

A single, eighty-year-old woman, Myrtle was referred for a social work assessment following the death of her sister. The two women had lived together for their whole lives, and cared for their mother who had died when the sisters were in their sixties. Myrtle was, not surprisingly, distressed at the death of her sister, but her worry on

continues

the first day of our meeting was what to do with the sister's body, as the two had both decided that their bodies should be donated for use by medical science. Ensuring that this occurred on her behalf brought her significant relief.

Subsequently, over some years of contact we explored her loss, and revisited much of her life story. Myrtle wrote little notes to herself to remind herself of what she wished to discuss with me on my regular visits. On one such occasion the note revealed the question 'When I go [she had no fear of dying, now that her sister was gone] who is going to turn off the fridge?' I viewed this question as having multiple meanings, and in answering her practical question was able to also begin to deal with the larger question of what will happen to what remained of herself and her sister.

Starting with where the client is at sounds like a relatively unproblematic positioning. Some challenges, however, include:

- cultural differences—how do we know, as the worker, where the client really is at or is it sometimes more of a case of where we *think* the client is at?
- communication barriers—how do we ensure that the client's perspective is heard and understood, when communication barriers are present, such as language differences or hearing impairments?
- disagreements with where our client is at—how do we ensure this positioning of starting with where they are at, respecting their humanity, when it may be so fundamentally opposed to our own worldview, as in the case of a perpetrator of violence or sexual assault?

This is where some of the skills we will look at in Chapters 7 and 8 come into play as ways of exploring these dimensions and ensuring, as much as possible, that the client's views and preferences remain central.

People's unique communicative styles should be attended to, either directly or indirectly, in this time of relationship formation. Koprowska (2005) identifies experiences of deafness, visual impairment, learning difficulties and dementia as influencing communication, and the engagement process is about finding ways to work with these dimensions and establish a working relationship.

The degree of cultural congruence (Dean 2001) is an important consideration in initial contact. As Jane highlights in her earlier example page with the bereavement group, sensitivity in relation to culturally safe practices is important. Decisions about initial interactions may relate to whether to engage in a formal handshake, or who to address in a group. These issues can always be enquired about in the initial encounters. For example: 'I would like to talk with you, but I'm wondering if we should have someone else here with us from your community?'

Cultural identities also influence engagement experiences; for example, when a female worker is engaging with a male client, and the client's cultural background does not permit contact with women. Other differences will be more fundamental, but perhaps more subtle, in relation to different worldviews and beliefs. Furlong and Ata (2006) were cited in the previous chapter in relation to naming cultural diversity and how this may not be enough. These are the complexities of a multicultural community and require sensitive negotiation in the context of a predominantly Western culture in Australia.

Confidentiality

Maintaining the confidentiality or privacy of a person's information is an important professional requirement, primarily in relation to creating a 'safe' space to talk about concerns. Agencies will have different practices, however, in relation to expectations of reporting and accountability around client information. Agencies involved in writing court reports, for example, have different recording and reporting arrangements compared with more therapeutic and voluntary agency settings. Being aware of your agency's requirements and talking with your clients about mutual understandings of confidentiality from the outset are two vital practices.

Melissa provides an excerpt from a presentation she gave, based on her doctoral thesis, which examined people who were engaged in suicidal behaviours and the impact of an intensive support program (Petrakis 2004). She describes how the worker's decision might be influenced by the legal and agency context, as much as the immediate client–worker situation:

Focus on practice: acting on client disclosures of risk

Confidentiality is a 'fundamental requirement for keeping trust' (BACP 2002). With a client at risk, a therapist needs to utilise careful professional judgment about the balance between potential harm to the client of either disclosing information or maintaining confidentiality. A disclosure in the absence of a strong belief that the client presents an immediate risk to themselves potentially creates a situation in which the therapist could be sued by the client for breach of confidence (Bond 2000); however, failure to disclose when there is a strong belief that the client presents an immediate risk to themselves and subsequently takes their own life may lead a therapist to having to defend themselves against the accusation of failure in their duty of care (Daines, Gask & Usherwood 1997; Jenkins 2002).

Increasingly therapists and clinicians are concerned with the risk of litigation (Reeves & Seber 2004). The risk of clients harming themselves can debilitate the therapist from acting creatively and collaboratively, making their actions defensive and focused 'solely on risk assessment rather than therapeutic change' (Sharry, Darmody & Madden 2002). Understandably then, in an underresourced system, focus shifts to at least keeping these clients safe. The focus shifts to risk assessment.

Using self-disclosure

Establishing a good relationship relies to a large extent on the client's willingness and capacity to engage in it. Degrees of disclosure (Burstow 1987, p. 18) vary enormously between workers and their clients, as this example from a therapeutic context illustrates:

> Therapists, certainly, disclose now and then. Therapists sometimes make themselves very vulnerable indeed. Clients, however, do not just do this 'sometimes'. The clients' ongoing job is precisely to do this disclosing, to make themselves vulnerable, to uncover, live, and embrace those parts of self that we generally hide.

It is taken for granted that clients in most situations will disclose extensively about their life circumstances. The degree to which a worker self-discloses, however, is more controversial. To self-disclose is to explicitly talk about your own experiences with the client. **Self-disclosure** is 'loosely defined as what individuals verbally reveal about themselves to others (including thoughts, feelings and experiences)' and is seen to play 'a major part in close relationships' (Derlega, Metts, Petronio & Margulis 1993, p. 1). We are always revealing things about ourselves through both our verbal and non-verbal interactions, but our use of self mediates these decisions and provides some boundary around some information. Self-disclosure is relating more to your explicit use of your own circumstances, either past or present, as the following example illustrates:

Client: I'm just not coping anymore. I don't go out, I can't go out. I sit at home and cry and eat. That's all I do. I can't see how this will ever change.

Worker: When my Dad died, I found it really hard to go out too. It felt much safer at home. But I found if I forced myself to go out, I'd sometimes have an OK time. Gradually, it just got easier.

Client: So I'm not going crazy? This will change?

In this example, the worker is emphasising the skills they found helpful in overcoming a similar situation. It *may* help the client feel less alone and overwhelmed by their situation, as their response tends to imply. It may provide some modelling as to how someone else coped with a difficult and distressing time. On the other hand, the client may feel resentful that the worker is telling them that it will get easier, when that is not how they feel right now, and that the worker has been able to adapt to something the client feels they will never be able to adapt to. The use of self-disclosure is controversial because it highlights some of the major differences in expectations of the boundaries and purposes of helping relationships.

Some workers are adamant that self-disclosure should always be avoided, whereas others are just as adamant that it is one of the most powerful, equalising skills of practice. This raises questions as to why the field is so divided and whether an absolute position is possible to maintain over time and in all situations.

Consider the situation Suzie found herself in, in her work with clients and drug issues.

Focus on practice

It is inevitable in any counselling session that the client will ask: 'So, do you have any kids—do you really know what it is like for me?' or 'So, do you use drugs or what?'

I found that the first time this happened I had not given enough thought to what my response would be and it is the type of issue that requires thought, reflection and ongoing discussion within a supervision session. For me, the question I had to ask myself was, how useful would disclosing my personal experiences be, given that every person has such a unique set of circumstances that are individual to them. Sometimes by divulging and exploring your own experiences the focus of the session becomes diverted, and it is this diversion that is worth exploring with your client in more detail.

Suzie's examples of the questions she has been asked in practice about her own private life highlight the dilemma: To answer or not? Directly or indirectly? One way of understanding these kinds of questions is to ask whether they are questions about you, whether as a worker you will understand them or view them in a particular way? Will you understand what it is like to feel so overwhelmed as a parent, for example?

■ Reflective practice questions

How would you respond to the following questions?

- Do you have children?
- How old are they?
- Do you have a boyfriend/girlfriend?
- Do you earn a lot of money doing this job?
- What time do you finish work today?
- Where are you off to for your holidays?
- Have you ever had an abortion?
- How old are you?
- Where do you live?
- Do you believe in a divine presence like God or Allah?

1 Would you respond to all of the questions?
2 Who could ask these questions and get an answer from you? Why?

The key argument for the use of disclosure is that, in a professional context, self-disclosure helps to build trust and authenticity in a relationship. That is, the worker joins with the client through self-disclosure as another human being, facing similar challenges or successes. This sharing reduces inequalities in the relationship by reducing the sense that the worker is somehow outside of life's problems and challenges. The norms of reciprocity that operate in many relationships are considered to be enhanced by mutual disclosure and intimacy levels. Shulman's (1978, p. 167) study of perceived worker effectiveness found that the 'worker's ability to "share personal thoughts and feelings" ranked first as a powerful correlate to developing working relationships and to being helpful'.

The argument against the use of self-disclosure is that it detracts from the focus on the client's story. The purpose of the relationship is to hear and support the client's story, not to hear and support the worker's. Some argue that self-disclosure not only shifts the focus onto the worker, but in doing so also burdens the client with the worker's issues. Another argument is that self-disclosure can place you at risk in certain situations. Clients may find out where you live or if you have children, and use this information to threaten you or intrude into this private space. Once this information is known, it can neither be retracted nor controlled, and can lead to serious breaches of privacy and safety. The consequences of self-disclosure are in some ways 'independent of what the teller might intend' (Derlega et al. 1993, p. 9). Managing self-disclosure is about managing privacy and vulnerability—dimensions that differ from individual to individual, as well as cross-culturally. As with other relationships, over time, the capacity to tolerate or trust different levels of vulnerability or reciprocity within the context of a client–worker relationship can increase.

Melissa, a social worker in the mental health field and teacher of communication skills, recounts a discussion of self-disclosure in one of her classes, which highlights how she resolves these issues in practice. These conversations are presented with the permission of the students. Melissa was working with a group of students who were about one month into their first field placements. She presents her experience below.

Focus on practice

We watched a video showing a counsellor opening an interview. The counsellor stated their name, asked the client in an open-ended manner what the client hoped to gain from the interview, and then explained the types of questions they would ask in counselling and the rationale. The counsellor had described the *process* of counselling, but they had not disclosed anything about themselves, their qualifications or their life. I reflected on this with the students.

Exchanges with two students were particularly instructional regarding the issue of self-disclosure:

Student situation 1—wanting to disclose

Student: 'I know I shouldn't self-disclose, but …'

Melissa: 'It feels as though self-disclosure would help with rapport.'

Student: 'Yes.'

Melissa: 'What was the context?'

Student: 'I am working in a mental health setting. We go out on home visits to families with a member with a mental illness. My brother has bipolar.'

Melissa: 'It feels as though it could help to share this information.'

Student: 'But I know I shouldn't.'

Melissa: 'It sounds as though you know there is a rule but your gut is telling you something else.'

Student: 'I guess so.'

Melissa: 'I'm a big believer in following our gut in counselling, but when we start out our gut isn't trained yet to how counselling is different from everyday conversations. In everyday conversations we assume two equal parties who can contribute confidently and assertively. Counselling is not like that. For one party they are feeling very vulnerable and being asked to reveal something they have tried to resolve by themselves, and often with the help of family and friends and even other professionals, yet they are still very troubled. They will feel embarrassed about sharing and unsure what we will think of them if they tell us everything they are thinking. If we talk about ourselves the client will gladly let us, relieved they are off the hook, at least for a while, and that the spotlight is no longer on them. This is not good, because we have missed this early opportunity to show our curiosity and concern for them, and to indicate that we can focus exclusively on them in this space because we consider them and their experiences important.'

Student: 'Yeah, I don't want to make it about me.'

Melissa: 'There's just one other thing, too. It might be that if the family's experience is similar they *do* feel a quicker rapport established by our self-disclosure. However, quickly it will become evident that our experiences are not exactly the same; it might be that the gender of the family member with bipolar is different, that age of diagnosis was different, that level of chronicity is different, that our families differ in financial resources or social supports available … Suddenly the family can feel betrayed that they thought we understood, however we don't understand at all.'

continues

Student situation 2—not having the experience to disclose and share

Student: 'My situation is different. My lack of experience makes me feel less skilled to help my clients.'

Melissa: 'Tell me how self-disclosure would help with feeling less skilled.'

Student: 'I am working in a women's health service where all the clients are pregnant. My supervisor has two children.'

Melissa: 'So it feels like your supervisor has legitimacy or expertise because she has been pregnant before, like these clients, while you have not.'

Student: 'Yes. I feel like I don't have that knowledge to offer.'

Melissa: 'You feel that the knowledge isn't something book-learned or learned through your work in the service, that you need to have gone through it yourself.'

Student: 'Yes.'

Melissa: 'This situation is not so different.'

Student: 'How do you mean?'

Melissa: 'Your colleague is feeling that in her setting, rules prevent her from disclosing when it would be helpful. You are feeling that in your setting rules would support disclosure, and it would be helpful, but you have no material to disclose.'

Student: 'Yes.'

Melissa: 'The dilemma is the same though. Our self-disclosure shifts the focus away from the client, and further is personal, specific and therefore limited. Even your effective supervisor, who uses her self-disclosure incidentally as part of her genuine use of self, will get in trouble sometimes because the client will note the differences in their experiences: that the gender of babies is different, there were differences in experiences of labour, the presence or absence of post-natal depression, the involvement or lack of involvement by a partner, spouse or extended family, cultural differences in diet, beliefs on childrearing practices, the question of circumcision, beliefs around religion and faith and rituals like baptism … We need to be very careful not to fast-track rapport at the expense of real empathy.'

The following questions may assist you in deciding whether or not to self-disclose:

- Is change possible without self-disclosure?
- Is the disclosure client-centred and client-focused or does it shift the focus to you and your circumstances?
- Is it a necessary condition of practice? Or is it always contextual?
- How does your use of disclosure change over time and what determines those boundaries?
- What are you wanting to disclose and, more importantly, why?

- Is it possible or desirable to generalise from the experience or distance from yourself so that a useful story can be told without creating the burden of it being your story for the client? For example, 'Some women have found …' or 'Some people have found …'

Chapter summary

In this chapter, we have explored some of the skills in establishing a client–worker relationship. This has included the skills of creating a safe and supportive environment in which to meet, the skills of an initial contact and the skills of active listening. In looking at engagement, the use of minimal encouragers, empathy and self-disclosure, it is apparent there is no one right way to be using these skills. Rather they need to be thought about in context.

Reflective practice questions

1 What have you learnt about:
   - empathy?
   - engagement?
   - minimal encouragers?
   - self-disclosure?
2 Which skills of engagement do you find relatively easy to apply and which not?
3 What do you notice about people's reactions to emotion in:
   - your family?
   - your community?

Key references

Bishop, A. (2002). *Becoming an ally: Breaking the cycle of oppression*. Crows Nest: Allen & Unwin.

Gibney, P. (2003). *The pragmatics of therapeutic practice*. Melbourne: Psychoz.

Goleman, D. (2005). *Emotional intelligence*. New York: Bantam Books.

Goleman, D. (2006). *Social intelligence: The new science of human relationships*. London: Hutchinson.

Additional resources

Daniel Goleman's website—Social and emotional intelligence: www.danielgoleman.info.

PACFA Ethical Guidelines: www.pacfa.org.au/scripts/content.asp?pageid= ETHICSPAGEID (see other professions' websites for similar guidelines).

Social Care Institute for Excellence: www.scie.org.uk.

PART 3

Basic
Skills:
Focusing the Communication

In the previous chapters, we have explored the ways in which we might approach practice and began to think about the process or relationship into which we are entering. In this next part of the book, some of the key verbal skills are identified that are involved in establishing what the situation is for a particular client and identifying an agenda for the work. This phase of work typically involves first using probes such as useful and relevant questions (Chapter 7), and then seeking further clarification and understanding of the situation through inviting, reflecting, paraphrasing and summarising (Chapter 8). So another dimension is added to the framework—focusing the communication.

Part 1—Framing the relationship:

- the purpose of human service work
- your value base
- your theoretical and factual knowledge.

continues

Part 2—Forming the relationship:

- your use of self
- your organisational context
- your ongoing support and professional development needs
- meeting the people involved
- opening the communication
- actively listening
- listening empathically
- using self-disclosure.

Part 3—Focusing the communication:

- establishing the story
- forming an assessment
- goal setting.

Establishing the Story

7

LEARNING GOALS

- Understand the purpose of minimal encouragers.
- Describe and use a range of probing skills.
- Differentiate the types of questions and their purposes.
- Understand the skills involved in using statements and making requests.

The task of establishing the story

As Chapter 1 outlined, your focus will be on building a multidimensional understanding of the client and their story. This means understanding the client's story in relation to their inner and outer worlds.

Specific verbal skills are used to support and encourage the client in telling their story. We look at minimal encouragers and probing skills in this chapter.

Using minimal encouragers

In Chapter 2, we looked at the verbal and non-verbal skills that enhance or inhibit a conversation. In order to keep talking in a conversation, we need some feedback from the other person that it is all right to continue. The verbal and non-verbal cues we give to another person are often **minimal encouragers**. That is, they are minimal in the sense of not being major statements or questions or reactions, but they encourage the person to continue in their talking. Minimal encouragers can be verbal or non-verbal. Verbal minimal encouragers include:

Yes!

Uh-ha …

Mm …

Right …

Sure.

Non-verbal minimal encouragers include all the facial and postural reactions we give—nodding, smiling or the raising of eyebrows—that inform the speaker that they are being listened to and should continue. Minimal encouragers are regarded as a way of keeping the conversation going. They are part of the conversation, however, and therefore their impact can be significant, both in intended and unintended ways. The following example highlights the unintended impact, when a minimal encourager was experienced as the end point of a conversation rather than an affirmation to continue:

Focus on practice

At a cross-cultural seminar, a woman from a severely war-torn part of the world spoke of the impact for her of minimal encouragers when she encountered professionals. When she advised them of her nationality, she was often greeted with a response of 'Oh'. She said she did not want that as a response to her communication, because she did not know what it meant. She was left wondering what the person was thinking and meaning by 'Oh'. Did it mean they assumed she'd been raped, that she'd been directly affected by the war, or that it was too hard to speak about? She wanted to know more of what the other person meant by 'Oh' rather than feeling as though she was on the end of someone else's assumption about her.

In this example, the meaning of the minimal encourager was not clear. Similarly, if the minimal encouragers 'right' or 'sure' are used, a very specific meaning as well as a general meaning can be conveyed. Unintentionally, someone can be affirmed in what they are saying, when their use is intended to affirm the continuation of the conversation, not the meaning of it. Minimal encouragers need to be well timed, appropriate and sensitive to the situation.

Using probes

Another set of these skills is termed **probes** because they are an active way of encouraging the client to relate the many dimensions of a problem situation. The verb 'to probe' means to 'examine or look into closely, especially in order to discover something; investigate; interrogate closely' (Brown 1993, p. 2362). This definition highlights both the strengths and the risks of these skills—the strengths being about discovery and investigation; the risks being that a client can feel interrogated.

Probes include questions, prompts, statements and even single words (Egan 2002, p. 120). Probes are one of the major groups of verbal skills that enable us to follow the client's story and get inside the detail of it. As Hepworth, Rooney & Larsen (2002, p. 155) state, focusing an interview is a complex skill, requiring three particular tasks. The first is selecting the topics for exploration, the second involves exploring the topics in depth and the third involves maintaining a focus and keeping on topic. The use of probes is one way of moving through each of these phases. These skills enable us to stay with the client's story and where they want to head with it. At the same time, we use these skills to diverge from the seemingly dominant story, and to expand the focus of the interview. Therefore, these probes are as critical for following the details of what the client is telling us as much as for exploring the unspoken dimensions of the experience; for asking about the history of an issue or to explore the range of impacts of a situation in terms of feelings, actions, thoughts and contexts.

Some scenarios were presented in earlier chapters for general discussion. Consider the ways in which each of these conversations would require very different opening statements or questions, and probing skills.

■ Reflective practice questions

1 How would you open the following discussions?

    a A child protection worker is making her way to meet with a parent, against whom allegations of abuse have been made. The worker, on arrival to the family home, notices that the parent is drug affected and not happy at all about the notification to protective services.

    b A housing worker is meeting with a group of concerned tenants to look at writing a letter of protest about the reopening of a road through a housing estate where children have been playing. Other actions may be developed after a community consultation.

    c A duty worker on a telephone crisis line receives a call from a young distressed woman who has been assaulted by her partner. She doesn't know what to do—whether to leave or stay.

    d A worker has been involved with one family for many years, since the time when their child was diagnosed with cancer right through to her death six months ago. The worker wants to invite the siblings to a sibling support group, which will involve contact with both the parents and the siblings.

2 What would be the first question you would ask and why?

3 Share your response with someone else—how different are your questions?

4 What questions would you want to ask?

What questions will I ask?

> The skilful use of questions is a potent device for initiating, sustaining and directing conversation (Dickson & Hargie 2006, p. 121).

In Part 2, we looked at the importance of understanding the agency context and the worker's role. Your context and role will strongly influence where, when, how and why you work with your client, and therefore inform the ways in which you will go about asking particular kinds of questions. How we ask and what we ask is inextricably linked with the purpose of the contact.

Questions, however, can be very intimidating—they can ask people to think about things that they have never thought of before or to recall traumatic issues and events. They can stigmatise and blame, inadvertently. If someone is questioned continuously, it can mean that they feel interrogated rather than heard—that it is more important that the facts be established than it is for the person to be heard. In the next chapter, we will explore the skills of paraphrasing and summarising as ways of minimising this outcome.

This discussion brings together some of the current thinking about the nature of questions in general. Questions can be effective in opening up an interview and gathering the necessary information, or they can alienate, marginalise or disempower people even further. Asking effective, empowering questions therefore is critical. The various aspects of questions are now considered.

Asking open-ended or closed questions

Questions can be open-ended or closed in their structure, influencing the kind of response that is elicited. An **open-ended question** is open in the sense that it invites the client to provide further elaboration of the details of their story. Questions beginning with the words 'how', 'what', 'why', 'when', 'who' and 'where' are all typically open-ended in that they invite some kind of descriptive, expansive response, not confirmation of information that has been provided by the person asking the question. For example:

When did you first notice these difficulties?

How many children do you have?

What do you think is the most important issue to work on right now?

Closed questions, by contrast, seek confirmation or disconfirmation of information—with a simple yes, no, maybe or other singular word response such as 'never'. They do not call for further elaboration on detail:

Have you spoken with anyone about this?

Can you get another job?

Do you think it will happen again?

Some authors suggest that any question eliciting a short answer is also a closed question—that a closed question is one where the topic is defined and the client's response is restricted to a few words or a yes or no response (Hepworth, Rooney & Larsen 2002, p. 142). A question as to how far someone had travelled could similarly be seen as a closed question, although this is moving to a different interpretation of confirmation or disconfirmation of information, which is typically considered to be the defining feature of a closed question.

Some questions, while structured as closed questions in a grammatical sense, can function as open-ended purely through our use of voice or intonation: 'Can you tell me about that?' can be understood as an encouraging **invitation** to talk some more about a problem situation rather than someone providing a 'yes' or 'no' response.

Closed questions can lead to more detailed, descriptive responses, but they rely on the client taking up the intent of the question and initiating further response. To illustrate how a closed question can lead on to further elaboration, notice the response here:

Worker: Have you spoken with anyone about this?

Client:　　No. But I think I need to speak with my boss about what's going on.

In some situations, however, these questions may not be the most effective approach, leading to monosyllabic responses and not much detail. The worker ends up doing a lot of the 'work' and it may not be a mutually satisfying encounter.

Worker: Have you spoken with anyone about this?

Client:　　No.

Worker: Do you think you should speak with someone, perhaps at work?

Client:　　No.

Worker: Isn't there anyone else?

Client:　　Maybe …

In this instance, the conversation is not getting far. Closed questions can present a number of other risks—the risk of getting the question 'wrong' or becoming too directive, and the risk of having to negate the other person, as well as the risk of lapsing into an interrogation, or of limiting the options.

The first risk, where the onus is on the interviewer to get the question 'right', means that the interviewer can end up becoming more directive of the agenda if the asking of closed question after closed question is not working to open up the discussion. In using closed questions to try to find the right lead, it can become a hunt for the right question—looking for a point of engagement. At these times, it may be more useful to reflect on what is not being heard in the situation or summarising where things are at in the conversation. It may be that the story has been difficult to establish because the client is not forthcoming—and why this is so is important to review. They may not wish to talk to you or trust you, they may not perceive you as competent, they may not be confident about their view of events, or they may not have the words to express what is going on for them.

If the question is 'wrong', too, the client is put in the situation of having to negate the person who has asked the question. For example:

Worker: Are you waiting to see me?

Client: Uh, no, I'm waiting to see [another person present].

In correcting the wrong assumption, the person has to negate the other person, whereas asking an open-ended question 'Who are you waiting to see?' would have led to the person indicating their wish to speak to a particular person. This may seem like a trivial example, but when a closed question is asked with more serious implications, the issue of having to negate another person becomes critical. In disempowering situations, we are less likely to have the confidence to negate someone else.

Closed questions can be coercive and manipulative, either intentionally or unintentionally. A closed question such as 'Are you going to leave?' presents only one option to the client. There may be many other options to consider, so an open-ended question such as 'What do you want to happen?' may not foreclose on these options.

Closed questions, however, have a very important role to play, both in assessment and intervention processes. They enable the clarification of the intensity of mood states or intentions, for example, or details of a past history that may be critical in understanding the current circumstances.

Focus on practice

Watch any of the nightly television programs showing court room scenes or police investigations and observe the way in which questions are often framed to force particular answers. In these situations, the answer is anticipated—a leading question has been asked. This is one of the major differences in human service work: we want to ask questions that will not presume to know the answers but instead encourage the client to discuss their circumstances as openly and fully as possible.

The use of open-ended questions tends to be encouraged more than closed questions in that they can be the more exploratory and less presuming style of the two forms of questioning.

Asking open-ended questions, however, can also present challenges. Some workers, for example, propose that 'why' questions should be avoided, on the basis that asking people for explanations of situations is too difficult and that these questions therefore can be experienced as 'accusatory and blaming' (Trevithick 2005, p. 163). In contrast, others argue that 'why' questions should be avoided because they tend to encourage the client to look for a pre-conceived response, which may even include 'excuses or rationalisations' (Geldard & Geldard 2005, p. 74). The other reason that 'why' questions may be difficult to answer is that when we are caught up in personal difficulties it can be very difficult to answer issues of causation or reason—that is, to understand why we are facing difficulties in the first place. Other schools of thought, however, see such questions and issues of explanatory power as a fundamental part of a person's story, which we will explore later in Chapters 11–14. For example, psychodynamic theory at its core looks at the connections and interpretations we make as to what is happening in the present. Similarly, narrative approaches emphasise the importance of what meaning we are making of particular situations.

Safer and more adaptable questions to ask are questions beginning with 'what', in that they are 'consistent with a systemic perspective that stresses that no one person is responsible for a problem or a difficulty that exists' (Trevithick 2005, p. 163). For example:

What do you think led to the argument?

What is your reaction to that situation?

These open-ended questions using 'what' are particularly useful in the narrative approaches, which emphasise externalising the problem.

Asking the opening question

An open-ended question is often used to start off a conversation—and it is the one question with which you can be relatively prepared. It is useful to think of the opening questions that appeal to you and why. Beginning with the very vague and open-ended question:

How are you?

The client may reply:

Not good at all. I've had some tests recently and it looks like I have cancer.

The question has worked as a vague, open-ended question to engage the client around the issue they wish to discuss. At other times, though, the question can be seen to be a social question we ask as a greeting rather than an authentic question of well-being. As an open-ended question, it is too vague and too socially anticipated. So the reply can be:

Fine. How are you?

And the conversation has not gone very far in relation to the specific issue. The client may not have seen this as an invitation to talk about their particular situation. Another open-ended question is required to get to the specific issues. Some other opening questions could be:

What's been happening?

What's going on?

These questions imply that something has occurred to trigger the contact with you as a human service worker, but they do not imply that the person needs or wants help in the way that other opening questions do:

What can I help you with?

What's the problem?

The questions about what has been happening or going on also do not imply that the person is the one with the 'problem'.

Asking succinct questions

A succinct question is a brief and concise one. Lengthy, imprecise questions often confuse both the worker and client. The worker can lose track of what the 'trigger' was for asking the question and the client can be left wondering what it is they are being asked. For example, how would you answer this question if you were the client?

Why do you think, I mean, what caused him to be so angry, or if not angry so frustrated when you spoke last with him, um, or was it, um, when he rang you up?

Notice in this question above, there is no hesitation to gather thoughts about what the question should be. The extraneous language used, such as 'I mean' and 'um', also breaks up the flow of the communication. Lengthy questions also can lead to multiple questions, where a client can be asked:

Do you talk with anyone about this? I mean, have you spoken with your family? Or your friends? What do they think?

In this 'question', there are now three different questions all wrapped up in the one delivery. It is as if the worker has found a flow and is rolling out all their thoughts in one go. The dilemma for the client becomes which of these questions to answer first. As a general rule, one question at a time should be asked.

Questions that are short and specific can provide a greater focus to the interview, even if it means pausing to work out exactly how that question should be framed. This momentary pausing and gathering of thoughts is often better than rushing headlong into a series of questions.

Asking relevant questions

Your agency context and purpose will determine what questions are relevant to ask. Even in a specific setting, however, each one of us will ask different questions. What we think is relevant is therefore a question of our subjective and objective positioning.

Focus on practice: group task

In a role-play, one 'client' is interviewed by a number of 'interviewers' (other students in the class) for about 10 minutes. The other students each take a turn at asking a question, and participants come to realise how differently they are thinking about the situation from the person sitting next to them. It is a good opportunity to reflect on why you wanted to know about certain issues and what you saw as relevant in this interview.

In our time-limited client contact, we need to be quite selective about what we ask and why we ask it. Armstrong (2006, pp. 19–20) states:

> When we know another person … there are often large blank spaces in their history … We may have only a sketchy—and probably one-sided—grasp of what occurred over substantial stretches of that person's life. And yet our encounter with them is not puzzling or missing something.

Armstrong is highlighting a fundamental process of engagement with another human being—that engagement is not about necessarily knowing the whole story, but about the narrative that is established together. Working with a client to establish their story is about building up an understanding of what has occurred in relation to specific events or experiences. It may be a sketchy picture, but the work together is about building as relevant a picture as possible, even though it is not complete.

Given that we gather selected information, the question of relevance therefore becomes critical. Important questions to keep in mind throughout all your practice are:

- Why am I asking this question?
- Who am I to this person and therefore is it valid that I ask these questions?
- For whom is the information important and/or relevant?
- Which elements of the story need to be clearly established, and which ones do not?
- What other sources of information are available—for example, through case file notes—rather than repeatedly asking the person the same questions?
- How would I feel about answering that question?

Another major dimension of relevance is cultural relevance. What cultural dimensions of this person's experience may impact on whether this question is relevant or not? For example, in many cultures, providing information about mental and physical health experiences is taboo. As Youssef and Deane (2006, p. 5) note: 'Social reputation ("soma") is a valuable asset in Arab culture and great efforts are made to avoid any shame that may threaten or compromise the family reputation.' An awareness of all of these issues is fundamental to sensitive and focused communication. Discussing these issues first may be more important than trying to move into a conversation that is experienced as culturally insensitive.

Relevance can be considered not only in relation to the nature or breadth of issues that are discussed but also in relation to the depth of questioning that occurs. One comment made frequently by students in role-play situations in debriefing afterwards is: 'I wanted to ask that question but I thought it might upset them.'

Clearly, this is an important consideration in all of our conversations—the intention is never to cause harm and distress. This highlights the importance of checking in with the client about their own comfort with such questions and the direction of the conversation, as well as us checking in with our own comfort levels and knowledge bases. What this hesitation may mean, however, is that if a worker avoids some questions for fear of upsetting a client, a client may not have the opportunity to tell their story. We live daily with the issues and preoccupations of our own lives, so telling a story is not necessarily distressing. It may seem overwhelming to the worker, but it may not be a new or 'out of control' experience for the client. Similarly, if the question does upset a client in inviting them to explore a part of their story they have perhaps not verbalised previously, this may not be *necessarily* a bad outcome, but rather a step in the process of establishing their story and their experiences.

In considering the depth of questions and their relevance, it is also important to consider some of the assumptions we carry as workers about the ease of answering questions. Working in the human services, we can become very familiar with a language of emotions and of the inner world, and often of valuing self-disclosure and self-reflection. These ways of being are not ways in which all people are comfortable, and yet we can expect answers to the questions we ask. The question of relevance remains crucial in determining whether we need to ask these types of questions.

Asking specific questions

As the worker in the situation, typically you have the responsibility to keep a sense of direction and purpose. This is about avoiding a sense of 'drift' (Trevithick 2005, p. 170). This drift can emerge when the direction and purpose of the conversation disappears and either the client and/or the worker is left wondering what the conversation is about.

The aim is to elicit specific information in relation to a client's story, not generalities. We need to know the detail of a client's experiences, which can then lead on to specific interventions. If we do not know how unhappy someone is, for example, we are not going to know enough about their current mental health to adequately undertake a **risk assessment** with them. If we do not know how difficult the financial circumstances are, we may not make the referrals or seek the assistance the situation requires.

In exploring stressful situations with clients, for example, it can be useful to think about the dimensions of events that make them stressful. Martin (1997) highlights the duration, timing, predictability and controllability of events as critical dimensions to understand. One example is of a client who reports spending a great deal of time in their room. Until an assessment of duration, timing, predictability and controllability can be undertaken, it is very difficult to discern what kind of situation this is, from the client's point of view. It may be extremely problematic behaviour, or it may be quite functional behaviour in the client's context as it gives them time and space to work out issues in their own mind or to avoid conflict in other areas of the family home.

This scenario highlights how critical it is to think about what is important in listening to a story. It is not about taking the response, at face value, as the information that is required. With the example above, further questions are required, such as:

When did this start?

How long do they stay in their room?

Why is it a problem?

Is this new behaviour?

What concerns you about it?

What do they say or think about it?

Only after asking some of these more specific questions can we begin to establish an understanding of how significant this is as a problem.

Asking specific questions can also mean raising taboo or difficult issues. Sometimes just asking a question gives permission to discuss a previously taboo issue or even, in some instances, the beginnings of a language to discuss it. In a recent conference presentation, Dora Black (Black & Trickey 2005) from the Tavistock Clinic in London spoke about her work with children recovering from experiences in family situations where one parent has murdered the other parent. Black's own therapeutic training had been within the psychoanalytic model, where specific questions were not asked. Interpretations of free associations or thoughts of the client were made, but questions rarely asked. In working with these children, and particularly in discussing the art work they created about what they had witnessed, she has discovered that because of their developmental stage at the time of the murders, these children did not actually have the language to name the experiences they needed to talk about. Thus, asking specific questions as well as commenting on the drawings was one way of bridging this gap in the client's story.

For many people, some specific questions can be highly culturally and personally inappropriate, as mentioned in the previous subsection. As individuals, we have different levels of tolerance for questions and privacy. Similarly, as families and communities we have spoken and unspoken rules in relation to information that is public and that which is private. For some families, saving face and not airing private problems is a primary value, whereas for other families, the boundaries of family extend to the community, and nothing is private. In asking questions, we can be intruding across the boundaries of another person's private world. When questions are experienced as intrusive, it is important that opportunities to decline questions are provided.

Building an understanding of the specifics of a person's situation is critical. What we do with the responses to questions therefore requires careful consideration so that we continue to develop detailed understandings of what the client has said. Sometimes we might only ask one question and regard that as having explored the issue. For example:

Worker: How does that leave you feeling?

Client: Oh, I'm just so disappointed.

Worker: What do you think you'll do now? Look for more work?

In this scenario, the worker has asked about the emotional state and has been told one specific dimension of this experience, but on hearing an answer, they have not explored it any further. They have moved on to the next issue, having spent only a moment focusing on the emotional response the client has expressed. One person's disappointment is very different from another's—one person might be very depressed in stating this but another might be quite dismissive. One answer does not necessarily provide the depth of understanding that might be required.

So, revisiting that situation, a follow-up question begins to provide some further elaboration on the disappointment:

Worker: How does that leave you feeling?

Client: Oh, I'm just so disappointed.

Worker: Tell me some more about that?

Client: Well, I thought the money stress was going to go away with these extra hours of work, but I'm still behind. It just isn't fair. Every time I try to get on top of things, they just keep on collapsing around me. I'm just useless!

Now the worker has a sense that the client is possibly feeling both angry about the situation and disappointed with themselves. A lot more exploration of this situation is required to really understand what is going on. Alternatively, the worker could have just used the word 'Disappointed?' to indicate a question and similarly encouraged further elaboration on the emotional experience of the client.

In many settings where you work, specific psychosocial or risk assessments will be used by your organisation to focus the information that is considered crucial. One of these specific assessment frameworks is a Mental State Examination (MSE; Bloch & Singh 2007). An MSE is designed to assess the cognitive status of a client in many different settings. It is included below as an example of a very specific set of questions that can be asked. Other agencies may have very standardised psychosocial assessment questions that are used—they ask specific questions so that specific issues of risk and protective factors can be addressed.

■ **Chapter 9 explores assessment further and presents more of these assessment frameworks.**

Focus on practice: the Folstein Mini-Mental Status Examination

Orientation
What is the year?
Season?
Month?
Date?
Day?
Where are we?
State?
County?
Town?
Hospital?
Floor?

Registration
I am going to name three objects and I want you to repeat them after me. [Interviewer: give one point for each correct answer. Repeat the objects until the patient can name them all—six trials maximum.]

Number of trials?

Attention and calculation
I am going to ask you to do some subtraction. Think of the number 7.

I want you to subtract 7 from 100. Now subtract 7 from that and keep on going. 100, __, __, __, __, __. Stop.

Alternatively, spell 'world' backwards.

continues

Recall
Please name the three objects that I had you repeat after me just a short while ago. [Interviewer: give one point for each correct answer.]

Language
Please name these for me [Interviewer: show patient a watch and a pencil].

Now please repeat the following: 'No ifs, ands or buts.'

Now I am going to ask you to do something for me: 'Take a paper in your right hand, fold it in half and put it on the floor.' Now I want you to read this and do what it says. [Interviewer: hand the patient a card that says 'close your eyes'.]

Now please write a sentence for me on this blank piece of paper. [Interviewer: give the patient a blank piece of paper and ask him or her to write a sentence for you. Do not dictate a sentence. It must be written spontaneously. It must contain a subject and verb and be sensible. Correct grammar and punctuation are not necessary.]

Visual motor integrity
Please copy this design. [Interviewer: on a clean piece of paper, draw intersecting pentagons, each side about 1 inch, and ask him or her to copy it exactly as it is. All ten angles must be present and two must intersect to score 1 point.]

Total score (30)

Interviewer: assess patient's level of consciousness along continuum:

alert   drowsy   stupor   coma

Source: Coulehan & Block (2006, pp. 222–3).

Specific questions, however, can be used to manipulate responses or they can also mean we miss out on critical information. In asking about 'x' and not 'y', we may then not realise that 'y' is the problem. Being too specific can mean that, because we do not ask the 'right' particular question, we do not establish what is going on or a particular detail of the circumstances. Again, using open-ended questions and clarifying responses further can help in avoiding some of these difficulties.

Asking neutral questions

Questions can be very loaded; that is, questions can carry very strong assumptions within their wording or expectations about the answer. Particularly in the early stages of a working relationship, minimising these assumptions is important, and asking questions that are more neutral in their language is a way of building the relationship and finding out the necessary information.

As discussed in earlier chapters, language can marginalise and stigmatise people. Questions need to be framed as inclusively as possible so that a client's story can be explored with as few barriers as possible. Assumptions about relationship status and sexuality, about financial capacities, about abilities and capacities, about beliefs and culture, about normative worldviews and a range of other dimensions of our lives can be made through the questions we ask or are asked. Rather than illustrate a whole range of possibilities, the reflection task below encourages you to think about the underlying assumptions that may be present in those questions.

■ Reflective practice questions

1 What underlying assumptions could be present in the following questions?
   - Have you talked to your friends about that?
   - What does your wife think?
   - Why didn't you write to them to lodge your complaint?
   - Are you going away for Christmas?
   - Can't your children help you?
   - Why didn't you move out?
   - Why don't you get Home Help involved?
   - Can you tell me about why you've been so upset lately?
2 How would you reframe each of these questions so that some of the assumptions in each question were minimised?
3 For the closed questions that are presented above, how would you reframe them as open-ended questions?

Some questions are very 'leading' in their intent; for example: 'Don't you think it really would be important to tell them what's going on?' In this type of leading question, the answer that the worker wants to hear is present in the question. Leading questions such as these have either the intention or the outcome of trying to 'coerce the other person into agreement' (Koprowska 2005, p. 84). For all these reasons, framing questions as neutrally but as specifically as possible is important.

Another way to address these issues is to clarify with the client whether the process of asking these questions is appropriate.

Worker: Is it OK to be asking these questions?

Client: Actually, I feel really uncomfortable.

Or alternatively, asking an open-ended question:

Worker: How do you feel about me asking these questions?

Client: It's fine. I just find it difficult to talk about these things.

Either of the answers could have been given to those questions—again, it is a matter of judgment as to whether you frame the question in terms of your role with the client or more as a question of how they are feeling in the situation. Depending on the reasons for the human service contact, this situation could be recontracted so that a mutual understanding of why such questions are being asked, and whether they are essential or not, can be reached.

Asking 'difficult' questions

In some areas of practice, very difficult questions need to be asked. They are difficult questions in that they relate to very extreme human situations and, often, ethical dilemmas. Many of these questions emerge in medical and legal contexts, such as the question as to whether a patient is consenting to resuscitation or not, whether a family is consenting to an organ donation of a deceased family member, or whether a child is a victim of abuse within a family. In these situations, some general principles (see, for example, Evans, Tulsky, Back & Arnold 2006) include:

- taking time to prepare in your own mind what the purpose of the conversation is about
- finding the optimal time to talk with the key people
- speaking clearly and slowly about the issues, even considering the possibility of using a warning or preface to what you are about to say
- being aware that on breaking bad news, very little is heard and remembered subsequently, so repeating and revisiting issues is essential
- checking in with people as to what they have heard, so that you can affirm that the message has been accurately conveyed.

Asking questions at an appropriate time

Sometimes a question may be an excellent question to ask, but the timing is wrong in the context of either the working relationship or the session itself. For example, we may not have established enough rapport with the client or we may be at a point in a conversation where it is inappropriate to ask such a question.

Carolyn identifies timing as a key issue in reflecting on her psychodynamically oriented practice, as outlined below, in the context of complexity too:

Focus on practice: helping clients face painful truths about themselves

One of the tasks of the psychodynamic therapist is to take in the verbal and non-verbal communications of their patients and to try to understand unconscious thoughts, imaginings and feelings about themselves, their relationships and their difficulties.

As some of our patients are struggling with experiences of lifelong losses, trauma and rejection, or painful realities such as disability, terminal illness or complicated mourning, our timing and way of making the 'unthinkable' thinkable is crucial.

With the therapist's support, their capacity to explore and integrate this aspect of themselves (and the attitudes of others towards them, which is arguably more difficult) will strengthen them and free them up to engage more with life. However, this may be a highly painful and confronting experience.

Discussing her clinical work with adults presenting with intellectual disability on a background of trauma, Sinason (1992, p. 319), describes this well: '[S]ome of their histories and life stories are extremely harrowing, and the process of recovering them has made me understand why their authors numbed their memories and minds for so long.'

Within the counselling literature, in particular, a great deal of emphasis is placed on the experiences of reluctance and resistance (Shulman 1999; Egan 2002). Reluctance, as in a hesitation, is seen to emerge when a client knows that 'managing their lives better is going to exact a price' (Egan 2002, p. 163) and thus is related to hesitating in the face of change. **Resistance** 'refers to the reaction of clients who in some way feel coerced' (Egan 2002, p. 165). A strengths-based approach is to understand these processes more positively as processes of timing and readiness—to focus on why a person might be able to look at change at one point as distinct from another.

Specifically regarding the timing of questions, some key questions to ask in relation to reluctance and resistance are:

- What's going on here?
- Am I as the worker adequately addressing the issues with this client?
- Are there barriers to good communication within the relationship in relation to effective engagement?
- Am I asking appropriate questions?
- Are there other problematic dimensions of this communication process—that is, not so much the focus of the interview but the way I am talking about issues or the language I am using?
- What is it about the timing of these questions that may be contributing to this reaction?

Asking questions that lead to new insights

We seek assistance primarily for new insights—to manage situations or emotions differently, to gain information or understand situations more fully, or to learn new skills and behaviours. Talking with someone else or in a group is an opportunity to see things differently.

Below, Karen describes her work with Max and a moment of new insight.

Focus on practice: challenging with creativity

It is sometimes important to have clients see the other person's viewpoint in order to recognise their own.

Max presented at the Community Health Centre at age 50, referred by the GP for 'support'. With a recent acrimonious marriage breakdown and estrangement, retrenchment from his role as bank manager and a serious health issue, Max was in need of much more than support. Max was suffering situational depression, sleeping problems, poor nutritional intake and financial difficulties. Over a number of sessions, Max reassessed some of his previously insignificant relationships and was able to regain some pleasure from a sporting interest, a daily walk and a 'cooking for one' class.

His relationship with his adult children remained thwarted by his former wife's bitterness, leaving him feeling embarrassed and belittled by the experience. This was compounded by a lack of status, and hence self-esteem, associated with the job loss. He felt unworthy of his son and daughter's offers of support and consistently refused them, although his ill health meant that he was unable to complete some tasks himself.

No amount of challenge regarding reciprocity in family relationships was effective in budging his view that, 'I am the father, I should be providing for my children and I don't deserve their help', until one day I asked him about his own role with his parents. He told me that for many years before they died he had maintained their house and garden.

Karen: 'So how was it that you did this for your Mum and Dad?'

Max: 'They weren't well, I am their son, and I wanted to help them stay in their home.'

Karen: 'What would it have been like for *you* if he had refused your help, because he felt he should have been able to cope?'

Max [hesitates, then bursts into tears]: 'My pride has got in the way of letting my kids be my kids!'

While we will look at these issues in greater detail in Chapters 11–14, this section raises the importance of questions that open doors for clients. Questions that lead to new insights can be oriented around previous perceptions and experiences of coping so that a client begins to reflect on their strengths and capacities. They can be oriented around what they think the future could be for them and what would need to change in order to bring that about. It is an important emphasis to maintain throughout a communication process, as questions so frequently focus on risk, problems and difficulties, rather than exploring protective factors, successes and strengths.

Below, Suzie's example from her practice highlights the use of these sorts of questions.

Focus on practice: the change process requires small manageable steps

Mac: 'Would you like to see some of the new pictures that I have done?'

Suzie: 'Yes, that would be great.'

Mac shows his drawings.

Suzie: 'They are excellent, I like this one in particular … you have a real talent there.'

Mac: 'I was asked to do a whole set of murals by this shop the other day—they have seen my stuff before, but I just can't. I think that's why I am an addict; I just think I am afraid of success.'

Suzie: 'What does success mean to you?'

Mac: 'Like doing something and then being expected to be able to repeat it again and again.'

Suzie: 'Can you give me an example?'

Mac: 'Like giving up H [heroin]. I have stopped before but that doesn't mean that it will last.'

Suzie: 'What if, with your drawing, you could do one wall or one section of the shop? Is it possible to negotiate dong something smaller, with no commitment to do any more—just that one piece of work? Is it possible to draw it first on paper until you are happy with it then show it to the shop owner and, if they like it, replicate it on the wall?'

Mac: 'Hmm, I am not sure. I never thought to ask them about that.'

Suzie: 'Sometimes it is helpful to take the things that have worked and replicate them in different situations, start with smaller steps and build up.'

Suzie says of this interaction: 'Concrete examples of problem solving can provide opportunities from which to draw parallels with other, more complex issues such as addressing substance use that a client is finding problematic.'

Advocates of a strengths perspective suggest asking the following types of questions (Saleebey 1997, pp. 52–4):

1 survival questions
2 support questions
3 exception question
4 possibility questions
5 esteem questions.

These questions will be looked at more closely in Chapter 13. The exercise below encourages you to think about how you use questions.

■ Reflective practice exercise: using specific responses

1 Conduct a 10-minute role-play with a 'client', having an observer present. Debrief around the probing skills you have used throughout the interview.
2 Then try to conduct the interview again using:
   • only open-ended questions
   • only closed questions
   • no questions—only comments or statements
   • only problem-focused questions
   • only strengths or problem-focused questions.

This exercise helps you to identify your preferred questioning style—for some of us, asking questions is easy, whereas highlighting and reflecting back emotion is more challenging and vice versa. This exercise highlights that we can use different questions to explore different dimensions of a situation. There is no one right way, but there are a lot of choices throughout an interview as to where we head with the conversation. It can be helpful to have a very active observer who will call a halt to an interview when certain skills are being demonstrated or not. This can be a useful way to begin to identify your style and skill preference.

What other verbal skills can I use to establish and clarify the story?

Questions are clearly not the only verbal skills used in exploring a story. Questions or comments using single words or statements also keep the conversation flowing. Without being formally structured as questions, by using tone of voice and non-verbal encouragers, the following can be used to establish further the detail of the client's situation:

You're angry?

It was due on Monday?

Disappointed?

Another type of probe is a request—an invitational or encouraging way of asking the client to explain more about their situation, in a genuine, interested way:

Tell me some more about that.

Go on …

Say some more …

Carl Rogers, the founder of person-centred counselling, appears in a well-known video interview with a client called 'Gloria' (Rogers, Ellis & Perls 1977). One of the striking features of this interview is that throughout the half-hour interview Rogers rarely asks a question. The rest of the interview is conducted using the skills of empathy, paraphrasing and summarising via which he clarifies Gloria's story and works with her towards a deeper understanding of her predicament. This interview highlights that questions are not always needed—that information can be shared through an engagement in a different form of dialogue. This is an important point. While many human service interactions are not going to be in the therapeutic context in which Rogers was working, many people tell their stories through means other than the more interrogative style of questions.

In the following chapter, we will explore the specifics of these skills of paraphrasing and summarising, again looking at their strengths and limitations.

Chapter summary

In this chapter, the key verbal probes for exploring a client's story have been described and analysed. The ways in which asking open-ended or closed, succinct, relevant, specific, neutral, well-timed questions that may lead to new insights have been explored, highlighting both the strengths and limitations of each of these questioning styles. The chapter then focused on the options of not asking questions but instead using other forms of verbal probes to achieve some similar outcomes. It depends on how the conversation then moves as to whether a further question is needed or whether an empathic observation is made. Conversation is created between people. Egan (2002) suggests that an empathic highlight should follow a question, but there is no rule. In a therapeutic context, more weight is given to empathic reflections and observations. The next chapter considers other verbal microskills such as paraphrasing and summarising.

Reflective practice questions

1   What have you learnt about:
    • some of the risks involved in asking questions?
    • the differences between an open-ended and a closed question?

- some of the key considerations in asking effective questions?
- the various types of probes?

2 What is your preferred style of questioning?

3 How do you think you will go about opening an interview or point of contact with someone?

4 What assumptions have been evident in some of your questions to date?

5 What are some of the key challenges for you in asking questions?

Key references

Egan, G. (2007). *The skilled helper: A problem-management and opportunity-development approach to helping* (8th edn). Pacific Grove: Brooks/Cole.

Hepworth, D., Rooney, R. & Larsen, J. A. (2002). *Direct social work practice: Theory and skills* (6th edn). Pacific Grove: Brooks/Cole.

Shulman, L. (1999). *The skills of helping individuals, families, groups and communities.* Itasca, IL: F. E. Peacock Inc.

Trevithick, P. (2005). *Social work skills: A practice handbook* (2nd edn). Maidenhead: Open University Press.

Additional resources

Breaking Bad News website—for strategies and guidelines: www.breakingbadnews.co.uk/.

Skills Cascade: www.skillscascade.com/index.html.

Wadsworth curriculum connector—online tutorials: www.wadsworth.com/connector/ViewConnector.do?connectorId=1&categoryId=13&resourceTypeId=2.

Paraphrasing and Summarising

8

Building the dimensions of people's experiences

In the previous chapter, we explored the use of questioning skills. Questions help to probe further into a person's story and to understand more fully some of the specific dimensions of thoughts, feelings, events and behaviours. However, you will need other skills to support people in the telling of their story. If you only ask questions, the conversation can become an interrogation, as if running through a checklist. You need other skills to open up the story further; specifically, you can encourage someone to elaborate on their story through the use of paraphrasing, reflecting and summarising skills.

In some ways, paraphrasing and summarising skills are the skills we use least in our everyday conversations. We tend not to actively reflect back to someone what we think we are hearing. Instead, we pick up the threads of a casual conversation. In a professional conversational context, paraphrasing and summarising skills are a critical way of ensuring a number of things are occurring. In reflecting and summarising, you can confirm the details of the story with the client. In doing this, you can confirm that you are hearing the story as they want and need you to hear it. This serves to confirm that you are listening, and, in particular, listening to the key dimensions of the experience.

Reflecting skills

■ Remember the model of communication presented in Chapter 2, where messages are encoded by the sender and decoded by the receiver. The skills of paraphrasing and summarising enable these messages to be confirmed or represented.

Reflecting skills are used in many ways—to affirm, challenge, clarify or normalise a person's situation. Generally speaking, 'reflecting' is a process of 'mirroring back to the interviewee what the interviewee has just said, as grasped by the interviewer' (Dickson 2006, p. 167). The term **paraphrasing** is similarly used to describe this process of relating back, in your own words, what you think you have heard the other person say. The risk in using the term 'mirroring' to define these processes is that it implies a fairly static and direct reflecting back of what has been said, which is not the aim of the skill.

A distinction that is sometimes made between the two types of responses—reflecting and paraphrasing—is that: '[W]hile paraphrases are restricted to what is actually said, reflections concentrate upon less obvious information frequently revealed in more subtle ways' (Dickson 2006, p. 171).

Paraphrasing is seen by others to be more typically reflecting 'cognitive aspects of messages rather than feelings' (Hepworth, Rooney & Larsen 2002, p. 141). However, these distinctions are not maintained by everyone, and the terms are often used interchangeably.

Egan (2007) refers to these responses as empathic highlights, as discussed earlier in Chapter 6. Being empathic and engaged in a story involves actively conveying that you are hearing how the person feels, as well as understanding the 'facts' of the story. The 'formula', as presented in the earlier chapter, for this active response is:

You feel … [state emotion] because … [state event, behaviour or condition].

Applying this, a conversation may go as follows:

Client: I'm exhausted. He's terrifying. He's so controlling of my every move, and any attempts I've made to break out of the situation, he's right there. When I moved out, he tracked me down and made me move back in. He threatened to beat the crap out of me if I didn't. And he would have if I hadn't returned. When I changed my phone number, he got it by tricking my best friend that there was an emergency.

Worker: You feel controlled and trapped by this guy because he's right there, wherever you turn in your life.

Client: Yeah, that's it. I'm trapped by him. It's useless trying to escape him.

In most situations, however, the essence of this formula is applied in a more abstract way. That is, we listen for the feelings and events that are at the heart of what is going on for the client, but we actively convey this using other responses; for example, in more abbreviated forms:

So he's trapping and controlling you, wherever you turn …

Alternatively, a more extended form would be:

And what I'm hearing is that while you're really trying to deal with this situation with this guy, whenever you do, he's able to get back in your life, and that's why you're feeling so tired and controlled.

Owning the reflection as the worker, through the use of such expressions as 'What I'm hearing', 'It seems like' or 'I wonder if ...', gives the client the opportunity to respond by refuting, correcting or agreeing with the view. If a reflection is correct, it is often greeted with the response: 'Exactly!'

Melissa's example of discussing self-disclosure was used in an earlier chapter. Below, notice her very natural integration of these paraphrasing skills in her conversation with a student.

Focus on practice: a discussion on disclosure

Student: 'I know I shouldn't self-disclose, but ...'

Melissa: 'It feels as though self-disclosure would help with rapport.'

Student: 'Yes.'

Melissa: 'What was the context?'

Student: 'I am working in a mental health setting. We go out on home visits to families with a member with a mental illness. My brother has bipolar.'

Melissa: 'It feels as though it could help to share this information.'

Student: 'But I know I shouldn't.'

Melissa: 'It sounds as though you know there is a rule but your gut in telling you something else.'

Student: 'I guess so.'

In most instances, a reflection should move the conversation in some way. For example, notice the lack of movement in the following conversation:

Client: I'm absolutely ropeable about this whole situation.

Worker: You're feeling ropeable about this situation.

This is merely repeating or mirroring directly, not reflecting what has been said. In some instances, however, this might be a useful thing to say, depending upon the tone of voice and the intent in saying it—it might help the client hear how angry they are in a particular situation. The risk is that the person may feel mimicked, and that the conversation has gone nowhere. In fact, the client could feel more frustrated and unheard:

Client: I'm absolutely ropeable about this whole situation.

Worker: You're feeling ropeable about this situation.

Client: That's what I just said.

It raises the question as to what conditions in the client–worker relationship enable us to feel most heard. It is rarely about repeating the story or echoing feelings, but more about what kind of purposeful response we give and receive.

In some instances, however, reflecting is used to just 'sit' with the emotion or the experience that is being described. Rather than finding out more detail through the use of questions, or challenging perceptions through reflections and summaries, sometimes reflecting back the emotion—be it heartache, exhaustion or excitement—is a way of sharing in the reality of the client's experiences. Returning to the case example from earlier, in this instance, the response would be different:

Client: I'm exhausted. He's terrifying. He's so controlling of my every move, and
            any attempts I've made to break out of the situation, he's right there.
            When I moved out, he tracked me down and made me move back in.
            He threatened to beat the crap out of me if I didn't. And he would have if
            I hadn't returned. When I changed my phone number, he got it by tricking
            my best friend that there was an emergency.

Worker: It sounds really tough, and exhausting and frightening.

Client: It is. It's lonely, it's frightening and I can't see it ever ending.

Here, the events or the feelings are not drawn out in any extensive way. An affirmation of how the client may be feeling is reflected in a short, empathic statement. This type of response is more of a normalising response.

Normalising is a skill of affirmation. Typically, it draws upon a wider pool of knowledge or experience to place a person's experience in context. For example, in grief situations, many people report that they feel as if they are going mad, given their experiences of auditory or visual hallucinations, or disturbances to their sleep or capacity to function as they had prior to the loss (Raphael 1983, pp. 40–3). Normalising is used in these instances to reassure people that these experiences are shared human experiences. Normalising can focus on experiences, such as these grief experiences, or on coping strategies. For example, this conversation shows how the focus is on normalising the experience following the death of a child:

Client: It's just stupid, stupid stuff. I hate feeling so disoriented. I feel as if I'm
            losing my mind. It's as if she's right there beside me and it drives me
            crazy. Am I crazy?

Worker: You're feeling like you're crazy because of these different experiences of
Shawana. Many people who have been through a major loss, like you have,
experience similar things and find that they ask themselves these questions.
It seems to be part of the 'making sense' of it. They're not mad, nor are you.

Normalising provides a useful reflection and reminder that people are not alone in their distress and difficulty. For some people, however, this is not what they need or want to hear. Their experience feels unique to them and any attempt by people to presume to understand it is deeply offensive. Workers have different competencies and inclinations in using these particular skills. The potential for the least authentic interaction is high in the case of paraphrasing, as is the potential to offend with normalising. The potential to deepen understanding and empathy, however, is also high and this is why these skills are encouraged.

In using reflecting skills, thinking about why you are using these skills is important. A major argument for the use of these skills is that they actively convey that you have understood where the person is coming from. These responses do more than simply clarify (Hargie 2006a). These responses can lead to new insights because people:

1   can feel heard, respected and affirmed in what they are experiencing
2   may not have thought about the situation in that way or listened to what they were really saying before. The listener can hear a different account of things because of their experiences, their listening or their distance from immediate involvement in the situation. This is so often why someone is sought out as a listener.
3   may not realise what they were saying in terms of its implications
4   may not realise the levels of contradiction and complexity in their situation, which can be often hard to hear or to articulate. Reflecting or paraphrasing often normalises these complexities of emotions and experiences, through naming them and recognising them as significant dimensions.

These skills are primarily about acknowledgment and provide a way of actively demonstrating the values discussed in Chapter 1.

Sometimes you will be aware of the other layers of the conversation or interaction. For example, someone can be talking about their sadness, and in describing their feelings of sadness—both verbally and non-verbally—you hear that they also seem to be feeling helpless or angry or ambivalent. This is why it is so important to be 'reading' the total communication message in any conversation: the message involves both the verbal and the non-verbal in fundamentally important ways.

Like questions, reflecting and paraphrasing skills highlight the influence of your own opinion and worldview in the interview. Your choice of response will depend on what you are listening for, as the following exercise highlights.

Focus on practice: a group role-play

If you are working in a supportive small group learning context, a group role-play or discussion can be a useful way to explore this issue of how you use particular responding skills and what connections they may have with your initial exploration of the story and assessment from the start of an interview.

One person can role-play the client. Alternatively, you could watch a short piece of a DVD conversation where someone is describing their situation.

The whole group, with the exception of the role-playing client, becomes 'the worker' in that each person is invited to state what they would reflect back to the client.

1 From the client's perspective, which response did they prefer and why?
2 How diverse are the responses your group has formed?
3 What was the focus of the responses?
4 What are the consequences of this focus? Think in terms of the direction of the interview, the impact on the client and the theoretical assumptions underpinning this focus, for example.

Overemphasising the skill of paraphrasing can mean you have conveyed that you are listening, but you may have established little of the 'facts' of the story, so are lacking the information to assess what's going on. Again, it depends upon your context and purpose as to whether you need to be probing for details or adopting a more reflective approach.

Summarising skills

Summarising skills are used in a conversation to draw together the various issues that have been discussed. While reflecting and paraphrasing skills are used throughout an entire interview, the use of summarising skills is connected to some important timing issues. A summary can be used after the initial overview of the issues with which someone is grappling:

Worker: So you're saying you've been into Centrelink, you've spoken with the duty worker there and they've referred you to me, to follow through on your complaint?

Client: That's right.

It can also be used when you feel stuck or as if you are not able to really hear what is going on. It enables clarification, through a summary rather than a question:

Worker: So you're saying you've been into Centrelink, you've spoken with the duty worker there and they've referred you to me, to follow through on your complaint?

Client: No, that's not what I said. I spoke with someone on the phone and they said I have to go into Centrelink after talking with you to put in my complaint.

This establishes the details of a complex sequence of events, which the worker had misunderstood. Had he or she not summarised their understanding at this early point in the conversation, the misunderstanding could have caused major confusion. Clarifying statements like 'Let me see if I have this right …' can also be added to actively seek the client's view on what you are summarising (Trevithick 2005, p. 166).

A summary also can be used as a way of setting the direction of the next stage of conversation. It can close off some issues, too, and enable a focus to be agreed upon for the rest of the discussion:

Worker: So we've talked now about what's going on for your parents, and how bad you think their housing and care situation is. You've said how urgent your father's health is at this point in time and that things need to change. What do you think we should focus on now?

A summary can also be used at the end of a meeting to bring together the essence of the conversation:

Worker: We've talked about a lot of things today—your job hunting, those really difficult interviews, and your thoughts about what's next. We've decided that talking with the financial advisor could be a good step and you're going to give that some thought. We'll talk again in a few days about whether that's something you'd like to do.

In general, a summary should be short. A long or mistimed summary can seem laborious. A long summary can sound as if it is just repeating what the client has said or presenting them with a 'shopping list' of issues, rattled off one after the other. A summary should aim to pick up on the complexity of issues to date and typically open up the next phase of the discussion. In addition, conveying accurately the language and emotional intensity of the client is important. A mismatch of emotional intensity can leave people feeling very misunderstood or misrepresented:

Client: [having discussed in detail their sexual harassment case and the need to access legal representation] So I'm a bit concerned about what this is all going to cost.

Worker: So with all this hassle of finding a lawyer, the ongoing complications at work with seeing this person each day, your ongoing difficulties at home, you're now also really overwhelmed by the enormous cost of the lawyers.

In this instance, the worker has used overly intense emotional language—the client said they were a 'bit concerned' and the worker has said 'really overwhelmed'—and the client has been inundated by all the issues they have described, when in fact they were needing to focus on the cost issue.

Summaries are particularly important in situations where cultural or linguistic misunderstandings can occur. For example, when working with interpreters, it is sometimes difficult to know what has been communicated to the client, in the sense of what they have heard you say and vice versa. Summaries by both the client and the worker can mediate some of this verbal difficulty, checking out regularly with each other as to what has been heard and understood.

Chapter summary

In this chapter, some of the skills you can use to consolidate the details of a person's story have been overviewed, with an emphasis on reflecting and summarising skills. These skills help to establish a common understanding of a conversation, and the overall work. They are skills that we tend not to use much in our everyday conversations, but they are one way of ensuring that the client's story is heard accurately and from their point of view.

Reflective practice questions

1 When would you use reflecting and summarising skills, and when would you not?
2 When have you experienced the effective and/or ineffective use of these skills?

Key references

Egan, G. (2007). *The skilled helper: A problem-management and opportunity-development approach to helping* (8th edn). Pacific Grove: Brooks/Cole.

Hargie, O. (2006a). Training in communication skills. In O. Hargie (Ed.), *The handbook of communication skills*. New York: Routledge (3rd edn, chap. 20, pp. 553–65).

Rogers, C. (1967). *On becoming a person: A therapist's view of psychotherapy*. London: Constable.

Additional resources

Person–centred links, University Counselling Service, University of East Anglia: www.uea.ac.uk/menu/admin/dos/couns/training/person_centred.htm.

Three approaches to psychotherapy (Rogers, Ellis & Perls 1977) This video in particular shows Rogers working with a client, Gloria, using primarily reflecting and summarising skills.

Forming an Assessment— Setting the Agenda

9

LEARNING GOALS

- Understand the purposes of assessment.
- Consider some of the inherent challenges in assessment.
- Understand the focus of assessments.
- Describe the process of setting goals for the work.

In the previous chapters, we have focused on some of the ways in which you can meet with people, engage in conversation and begin to explore the circumstances that have led to your contact. Each time you ask a question, or reflect back to someone what you have heard, you are making decisions about what to respond to, what to hear (but not actively address) and what to remember from the conversation and perhaps address at a later point. You are beginning to focus more on particular dimensions of their situation. You are forming an assessment of someone's circumstances and how they are placed within those circumstances. The example below highlights that an interview or conversation will need to move to a particular focus after an initial period of exploration of the issues and concerns.

Focus on practice: moving from the story to an assessment

Your client, Mohammed, has described his difficult transition to life in Australia. He arrived several months ago on his own, after 14 months in a refugee camp adjoining his home country. He has some distant relatives living in Australia, but not locally and contact has been difficult. His wife and two children are back in his home country and he is working towards bringing them to Australia, but it is not an easy process, especially given the language and financial resources required.

Mohammed has found accommodation, but is experiencing great difficulties in adapting to Australian life. He has come to your service for assistance with a number of urgent issues:

- his housing circumstances, which are appallingly overcrowded
- his health—given both his lack of financial resources and therefore adequate nutrition—and his traumatic memories, which combine to keep him from sleeping
- his difficulty finding employment.

1 What else would you want to know about Mohammed and his situation?
2 What would you see as some of the major issues to address and how would you go about setting the priorities?
3 Are there other issues you would want to explore and possibly focus on in your conversation?

The term **assessment** is very broad, meaning different things to different professions. In Chapter 1, we looked at the general purpose of human services: working with people to alleviate adversity and oppression, and to promote well-being and health. Assessment, therefore, focuses on exploring how people are functioning and how optimal functioning and well-being can be enhanced through the provision of specific resources for their inner and outer worlds.

The type of assessment required varies according to your agency context. In work that is oriented towards a social care agenda, where change is a mutual goal, the assessment process focuses on setting goals for the work that will be engaged in together. Where you may be in a position of imposing a change agenda, assessment may be driven more unilaterally by you. You will be making judgments and decisions about coping capacities, about risk and about resources. This work will still focus on change as the outcome, but it may not be so mutually determined.

The processes and purposes of an assessment are filtered by the influences we have discussed in earlier chapters: your values, knowledge bases, skills and organisational context. You can see in the following scenario that you would be dealing with a number of different points of view throughout the assessment process and needing to juggle these.

■ Remember the values, knowledge bases and theoretical perspectives explored in Chapters 1–3. These provide the basis for your assessment.

Focus on practice: Mr and Mrs Willis

Mr and Mrs Willis have been living in their own flat for thirty-two years. They have strong connections with a number of neighbours, and their local RSL club. Mr Willis fell last week when he got up to change the TV channel. He is currently in the local hospital with a fractured leg and wrist. Since his admission, the nurses have become very concerned about his memory, and organised for an assessment, which has confirmed that he has dementia. The worker is to talk with them about a range of home-care options, including the possibility that he move into a supported living arrangement. Mrs Willis is distraught about the diagnosis and the possibility that he might move out of their family home, where they have lived for so long. She has made it very clear that she wants her husband to come back home and live there. In her mind, this admission is about his physical recovery only and she is terrified of any suggestion that he no longer live with her.

Reflections

1 What would you see as some of the immediate issues that would form part of your assessment?
2 How would you go about exploring these issues with the people involved in this situation?

In this scenario, the focus has moved from the initial presenting problem or concern (Mr Willis's hospital admission) to establishing some underlying concerns. In this instance, the presenting and underlying problems are quite different depending on who it is you talk to about the situation.

Who is the assessment for?

Ideally, an assessment process enables the establishment of a mutual agenda for future action. In exploring the story with the client, the assessment process provides the step towards establishing the basis for further work and the ongoing purpose of the relationship. It is about moving from 'starting where the client is at' to working towards where the client wants to be, or, in more mandated circumstances, where others consider the client should be.

The different formats and requirements for assessments raise some major challenges in the assessment phase, depending upon who the assessment is really for. For example, the following assessment formats are identified by Lloyd and Taylor (1995, cited by Trevithick 2005, p. 130):

- third-party assessments
- investigative assessments
- eligibility/needs assessments

- suitability assessments
- multidisciplinary assessments.

In addition to this are assessments within the context of a more therapeutic client–worker relationship, where the assessment is conducted to ascertain what should be the focus of the work together. Some of these challenges raised in the assessment process are described now, before moving into an exploration of assessment frameworks.

What are some of the challenges in the assessment process?

Forming an assessment is a challenging task. An assessment needs to capture the diversity of a client's life and the complexity of their unique and current situation. An assessment can have a profound impact on a person's life; for example, if it denies them eligibility for a service, or concludes that their child can no longer live with them. In the scenario outlined above, an assessment may lead to a strong recommendation that Mr Willis does not return to his home. A comprehensive assessment, therefore, is critical. Some major challenges inherent in the process of assessment are briefly discussed, including the focus of the assessment, the adequacy and accuracy of the information gathered, the fluidity of assessment, who is setting the agenda, and cultural diversity.

Assessing for risks or strengths?

In the context of resource limitations and a focus in Western society on risk management (Webb 2006; Lupton 1999; Giddens 2002), many assessments remain risk assessments, adopting a primarily pathogenic approach to understanding people and their circumstances. Morley (2004, p. 127) defines a risk assessment as a 'process of categorising and recording particular information about clients to make predictions about the likelihood of particular future events occurring'.

Assessment is, therefore, often about highly subjective predictions being made (Webb 2006; Lupton 1999; Giddens 2002). A focus on capacity building, both within the person and within their wider families and communities, is also an essential component of an assessment. A comprehensive assessment should incorporate both a risk and a strengths perspective.

Adequate and correct information

In some situations, a systematic, detailed assessment may be possible. This enables an in-depth discussion of many dimensions of a person's life. Assessments, however, are often conducted quickly with people in less than optimal conditions. The available time and place can impact, therefore, quite profoundly on the outcome of an assessment. Similarly, what clients know of you—and what the information they give you will be used for—influences willingness to disclose, or even the perception that disclosure of certain information is relevant or required.

Fluidity of information

People and circumstances change over time, sometimes very rapidly and sometimes more slowly. For example, poverty is an experience that, in Western contexts, often shifts for people across their life span, rather than remaining a constant (Room & Britton 2006). People acquire different coping capacities or different stressors. Assessments can be written up and placed in client files, and become the source of information about the client over many years, without ever being revisited or verified. Details of a client's life can be handed on as 'fact' when it may long since have changed yet again.

As a worker, too, you will change over time as you develop your knowledge base and practice wisdom. Perceptions of risk, for example, may change the more you are confronted with people in a particular setting. You may realise you were more cautious or liberal in an assessment of an earlier client situation as a result. The information gathered in any assessment process therefore necessarily changes over time.

The monitoring of changing needs and issues is important in situations where ongoing contact is maintained. Thus, assessment is both a one-off process often done in a first interview and an ongoing process throughout the length of any contact with someone.

Who is setting the agenda?

Your aim is to set a mutually agreeable agenda for the work to be done together. At another level, you as the worker, and as part of a particular agency, influence that assessment and agenda, either implicitly or explicitly.

Depending upon the context, you and your client may disagree in your assessments of a situation. For example, different perceptions often arise as to whether someone requires an involuntary hospital admission, in acute psychiatric service settings; whether a parent should be allowed to continue living in the family home following allegations of sexual abuse; or whether a young person's non-attendance at school is indicative of more serious underlying problems at home or at school.

Making an assessment with clients in involuntary circumstances is a more fraught process. Important information is likely to be missing if a strong engagement and rapport has not been able to be established. It is also critical to explain why the assessment process is important—that is, clarifying the role

> ▪ Remember the example of the research conducted at the Alfred Hospital where people told very different dimensions of their story to the researcher because of the perception of her role as researcher rather than social worker.

▨ Reflect back on Mohammed's situation earlier in this chapter, and on the ways in which your assessment may be influenced by an agency's resources.

accurately (Trotter 2006, p. 18). This can be done through ongoing, honest discussion. People's experiences of trust in both personal and professional relationships may have been poor, and so this is an opportunity to promote collaborative problem solving (Trotter 2006, p. 21).

An organisational context will also impact profoundly on what assessment can be made and what subsequent interventions can occur. Thus an assessment may be limited by what resources are available rather than what the person actually needs or has a right to access (Ife 2001; Trevithick 1995, p. 130).

Diversity

Assessment processes have the potential to amplify all sorts of assumptions of worldviews that are made. Assumptions about consent, agreement and commonality of goals can be imposed without a worker realising it. Assumptions about ways of living and perceptions of coping and adaptation (Rigney & Cooper 2004; Smith 2001) similarly can be imposed. You can build optimal understanding by asking open-ended questions about the meaning of events or actions and using paraphrasing. Workers have a professional responsibility to develop and sustain cultural awareness in relation to all diversity issues—including sexual, religious and cultural diversities—and to their own prejudices and assumptions. As Miller, Donner and Fraser (2004, p. 380, citing Goodman 2001) note: 'Most people with agent status do not view themselves as having power and privilege.'

▨ Remember the diagram reflecting the communication process in Chapter 2. In any assessment process, the worlds of the worker and the client are present.

What assessment frameworks are used?

As we listen to someone speak, we begin to form an assessment. In this sense, assessment begins as the work begins. Typically, though, after an initial exploration of the client's story, the communication needs to become focused in a purposeful way around specific issues of concern and action. Given the specifics of each particular context, no single assessment framework exists. Many agencies have standardised intake and assessment forms and procedures, reflecting the assessment of the particular dimensions they focus upon in service delivery.

Why we come to emphasise some dimensions and not others within these assessment processes is an important question to reflect upon. The theoretical dimensions we privilege as a worker and/or as an organisation profoundly influence the listening. As Fook (1993, p. 74) states, assessment is 'the phase of casework helping where a theory is formed about the particular causes of a particular person's particular situation'. This returns our discussion to some of the earlier chapters, when theoretical perspectives influence what we hear and why.

Many assessment frameworks focus primarily on a client and their inner-world dimensions. Their personal stories and circumstances are understood as follows (Egan 2002, p. 77): 'Stories tend to be mixtures of clients' experiences, behaviors and emotions. Traditionally, human activity has been divided into three parts: thinking, feeling and acting.'

From this theorising of human experience, a framework for listening includes the following questions.

Focus on practice: a framework for listening

1   What are the main points?
2   What experiences are most important?
3   What themes are coming through?
4   What is x's point of view?
5   What is most important to them?
6   What does he/she want me to understand?
7   What decisions are implied?
8   What is she proposing to do?

Source: Egan (2007, p. 89).

This framework will enable the worker to listen to the priorities in the client's story. It provides an insight into the inner world of the client by linking their thinking, feeling, behaving (both in the past and the future) and events. These dimensions begin to provide the basis of 'what' to listen for.

What is underemphasised at this point is a sense of the client's circumstances in relation to their outer-world connections—their relationships, their social and cultural context, and the nature of their **structural context**. As Fook (1993, p. 75) notes: 'The structural element will always interplay with personal factors such as biography, current life events, emotional and psychological characteristics, genetic inheritance, physical health and so on to create a unique personal situation.'

This shifts an assessment from focusing only on thinking, feeling, behaving and events to include the mediating dimensions of context.

A multidimensional assessment framework

A multidimensional framework includes these other dimensions of the social, structural and cultural context. The ways in which the environment enhances or inhibits coping become part of the assessment. Frameworks that assess behaviours, thoughts and feelings place the individual at the centre of the construction of the problem, as distinct from being acted upon by external forces

This is one way of thinking about assessment that focuses primarily on the individual and their inner world. Other assessments consider outer-world dimensions that impact on these experiences, taking into account such factors as poverty and marginalisation. Later chapters will elaborate on these themes in greater detail.

or circumstances. Assessment within the human services involves inquiry about these external dimensions as much as the internalising of situations and events.

As outlined in Chapter 3, a multidimensional approach seeks to understand both the inner- and outer-world dimensions of a person's circumstances. The inner-world dimensions include the biological, psychological (thoughts and feelings) and spiritual dimensions. The outer-world dimensions include the relational, social, structural and cultural dimensions. A broad, multidimensional assessment framework may include, then, each of these specific dimensions (Anglem & Maidment 2004; Fook 1993, pp. 153–5; Harms 2005; Hepworth, Rooney & Larsen 2002).

Exploration of each of the dimensions in the box below includes an assessment as to whether they are significant sources of stress and vulnerability, or significant sources of protection and resilience. In some instances, you may need to ask very direct, closed questions to establish an understanding. In others, you may develop your understanding from a more descriptive conversation, so that specific questions do not need to be asked. Each of these dimensions can become the focus of further exploration and intervention.

Focus on practice: exploration of the client's physical dimensions

In what ways do the following dimensions impact upon a person's current circumstances and coping capacity:

- age
- sex
- general presentation and appearance
- general health or medical status—drug and alcohol use
- housing environment
- physical changes and their impact on well-being
- sources of physical stress
- physical coping strategies and resources?

At the end of this chapter, links to other specific websites with assessment tools are provided.

Depending upon the circumstances, a range of other questions about specific dimensions may be relevant. Within the physical dimension, specific assessment tools are available to assess drug and alcohol use and abuse (National Drug and Alcohol Research Centre 2007) or general health (Goldberg 1978), for example.

Thousands of scales have been developed to assess a person's psychological functioning. For example, scales are available to measure intelligence; emotional intelligence; the impact of trauma, stress and grief; and personality traits. *The Diagnostic and Statistical Manual of Mental Disorders* (APA 2000) is a major collation of psychological assessment guidelines used in many mental health settings. For any psychological phenomenon, a scale seems to be available.

Remember, in Chapter 7, a mini-Mental Status Examination was presented as one example of an assessment tool.

Focus on practice: exploration of the client's psychological dimensions

In what ways do the following dimensions impact upon a person's current circumstances and coping capacity:

- intellectual capacity
- language capacity
- self-image, self-esteem
- sense of agency and motivation
- mental health status
- subjective perceptions of the problem situation
- psychological changes and their impact on well-being
- sources of psychological stress
- psychological coping strategies and resources?

Similarly, spiritual dimensions of a person's life can be measured using a range of assessment tools, such as Fowler's faith development framework (Parker 2006), as described below.

Focus on practice: exploration of the client's spiritual dimensions

In what ways do the following dimensions impact upon a person's current circumstances and coping capacity:

- importance of spirituality
- spiritual practices
- importance of religion
- religious practices
- spiritual changes and their impact on well-being
- sources of spiritual stress
- spiritual coping strategies and resources?

Many dimensions of a person's social network also can be analysed, using a range of available tools.

Focus on practice: exploration of the client's social dimensions

In what ways do the following dimensions impact upon a person's current circumstances and coping capacity:

- qualities of relational networks with partners and family
- qualities of social networks with neighbours, friends, colleagues, clubs, church groups etc.
- perceived and received social support
- significant power relationships
- qualities of social roles the person engages in
- occupation—education, schooling, university or paid/unpaid work
- major family and life events and history
- sources of social stress
- relationships with social institutions (past or present)
- social changes and their impact on well-being
- sources of social stress
- social coping strategies and resources?

A comprehensive assessment of a client's social dimensions or environment networks can be undertaken by talking through and drawing an ecomap, for example. In an ecomap, you document each relationship a person has with those in their immediate networks, according to its particular qualities or resources. You can also show the interconnections between people in a person's network. Each relationship can be illustrated by using different connecting lines, according to the legend in Figure 9.1:

An ecomap can also identify workers in various organisations who may be contributing to a particular situation. In this sense, they are the front line of the structural dimension; that is, the broader systems that impact profoundly on a person's coping capacity, and indeed, often create the difficulties in the first place. Thus it is equally important to assess the structural and cultural dimensions that impact on people's lives.

The assessment tools for the structural dimensions are less utilised in many organisations, and are often more the focus of discussion than formal assessment.

Figure 9.1   Mapping a client's social network using an ecomap

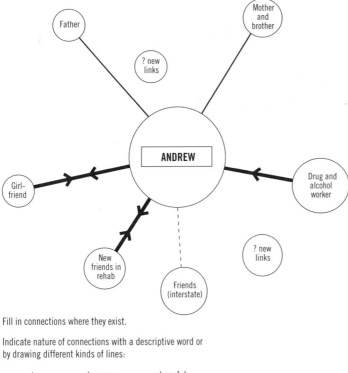

Fill in connections where they exist.

Indicate nature of connections with a descriptive word or
by drawing different kinds of lines:

━━━ strong ——— tenuous ┈┈┈ stressful

Draw arrows along lines to signify the flow of energy, resources etc.
Identify significant people and fill in empty circles as needed.

Source: Harms (2005, p. 37).

Focus on practice: exploration of the client's structural dimensions

In what ways do the following dimensions impact upon a person's current circumstances and coping capacity:

- financial circumstances
- legal circumstances
- socio-economic status and roles
- political circumstances
- gender roles
- occupation and education level
- structural changes and their impact on well-being
- structural sources of stress
- structural resources?

Cultural assessment tools are also available, and address a range of issues within this critical dimension. For example, the checklist of social dimensions (Fook 1993), cited earlier, provides a way of reflecting on the dimensions not only of your social identity but also those that may be influencing your client's experience. Other possible areas of assessment are outlined below.

Focus on practice: exploration of the client's cultural dimensions

In what ways do the following dimensions impact upon a person's current circumstances and coping capacity:

- culture and ethnicity
- culture and sexuality
- subculture or cultural minority status
- socially held beliefs and myths
- cultural changes and their impact on well-being
- cultural sources of stress
- cultural coping strategies and resources?

A sound assessment should focus on both the risks and strengths in a client's circumstances. Listening for strengths is critical in any assessment process. While such a focus by no means diminishes the difficulties a person has been encountering (Saleebey 1996, 1997, 2001), understanding how someone is addressing or coping with other demands or similar demands has been an important inclusion in understandings of change and adaptation.

Focus on practice: unexpected strengths

Many practitioners within antenatal care services have been concerned with women's non-attendance at clinics when substance abuse issues have been identified. However, a study of twenty-three women attending a major women's hospital, combined with a data analysis of 1250 hospital records, found that:

- 'Contrary to popular opinion, less than half (47%) of the women identified that a lifestyle preoccupation with drug and alcohol issues posed a barrier to attendance for pregnancy care.
- The overall attendance rates for women with substance abuse issues … do not differ greatly from those without substance use issues' (Tobin 2005, p. 7).

These findings have enabled workers to rethink their understandings of women's efforts to attend antenatal care, while also dealing with drug and alcohol issues.

An assessment process can vary from a very brief discussion and assessment of needs or rights, through to a planned assessment period over a specified time period or number of sessions. For example, the Metta Youth Psychotherapy program (Harms & McDermott 2003), which provides intensive psychotherapeutic support for at-risk young people for up to three years, has a four-session assessment period, at the end of which both the client and the worker discuss the continuation or cessation of therapy.

What interventions are used?

At the end of an assessment process, possible interventions typically are discussed. A 'contract' is sometimes formally undertaken, in that there is agreement around the problem areas or difficulties, and the ways of addressing some or all of these issues. Typically, you will discuss:

- the perceived areas of work for change
- how that may be achieved
- your mutual responsibilities and commitments as the worker and the client
- the time limits on your work together.

From this, a plan for intervention emerges. Interventions can address resources in the inner and/or outer worlds of the person. For example, inner-world interventions can help clients develop new ways of coping with behavioural or belief restrictions that they impose on themselves, or others impose on them. Intervention strategies include counselling, **psychoeducation**, social support strategies and group work. Outer-world interventions can help clients manage and change the structural restrictions in their worlds, and may involve very active worker action to bring this about with the client. Intervention strategies include resource provision, referral, liaison, advocacy, capacity building, group work and community development.

How do we set the goals for the work?

Whereas the assessment process establishes the overall problem and strengths areas in a client's circumstances, and resource requirements, contracting and **goal setting** are important processes in establishing the priorities for intervention, both from the client and worker perspectives. That is, when you have explored with your client the key themes of their difficulties, priorities need to be set as areas for work. It is not possible to address everything at once, and a process of goal setting enables a plan to be developed around the tasks and timelines.

The goals for the kind of intervention need to be articulated and ultimately, even if only in a small way, mutually satisfactory. Burstow (1987, p. 21) recounts her own experience of encountering a therapist who worked in such a different way from what she was wanting and needing by way of intervention at a particular point in her life:

Focus on practice: mutual goals

From a client's perspective, Burstow said: 'I was in the process of making a major move and found myself panic-stricken. The therapist I sought help from was client-centred. He was very empathic, very kind, very respectful, but he gave me nothing on which to hold. He offered no clue about what I might do in a situation that demanded that I act almost immediately and in which I was paralysed. I emerged from the session more terrified than ever and by now markedly suicidal. Eventually, I did what I should have done in the first place. I sought help from someone who would offer me what was missing in myself, who half-gave-me, half-helped-me-find some preliminary sense of direction. I sought help, that is, from a helper who did not ask me to be an equal at a point where I clearly could not be.'

Reflecting on this experience, Burstow reflected that the therapist 'failed' because:

1 He did not acknowledge or understand how vulnerable she was.
2 He assumed that everyone at all times was equally able to get their needs fulfilled, as long as the therapist is empathic.
3 He did not take an active leadership role when such a role was required.

■ Remember Mrs B's work with Nicole in Chapter 6 and their ability to reset the goals of their relationship.

One possible explanation for why this situation occurred was that the client and the worker did not explicitly discuss the goals of the work. An opportunity to discuss goals together is vital.

Goal setting occurs in a number of ways, depending upon the context and the theoretical orientation of the worker. Goal setting is also influenced profoundly by the client's engagement in the change process. Some general views on the nature of the goal/s that are set are expressed by Marsh and Doel (2005, p. 117):

In common with the selected problems, the chosen goal should be one which is feasible and desirable for the person to achieve within the agreed time limit, relatively specific, something they feel motivated about, and a clearly understood link between how the goal will alleviate the problem.

Breaking this down further, an emphasis is often placed on developing SMART goals (Marsh & Doel 2005, p. 36), where the well-known acronym SMART stands for specific, manageable, achievable, realistic and timely.

1 *Specific*—Goals should be very focused on particular issues, not generalised states of being, for example. This may involve transforming the following statements, where the worker is talking with his client about his goals in moving in with his new partner and her two children from another relationship:

Worker: What would your goal be with these kids?

Client: I really want to be a good dad to these kids [Goal statement 1].

Worker: How would you know when you're being a good dad?

Client: I'd be doing things that would be natural, like taking them to the park that's just around the corner, and those things that I know we already share. But I'd also be able to be clear with them when they start mucking around and not having to worry that they're 'not mine' [Goal statement 2].

The first goal statement is very global and it may be hard to know when it has been achieved. Notice the second goal statement is much more specific to certain situations, so the client will know when he has, by his criteria, met his goals.

2   *Manageable*—Notice the goals set in the above scenario are manageable goals, in that they involve some small steps about the kinds of changes he wants to see. Many people set unmanageable goals, in a number of different ways. They may take too long, or require resources that are unattainable, for example. Goals need to be manageable in the sense that adequate resources are available—be they time, energy, condition or personal resources (Hobfoll, Ennis & Kay 2000).

3   *Achievable*—The client in this scenario can probably easily achieve these goals, in that he has specified two ways in which he can make immediate, tangible changes in his interactions. Many people set unachievable goals in that they are incompatible with where they are at. The goal may be too ambitious or require too much of a major change in too many dimensions of someone's life. For women leaving situations of violence, a major barrier is often the prospect of leaving so many dimensions of their life, including sometimes children, to ensure their own safety.

4   *Realistic*—This client is talking about realistic goals in that visiting a park is probably possible in a local community during the course of a week. Realistically, he recognises that differences in parenting style may be a source of difficulty in the new family arrangement. He is not setting ambitious goals, for example, by promising a trip to Disneyland or that he is always going to be able to maintain his commitment without fail.

5   *Timely*—His goals seem to be appropriate in terms of timing in that he is anticipating moving into a new situation. If he was presenting in the midst of a high conflict situation around parenting issues, these goals may not be so timely. They may be too late! The timeliness of goals is an important determinant of their success.

■ Reflective practice questions

1   Think of a time when you have wanted to change a specific dimension of your life. What was your goal?
2   In retrospect, would you describe it as a SMART goal, using the definition above?
3   What were the challenges or barriers to making the change in the first place?
4   How did you go about trying to make the change?

5 Did it work? Why or why not?

6 What would you do differently if you were looking to make that change again?

Egan's problem-management and opportunity-development model has been used internationally as a framework for an interview, or series of counselling sessions with clients. It is based on a process of goal setting, and includes the following questions within each stage of the model:

Focus on practice: the Egan model

Stage 1—problem clarification and ownership

What's going on? What are the problems, issues, concerns or undeveloped opportunities I should be working on?

- Help clients to tell their story.
- Help clients break through blind spots.
- Help clients choose the right problems/opportunities to work on.

Stage 2—goal setting and commitment to goals

What solutions make sense for me? What do I need or want?

- Help clients use imagination to spell out possibilities for the future.
- Help clients choose realistic and challenging goals that will equal real solutions (agenda for change).
- Help clients find incentives—what am I willing to pay for what I want?

Stage 3—strategies for accomplishing goals

What do I have to do to get to what I want?

- Help client see possible actions—many ways to achieve goals.
- Help client choose best fit.
- Help client to craft a plan.

This is a very structured way of working and, in some settings, can be applied fully. Processes like these enable us to talk through goals with clients or to even write them down on paper or on a whiteboard so that they are clear and can be easily remembered.

One way of opening up further the goal-setting process is through brainstorming. Brainstorming involves either verbally or in written form proposing every possible solution or course of action relevant to the current situation. The important feature of a brainstorm is that it is done without any censoring of ideas. Brainstorming enables the opening up of new possibilities. In some situations, the lack of new coping strategies is part of the problem. As a discussion between the client and worker, brainstorming enables a pooling of resources, without any pressure towards a particular option at this point in time.

Worker: Let's think about what the possibilities are here, without putting any limits on at this point. What have you thought about doing?

Client: I'm stuck. I can't think of anything.

Worker: OK, that's one option. To stay stuck, to keep things as they are!

Client: [laughs] I hadn't thought about that! No way, I couldn't bear that. You know, when I felt more on top of things, I did half wonder about going back to school and finishing that.

Worker: And what would you then do?

Client: Well, I'd be able to work, you know. Get a job. Get out of the house, get some money. Have some time out from my kid who drives me nuts sometimes.

Already in this scenario, six different goals have possibly been identified, all of which would need some further exploration:

1   not doing anything
2   going back to school
3   seeking a job
4   seeking a job after a further educational experience
5   getting out of the house—either through employment or through other options like community involvement
6   time out from the children.

Not changing is equally a possible goal to explore with a client, when so much of the emphasis is on changing. It provides a safe place to explore why change really is so often necessary, and emphasises that any change beyond staying the same is challenging and possibly new territory.

Some goal setting will require negotiation and possibly compromise, where the goals with clients are not mutually agreeable. Some actions will be imposed on clients, as a result of court orders, and in these situations the goals needing to be met are not always mutually agreeable. Working through the SMART dimensions of goals, however, can go a long way in finding mutually agreeable grounds for continuing the work together.

Chapter summary

In this chapter, the assessment process has been explored, highlighting its usefulness in focusing the client's story on intervention and action. A multidimensional assessment framework was presented as a very broad way of understanding a client's situation and resources. The risks inherent in assessment have also been examined, particularly in relation to perpetuating fixed and assumptive assessments of people and their circumstances. The chapter briefly outlined some of the interventions human service workers use in relation to both outer- and inner-world change for clients. The chapter concluded with an exploration of the process of goal setting, often used in practice to set the agenda for action and intervention.

Reflective practice questions

1 What have you learnt from this chapter about:
   - assessment processes?
   - interventions?
   - goal setting?
2 What are the dimensions you find relatively straightforward to ask about in an assessment process and what do you find more difficult? Why?
3 What are the risks in an assessment process?
4 How often do you consciously use goal-setting processes to work through issues? What impact do you think this has on your practice?

Key references

Anglem, J. & Maidment, J. (2004). Introduction to assessment. In J. Maidment & R. Egan (Eds), *Practice skills in social work and welfare: More than just common sense.* Crows Nest: Allen & Unwin (chap. 8, pp. 112–26).

Hepworth, D., Rooney, R. & Larsen, J. A. (2002). *Direct social work practice: Theory and skills* (6th edn). Pacific Grove: Brooks/Cole.

Trotter, C. (2006). *Working with involuntary clients: A guide to practice.* Thousand Oaks: Sage Publications.

Additional resources

American Psychiatric Association and the DSM IV: www.psych.org/.

Australian Drug Information Network: www.adin.com.au.

Beyondblue: The National Depression Initiative: www.beyondblue.org.au/.

David Baldwin's Trauma Information Pages: www.trauma-pages.com/.

National Drug and Alcohol Research Centre: www.ndarc.med.unsw.edu.au.

Published International Literature on Traumatic Stress database via the National Center for PTSD (USA): www.ncptsd.va.gov/ncmain/index.jsp.

Victim's Web at Swinburne University, Centre for Neuropsychology: www.swin.edu.au/victims/index.html.

World Health Organization: International Classification of Diseases (ICD): www.who.int/classifications/icd/en/.

Assessing Risk Situations

10

LEARNING GOALS

- Understand the dimensions of situations of conflict.
- Review your safety and appropriate responses
  when you are threatened by others.

Working with conflict

In Chapter 4, we looked at the concept of your 'use of self'. The focus in that discussion was primarily on how you engage as a worker in empathic and supportive work. In many situations, this is the case. For many workers, though, the work is characterised by frequent or occasional incidents of physical and/or verbal abuse. You need to respond to these situations with some additional priorities, using some different communication skills.

To date, the examples we have looked at have been focused on interventions where a relatively positive engagement is possible, even if not in the initial stages of working together. Below, David describes one such practice experience where initial engagement seems to be progressing relatively smoothly.

Focus on practice: David's example of working with conflict

When I was working in a prison mental health unit, I was the case manager for a client with an acquired brain injury and English as a second language. He was charged with a serious offence and was distressed about a discussion he had with his solicitor regarding whether he should plead guilty or not guilty at court. He asked to see me and I decided to see him in an open area rather than an enclosed office as he appeared quite agitated. We talked through his concerns for some time and he gradually became less distressed.

1   How do you think David approached this conversation to help reduce his client's agitation?
2   What do you think you would feel and do in this type of situation?

At this stage, David and his client have managed to engage together in conversation. The client seemed to be experiencing a highly agitated physical and emotional state, influenced not only by his stressful circumstances but potentially through the communication difficulties and cognitive difficulties created through his brain injury. Some of the skills David may have used at this time include:

- Speaking slowly and calmly, avoiding getting caught up in the emotion of his client's agitation.
- Speaking clearly and in plain English so as not to compound his client's disempowerment through use of a second language.
- Emphasising an alliance or joint problem-solving relationship, alleviating the isolation that the client may have been experiencing—for example, focusing on statements like: 'Let's see what we can sort out together here.'
- Containing the emotion, through not mirroring the distress and agitation of the client but mirroring a calmer state of being that may reduce the client's agitation; and, in some instances, maintaining a distance so that the client does not feel enclosed or trapped, and maintaining a steady eye contact to help engage them in a different mood state.
- Establishing an appropriate and structured agenda for the conversation. If someone is feeling overwhelmed by their circumstances, remember the goal-setting tasks outlined in the previous chapter, where goals are SMART. In this instance, a very small goal may need to be set in discussion to establish a focus in among the chaos.
- Using repetition: the 'broken record' technique encourages the use of one message until it is heard by the other person. In David's situation, he may say something like: 'Let's just sit over here and talk.' And he would repeat

> ▨ In Chapter 12, we explore containment skills more fully.

that one statement calmly until that can happen. In some situations, this can be inflammatory, but in others it helps restore a focus and an agreement on the next step in the conversation.

All of these skills are examples of **smoothing skills**. They aim to reduce agitation and the emotional escalation in a situation that can make communication difficult to sustain. David also took steps to ensure his physical safety, and potentially that of his client. It is not always appropriate to move into private spaces if you have concerns for yourself and/or your client. Thus, his responses were active, assertive responses. Despite all of this, the situation escalated into a more violent one. We will return to this situation in the next section for further discussion.

The situation to date, however, highlights the differences between passive, aggressive and assertive responses. Workers need well-developed assertion skills, particularly in response to aggressive encounters. The advantage is that assertion:

> … unlike aggression, respects the other person's rights and dignity through the use of non-hostile verbal content and verbal attributes. Assertion is expected to produce strong relationships and relatively few negative emotions, whereas aggression is predicted to result in a strained, emotionally charged relationship (Rakos 2006, p. 348).

Rakos (2006, pp. 350–1) identifies four behavioural components of what he terms 'conflict assertion'. Related to the above situation, they include:

- The content of the conversation—that is, what David says in response to his client's distress and agitation.
- Paralinguistic elements, or how the communication sounds to the other person—that is, does David speak loudly, warmly or gently, for example?
- Non-verbal behaviours or how people appear to be physically reacting— does David bear in on his client's personal space or step back and allow him some space?
- Social interaction skills—Rakos (2006, p. 351) identifies 'the timing, initiation, persistence and stimulus control/skills that enhance the impact of the verbal behaviour'; what does David choose to do by way of focus in the conversation, for example?

Assertive feedback is characterised therefore by:

- 'I' statements—as the worker, you clearly own your feelings, beliefs or thoughts. The other person can disagree with your view.
- Behaviour focused statements—you provide feedback or criticism of the behaviour not the person. Behaviour can be changed.
- Seeking a response back from the person—through asking, for example, 'What do you think?'

Other strategies can be used to deal with criticism and feedback that is directed towards you, as indicated below.

Focus on practice: dealing with criticism

If it is accurate	accept it
If it is clearly wrong	disagree and affirm yourself
If it is unclear	clarify it
If it is about you rather than your behaviour	accept the behavioural part if it is true reject the personal label
If it is nagging, too frequent or destructive	use fogging techniques
If you are stunned, overwhelmed or confused by the criticism	delay your response

Source: Kotzman (1995).

In managing conflict, it is important to consider what the best strategy may be. If the situation is too emotionally confronting or unexpected, it may need to be dealt with at a later time. Opportunities for direct conversation about a conflict should be normally offered, however, as one way of escalating tension is to deprive people of opportunities for open albeit difficult communication. Clients have often experienced major disadvantage and oppression in prior circumstances, and the opportunity for them to be heard and for a solution to be worked towards is critical. Intense emotions can be compounded through a lack of resolution mechanisms. Mediation, in some instances, can facilitate a resolution.

Threatening behaviour towards ourselves

As mentioned above, David's situation with his client escalated further. The scenario continues from where it left off above.

Focus on practice: the next step in David's work with a client

David reflects on the next steps in his contact with his client: 'We talked through his concerns for some time and he gradually became less distressed. We started to discuss if it might be useful to arrange for the solicitor to visit again, when as part of a stream of conversation he focused on my use of the word 'guilty'. He became highly agitated, believing I was now accusing him of being 'guilty', and he started to become aggressive and threatening before storming off. The situation was becoming quite tense and I decided to remove myself from the area to avoid it escalating any further.'

This example reinforces how factors such as a disability and limited language skills can inhibit clear communication, and the importance of assessing potential risk from both verbal and non-verbal cues prior to and during work with distressed and agitated clients.

1   What is your immediate reaction to the situation David and his client were in?
2   What do you think you would do in a similar situation?
3   What cross-cultural issues could be influencing this situation?

David's example is one where finding common ground just was not possible. David's safety, the client's safety and the safety of others in the environment became the most immediate issues of concern. In reviewing the situation, some conclusions may be that:

- It was an unsafe situation to stay in and physical evacuation was needed. In some instances, police may need to be called.
- The client's agitation was indicating something very important about what was going on for them—the disempowerment, frustration and anger they were experiencing.
- He had a low frustration tolerance—in this case, as a result of the brain injury.

In this instance, the client returned later and smashed furniture in the reception area, and the police were called to manage the situation.

Unfortunately, many human service workers face circumstances of **violence**, stalking or threatening behaviours (Ogloff 2006; Warren 2006). Some key principles or skills for these situations include maintaining:

- a high alertness for your own safety, both physical and emotional and trusting any intuitions about a lack of safety, even if not manifest in a situation; the situation may be physically unsafe and you may need to leave
- reporting and accountability requirements, including always alerting someone in your organisation as to your whereabouts
- high levels of proactive planning, and preventive strategies in relation to concerns for your safety and well-being through supervision.

Revisiting confidentiality

In reflecting on situations of risk, it is important we briefly revisit the issue of confidentiality. Reflecting back on Mark's situation outlined in Chapter 4, and his expressed suicidality, or considering David's client who was threatening violence and indeed became violent, some additional considerations in confidentiality come into play. In situations like these, it may be necessary to breach the usual confidentiality standards we adhere to in low or no risk situations. Within the ethical guidelines of various human service professions, this 'duty to warn' is identified as: 'The responsibility to report threats made by a client, if the social worker believes that the client will carry out such threats and that they will result in danger, harm or injury to the client or others.' This example is from the Australian Association of Social Workers' *Code of Ethics* (2002, p. 26). In becoming aware of a public safety risk, social workers, in this instance, 'will be excused from breaching confidentiality where they disclose information about the risk in order to protect the public'.

At times when you have concerns about a client's safety, or the safety of others because of what the client is saying, a careful consideration of whether to breach confidentiality is required. If possible this should always occur with the support of a supervisor or manager, and, if safe to do so, the client can be advised of your intended actions. For example, this may involve a conversation with Mark about his suicidality and then a discussion of your concerns for his safety before contracting together on a safety plan. The safety plan may involve discussions with other significant people in his environment, or it may involve a crisis assessment and treatment team if the danger of self-harm or suicide is high.

Further information about suicide risk assessment and managing physical or verbal violence is available, and some useful links are included at the end of this chapter.

Chapter summary

In this chapter, some of the key strategies for dealing with high-risk situations have been overviewed and critiqued. These strategies are not prescriptions for success; rather, they provide some ways of thinking about what to do in certain situations that have been found to be effective in situations in the past. The risk situations of suicidal behaviour, threatening behaviour and conflict have been explored briefly and you are encouraged to expand your reading, supervision and awareness in practice in relation to these experiences. Risk cannot be eliminated in the work that we do—people in stressful situations often respond unpredictably, and that relates to ourselves as much as our clients. Good ongoing support and supervision are two ways of working preventively, but they are also critical buffers in the aftermath of high risk situations.

Reflective practice questions

1   What have you learnt about assessing risk situations from reading this chapter?
2   What are some of the personal and professional dilemmas that such risk situations raise for you?

3 What do you see as some of the essential skills required in dealing with risk situations?

4 Reflect on situations of conflict or risk that you have been in and on the ways in which you have responded.

Key references

Laming, C. (2006). *A constructivist approach to challenging men's violence against women.* The University of Melbourne, Melbourne.

Morley, C. (2004). Conducting risk assessments. In J. Maidment & R. Egan (Eds), *Practice skills in social work and welfare: More than just common sense.* Crows Nest: Allen & Unwin (chap. 9, pp. 127–45).

Ogloff, J. (2006). Advances in violence risk assessment. *InPsych, 28*(5), 12–16.

Trotter, C. (2006). *Working with involuntary clients: A guide to practice.* Thousand Oaks: Sage Publications.

Additional resources

Australian Government—Mental Health and Wellbeing publications: www.health.gov.au/internet/wcms/publishing.nsf/content/mental-pubs.

Beyondblue: National Depression Initiative: www.beyondblue.org.au.

Domestic Violence and Incest Resource Centre: www.dvirc.org.au.

Orygen Mental Health Services: www.orygen.org.au.

SPINZ: Suicide Prevention Information New Zealand: www.spinz.org.nz.

PART 4

Applying
the Skills:
Focusing the Intervention

In this next part of the book, we explore briefly some of the specific tasks and skills of human service practice. This book is not primarily about theoretical approaches to working with people; however, we will examine some of the specific skills emerging from the eight theoretical approaches introduced in Chapter 3.

In Chapter 9, human service interventions that target change within the inner and/or outer worlds of people were identified. Change strategies that focus on people's inner worlds—strategies of counselling, psycho-education, social support and group work—can help clients develop new ways of coping with behavioural or belief restrictions that they impose on themselves, or others impose on them. Change strategies that focus on people's outer worlds—strategies of resource provision, referral, liaison, advocacy, capacity building, group work and community development—can help clients manage and change the structural restrictions in their worlds, and may involve very active worker action to bring this about with the client.

Each theoretical approach has a long tradition informing its current understandings and use of skills. It is beyond the scope of this book to explore the rich tradition and the developmental processes that inform that tradition, but resources are provided at the

continues

end of each chapter for you to follow up on this reading. The aim here is to provide you with an introduction to some of the direct practice skills.

The emphasis throughout these next four chapters is on how these skills can be applied in different settings. Some workers adopt a 'purist' theoretical approach; that is, they are a psychodynamic or a feminist worker. Most workers, however, incorporate a range of skills into their practice, drawn from a range of theoretical perspectives—in this sense, they are eclectic in their theoretical base. That is why the skills are presented, rather than the overall approach. The overall aim of these four chapters is to illustrate how the choice to use these skills will impact on the work you do.

So another dimension is added to the framework—focusing the intervention.

Part 1—Framing the relationship:

- the purpose of human service work
- your value base
- your theoretical and factual knowledge.

Part 2—Forming the relationship:

- your use of self
- your organisational context
- your ongoing support and professional development needs
- meeting the people involved
- opening the communication
- actively listening
- listening empathically
- using self-disclosure.

Part 3—Focusing the communication:

- establishing the story
- forming an assessment
- goal setting.

Part 4—Focusing the intervention:

- drawing on theoretical perspectives
- doing the work.

Task-centred and Crisis-intervention Skills

11

LEARNING GOALS

- Identify the core skills of task-centred and crisis-intervention approaches, particularly in relation to the establishment of the relationship between a worker and client and specific interventions.
- Understand the strengths and limitations of these approaches.

Core skills of task-centred practice

The Ahmed family have arrived at your agency, seeking assistance with their multiple stressors. Depending on what agency the Ahmed family presents to, the focus of the work will differ. As you will see from the account below, they are dealing with many stressors. Some are outer-world or practical tasks associated with living in Australia, whereas others are clearly inner-world tasks of adapting to life in a new country and culture.

Focus on practice: immediate needs

The Ahmed family arrived two years ago from Somalia. They have five children—three attending school, a three-year-old and a one-year-old infant. They are living in shared housing with another family, all who have been granted refugee status. They have been able to connect with the local school but miss many aspects of life back home. They have been able to build connections with other members of the Somali community.

continues

They feel emotionally torn about their migration. They have left behind family and many friends. They are learning English but finding that it is still very difficult to fit into Australian culture. Being unemployed, they are also finding it difficult to afford the expenses of daily life.

Mrs Ahmed has found it much easier to connect with Australian life—she enjoys being in the shared house situation, and the ways in which she can share the cooking and domestic duties with the other family with whom they live.

Mr Ahmed is frustrated by his difficulties finding work. He sees himself as the one responsible for earning the family's income, and feels deep shame that he has not been able to do this so far. He has become very withdrawn and depressed.

Source: adapted from Harms (2005, pp. 68–9).

Establishing and sustaining the relationship

From a task-centred perspective, your engagement with your client is established through the focus on task and goal setting. Given the multiple concerns for this family, this may need to occur through providing a culturally empathic space for exploration, with adequate time and space for a full exploration of their circumstances (Marsh & Doel 2005, p. 115). In order to engage in problem solving, the main aim of task-centred practice, a worker typically engages using high emotional warmth, an optimism about finding solutions and, in some situations, considerable **assertiveness**. Engagement is with the details of the person's circumstances and the possibilities for solution.

A major criticism of task-centred approaches is that they fail to acknowledge the importance of the client–worker relationship. This is seen to be a misrepresentation of the centrality of this relationship, as Marsh and Doel argue (2005, p. 119), with the relationship emerging:

> … from the doing, rather than the doing arising from the relationship. We believe this mirrors what happens in our everyday lives, just as a complete stranger can feel like a lifelong friend if you happen to find yourselves mutually dependent in a short, intense crisis.

However, the relationship is seen primarily as an active and 'doing' relationship, which is in contrast to some of the other approaches described in the next few chapters. Thus, your knowledge of resources possibilities is as important to bring to this interaction as your interpersonal engagement skills.

Specific interventions

Task-centred practice has emerged from a more pragmatic approach to human service delivery. It is a time-limited, contracted and highly structured approach, and therein rests both its strengths and limitations. Interventions focus on 'doing'—on activities, either within the context of the contact itself or outside as homework (Marsh & Doel 2005, p. 38).

The skills of task-centred practice relate to the Task Planning and Implementation Sequence (TPIS), first outlined by Reid and Epstein (Marsh & Doel 2005, p. 78; Tolson, Reid & Garvin 2003). As seen below, once the circumstances have been explored, the six steps are followed, drawing on the exploration and goal-setting skills we have looked at in previous chapters.

Focus on practice: the six steps of task-centred practice

1 Task selection

Drawing on the probing, paraphrasing and summarising skills discussed in Chapters 7 and 8, you work with the Ahmeds to identify a key task to work on. In this instance, it could be to address Mr Ahmed's isolation and lack of income possibilities, or to link them in with others in the community during the day, for example. It involves asking the question: What do you think you might be able to do about this problem?

This question then serves as a brain-storming exercise to find possible solutions.

2 Task agreement

Talking with the Ahmeds about the possible goals, you then talk through each one to arrive at one task that you all think will be the most achievable.

3 Planning specifics of implementation

An implementation plan is then discussed—'how, who, where, when and why' are often important questions to explore throughout this phase.

4 Establishing incentives and rationale

In this exploration, you look together at why the change should occur—what are the motivations, and why is it necessary?

5 Anticipating obstacles

In this exploration, you turn the focus around from that above, to look at all the potential barriers to the successful achievement of the goal. Both inner-world and outer-world barriers are important to explore. This is about exploring the 'what if' questions (Marsh & Doel 2005, p. 78).

6 Simulated and guided practice

Talking through a process is important—the techniques of rehearsal prepare us to put into practice new skills and help us to experience some of the potential new emotions we may experience in a situation. We can learn how we might react to a number of different dimensions in an experience.

continues

A final seventh step might happen in another session: task review. Review and evaluation is critical in a task-centred approach. What worked and what didn't work? Why? It enables a review of goals and whether they were SMART goals or not.

Healy (2005, pp. 113–15) outlines eight practice principles relating to this very structured approach, which translate further into the skills you could use. Each of these is applied to understanding the Ahmeds' situation.

1   *Seek mutual clarity with service users*—This involves exploring the story extensively, and coming to understand the story fully from the Ahmeds' perspective and your own, using the skills we have looked at in Chapters 7 and 8. Shared concerns would be raised and a particular emphasis on cultural empathy would be required. A cultural consultant may be a very useful ally for the Ahmeds and you in this situation, so that solutions are culturally sensitive and appropriate.

2   *Aim for small achievements rather than large changes*—With the Ahmeds, so many changes are being expressed by them as necessary that it could feel overwhelming both to them and to you as a worker. Achieving small steps helps to build a sense of efficacy and accomplishment (Bandura, Caprara, Barbaranelli, Gerbino & Pastorelli 2003), building in turn a confidence and capacity to continue to make changes.

3   *Focus on the 'here and now'*—This is one of the major differences from other approaches, in that the problem is seen to be in the present: not in the past, or even the future, as other approaches might locate them. Change is brought about in the present to enhance current coping and functioning, and to build coping capacity for the future. In this sense, a way of coping is being taught or developed further with the client.

4   *Promote collaboration between the worker and service users*—You can establish a sense of collaboration with your client through sharing the solution-focused process; using collaborative language such as 'we' or 'when we have done that'. The solution becomes shared so that a sense of isolation can be somewhat reduced for people in overwhelming situations. The collaboration, however, must be authentic and viable, rather than becoming a series of false promises.

5   *Build client capacities for action*—As Healy (2005, p. 114) notes, '[w]hile acknowledging that the problems may have their origins in other "causes" such as "deeper" psychological problems or unjust structural conditions' these are not the focus of task-centred interventions. The focus is on dealing with an identified problem and targeting immediate practical or psychological resources to solve them. Capacities for action emerge from the provision and receipt of resources (Hobfoll, Ennis & Kay 2000).

6   *Planned brevity*—Task-centred approaches are short-term and time-limited approaches, not extending beyond fifteen sessions. You may even focus on

task-centred work within the context of a single session with someone. The Ahmed family would be advised of this in your initial contact, and a close scrutiny of these time limits would be maintained, once the goals for the work have been set. This approach is consistent with a strengths perspective, which sees people as capable of influencing their own lives and functioning when adequate resources are in place.

7 & 8 *Promote systematic and structured approaches to intervention, and adopt a scientific approach to practice evaluation*—These last two principles highlight that the model outlined above gives you and your clients a very clear map of how you will work together and what you will aim to achieve. In this sense, the Ahmeds are empowered in the process as they are informed of the process. Healy (2005) identifies the **mutual clarity** and the 'external accountability' of applying a standardised practice model as two of the approach's major strengths. In contrast to the less structured and arguably less measurable interventions outlined in the following chapters, this approach is seen to use and provide an ongoing evidence base for practice.

In summary, the skills that are relied on extensively are:

- exploring, probing and clarifying skills
- contracting and problem-solving skills
- task-focused, strengths and solution-focused goal-setting skills
- teaching, advising and directing around resource use
- resourcing and referral skills.

We explore the process of making a referral in Chapter 15.

Core skills of crisis-intervention practice

The Willis family, presented in Chapter 9, are experiencing difficulties of a different nature. Given that Mrs Willis is experiencing an immediate **crisis**, task-centred skills could be successfully used, but crisis-intervention skills may be more appropriate. Here is their situation again.

Focus on practice: Mr and Mrs Willis

Mr and Mrs Willis have been living in their own flat for thirty-two years. They have strong connections with a number of neighbours, and their local RSL club. Mr Willis fell last week when he got up to change the TV channel. He is currently in the local hospital with a fractured leg and wrist. Since his admission, the nurses have become very concerned about his memory, and organised for an assessment, which has confirmed that he has dementia. The worker is to talk with them about a range of home-care options, including the possibility that he move into a supported living arrangement. Mrs Willis is distraught about the diagnosis and the possibility that he might move out of their family home, where they have lived for so long. She has made it very clear that she wants her husband to come back home and live there. In her mind, this admission is about his physical recovery only and she is terrified of any suggestion that he no longer live with her.

Crisis-intervention skills are based more on an understanding of the mood and cognitive state of the person at the time of the intervention; that is, the immediate context or state of the person determines the way of thinking and intervening at that time. As a result of this focus, your intervention is about enhancing the immediate functioning of people affected by the crisis, both practically and emotionally.

A crisis is typically defined as

> … an upset in a steady state (state of equilibrium) that poses an obstacle, usually important to the fulfilment of important life goals or to vital need satisfaction, and that the individual or family cannot overcome through usual methods of problem solving (Hepworth, Rooney & Larsen 2002, p. 382).

Critically, a crisis state is seen to be a temporary state, 'during which a person has the potential for heightened maturity and growth or for deterioration and greater vulnerability to future stress' (Poindexter 1997, p. 125). This understanding is vital, as Caplan (1990) and others have argued that crisis presents an opportunity for the development of new coping skills as well as threat and loss.

Establishing and sustaining the relationship

Like task-centred approaches, crisis-intervention approaches do not typically focus on understanding the nature of the relationship between the worker and the client to the extent that other approaches do. It is fundamental to the success of the work, however, and therefore is still regarded as being the 'glue'.

Intense and strong bonds often form during crisis, from a sense of the shared experience, and from (as others argue) the psychological regression and dependence that can occur in the midst of a crisis. The regression and dependence, however, are viewed as temporary, resolving typically within weeks of a particular crisis.

Early in the crisis period, particularly in disaster situations, the worker assertively fosters a highly directive and assertive role, expressing high warmth and a highly empathic engagement. Over time, as individuals resume their pre-crisis levels of functioning, the worker is no longer as directive or assertive.

Specific interventions

Crisis-intervention skills are about supporting people to cope in the immediate aftermath of traumatic or stressful situations. Based on understandings of how people cope in crisis, they focus on an immediate restoration of cognitive and emotional control, as well as resuming normal functioning as quickly as possible, through the re-engagement with daily tasks and defusing of mood and emotion.

Some of the key skills that are used are:

1 *A rapid assessment of functioning*—As a worker, you need to assess very quickly how someone is functioning. This is important as often in the midst of a crisis, serious decisions need to be made. If someone is unable to make decisions clearly, then different strategies may be required. Many formal tools are available for this assessment. For example, the Triage Assessment Form: Crisis Intervention (Myer, Williams, Ottens & Schmidt, as described in Myer & Conte 2006, pp. 968–70) has been developed, which establishes a person's functioning in relation to three domains of functioning: the affective or emotional domain, the behavioural domain and the cognitive domain, assessing them on a rating scale from 1–10. This helps to distinguish levels of functioning, and also changes over time.

2 *Reassurance of safety*—While Mrs Willis is in a safe situation, in some other instances you may be working with people who have been confronted with life-threatening situations, such as a sexual assault, road accident or violent incident. In trauma situations, reassurance of basic physical safety is often critical (Herman 1992), if it is able to be provided realistically.

3 *Maintaining a needs and rights focus*—Despite the above comments about coping capacity, decisions are often made for people during a time of crisis that they knew nothing. People affected by crisis can still remain very empowered throughout situations to make decisions for themselves and others. Overlooking this has been a major criticism of many debriefing efforts, where people have not been able to act in ways in which they wanted to (Crumpton-Cook 1996). Crisis intervention skills focus on empowering the affected person to make necessary decisions in a supported way.

4 *Validation of feelings*—As distinct from the task-centred approach, crisis intervention focuses on the often intense emotional state someone is experiencing. Mrs Willis may be experiencing an enormous range of emotions. A crisis intervention encourages the **ventilation** or expression of all these emotions. In this sense, it is connected with psychodynamic approaches; with the cathartic release of all emotions in all their complexity the first step in being able to consciously control them. Thus, listening and supporting, through probing, reflecting and paraphrasing, is important. The listening is characterised by validating all emotions. While a cognitive behavioural approach may then move on to challenge some of these feelings, assessing them as irrational or rational thoughts or emotions, crisis–intervention approaches see this as the first step in dealing with the disequilibrium that crises create.

The term **containment** is often used in relation to the ventilation of feelings and the skill of the worker to support the client in experiencing but not being overwhelmed by these feelings. The term originates from psychodynamic understandings, so the skills of containment will be discussed in Chapter 12.

5   *Information and resource provision*—Mrs Willis has been confronted with a lot of new information. Not only will she need to support her husband in his recovery from his fractures, but by her own admission she also knows nothing about dementia, nor of the processes involved in moving him to new accommodation. Similarly, she has been confronted with a range of new emotions and is finding it hard to cope with their disorientating impact. Crisis-intervention strategies are 'immediate, active and directive interventions such as education, clarification, and reassurance about the normative, expectable reactions to trauma' (Gelman & Mirabito 2005, p. 481) or crisis. Your knowledge of crisis and trauma, and the expectable immediate and longer-term reactions, is drawn on at this time. It may involve you making a normalising statement like the following:

> You said you're feeling really strange, as if it's all happening around you, but you're not part of this. You may find that over the next few days, these feelings come and go, and then pass. This is a normal reaction to the distressing information you've been given.

With these skills, you are providing a psycho-educational base for your client to understand their world. This is the difference between a more supportive or reactive approach in other situations of communication. Here, you are actively drawing on your knowledge base to provide resources for your client to draw upon.

6   *Direct influence*—In addition to the more active stance outlined in the previous section, in some instances you may use directive or influencing skills (Walsh 2006, p. 282). The person may not be able to make decisions because of the overwhelming nature of their circumstances. For example, after the conversation with the doctors about Mr Willis's newly diagnosed dementia, Mrs Willis may not be able think clearly about whether she should go home, ring her children or stay with him. In this instance, a worker might be quite directive about suggesting a plan if no priority seems to be emerging:

> How about we go and make the phone call to your children and see what they would like to do. If they decide to come in, you can wait here with your husband and meet them. If they can't come in now, we can think about how you will get home and what you might do tomorrow.

This sets some limits around what Mrs Willis needs to think about in the midst of this crisis. It is not taking away any of her rights or disempowering her, because it is clearly driven by what she wants to do. It is, however, containing those options when her emotional state is high and clouding her ability to think clearly.

In other situations, you might make some suggestions about what she could do if she is unable to make a decision. Remembering Maslow's hierarchy of needs is important in this kind of work—people in crisis often need the basics attended to, in relation to shelter, food, clothing and communication. Mrs Willis may forget that she hasn't eaten since dinner last night, and need support in ensuring these basic needs can be met.

As you can hear from the above example, the skills you employ are assertive and directive skills recognising that, in the disruption of life crises, people's usual coping capacities are similarly disrupted. A crisis-intervention approach does acknowledge that crises are both threats and opportunities, in that new coping strategies can be introduced when usual coping strategies do not work, and thus growth and development may occur (Caplan 1990; Poindexter 1997).

Maslow's hierarchy of needs was presented in Chapter 4.

Strengths and limitations of these skills

The skills outlined in this chapter have emerged relatively recently in recognition of people's immediate reactions to circumstances of trauma and crisis. Thus, in using these skills, you are aiming to resource people to cope with immediate circumstances, and to find active solutions to them. In this way, these skills are less pathologising of people's coping capacities. They encourage people to develop or regain a sense of control and empowerment as quickly as possible. Engagement with a supportive and encouraging worker is seen as a critical step, through becoming an ally and a resource through particular times of difficulty.

The skills within a task-centred approach are primarily task focused, whereas crisis-intervention skills are about both task- and emotion-focused strategies. In focusing on tasks, many criticisms have been levelled at task-centred approaches in relation to what is regarded as their conformity with a neo-liberal political agenda. As Webb (2006, p. 123) states:

> The danger with adhering to this kind of perspective is that it can result in crude unreflective instrumentalism, in the bid to water things down to tasks, to dilute difficulty, to make things so simple that they no longer carry any depth of meaning or value for service users.

In addition to this agenda, criticisms are made of both approaches in relation to the potentially disempowering location of the client in relation to the worker. Another concern is that the pragmatic, evidence-based nature of both approaches, and their tendency towards a linear approach to problem solving (Healy 2005), may be inconsistent with people who carry more cyclical notions of time and change; for example, Indigenous cultures.

In some instances, though, task-centred and crisis-intervention skills are clearly inappropriate. More insight-oriented problems require more insight-oriented skills and understandings. These are considered in later chapters.

Chapter summary

In this chapter, some of the key skills that are used in task-centred and crisis-intervention approaches have been introduced. The goal-setting and problem-solving skills of a task-centred approach were applied to the complex circumstances of the Ahmed family, to demonstrate how finding solutions is the focus of the work together. The emotion- and task-focused skills used with Mrs Willis highlighted the short-term, multidimensional emphasis of a crisis-intervention approach. These skills are primarily used in situations where communication is time-limited. They focus on optimising people's strengths and capacities in the face of the difficult circumstances of everyday life.

Reflective practice questions

1   What task-centred and crisis-intervention skills appeal to you? Why?
2   When would you find these skills helpful?
3   What are some of the strengths and limitations of these skills?

Key references

Brown, F. & Rainer, J. (2006). Too much to bear: An introduction to crisis intervention and therapy. *Journal of Clinical Psychology, 62*(8), 953–57.

Flannery, R. & Everly, G. (2000). Crisis intervention: A review. *International Journal of Emergency Mental Health, 2*(2), 119–25.

Marsh, P. & Doel, M. (2005). *The task-centred book.* London: Routledge.

Myer, R. & Conte, C. (2006). Assessment for crisis intervention. *Journal of Clinical Psychology, 62*(8), 959–70.

Tolson, E., Reid, W. & Garvin, C. (2003). *Generalist practice: A task-centered approach.* New York: Columbia University Press.

Additional resources

Australian Critical Incident Stress Association (ACISA): www.acisa.org.au.

National Center for Crisis Management (USA): www.nc-cm.org/index.html.

The Task-Centered WebPages: www.task-centered.com.

Psychodynamic and Cognitive Behavioural Skills

12

- Identify the core skills of psychodynamic and cognitive behavioural approaches, particularly in relation to the establishment of the relationship between a worker and client and specific interventions.
- Understand the strengths and limitations of these skills.

Core skills of psychodynamic practice

To illustrate some of the key skills within a psychodynamic approach, Karen describes her work with Julia, a forty–year–old woman:

Focus on practice

Julia requested counselling on the basis that her friends had told her she was depressed. The first, and many subsequent, interviews revealed a complex and detailed examination of a range of life events through the lives of all her family members, friends, work colleagues and extraneous others. It was impossible to gain any view expressed by Julia herself, and she was apparently incapable of identifying (or even experiencing?) a feeling or having an opinion without input from others.

It became clear that her unconscious expectation of the counselling was also to gain further insights from yet another person into her own situation. The challenge was not to be drawn into this pattern, and rather reflect it back and assist her to examine the position she placed herself in, in relation to others. The concepts of transference and countertransference were helpful in this instance.

continues

A further pattern that developed during this counselling contact was for the client to regularly appear in a chaotic state, with a range of apparent crises being reported from the previous week. Counselling sessions involved deconstructing and reframing these experiences to assist Julia to view them in a more positive light, and restore a sense of efficacy in her own capacity to act and interpret her own experiences. Due to her longstanding habit of having others define events negatively, particularly her mother, she found it quite challenging to break this habit and be prepared to have a hope for change.

This experience of **repetition** was challenging for me as the counsellor, but Julia began to learn how she could take control of her understanding of events.

1   What is your initial reaction to hearing about Julia and Karen's work?
2   What would you focus on in the work with Julia? Why?

Notice the emphasis in this scenario is on:

- lifelong patterns of behaving and relating
- family and significant others and their impact on her sense of self
- conscious and unconscious motivations and drives
- parallel processes occurring in the client–worker relationship
- transference and countertransference experiences
- working over time to address ways of behaving, thinking and feeling that keep repeating themselves
- developing insight and ultimately changes to an experience of self as chaotic.

Each of these will be addressed throughout this discussion of psychodynamic skills.

Establishing and sustaining the relationship

The client–worker relationship is central in any work with a strong psychodynamic orientation. The focus is on the relationship dynamics (Walsh 2006, p. 30). A client can resolve problematic issues from the past through experiencing a positive relationship in the therapeutic relationship or 'working alliance' in the 'here and now'. In this way, the relationship provides a 'corrective emotional experience' (McCluskey 2002), in that internal working models of relationships that a client may have developed through poor earlier relationships can be influenced for the better.

The relationship becomes the vehicle for change, as issues of unconscious motivations and desires, conflicts and anxieties repeat themselves in the client–worker relationship. The intention is that the client projects these conscious and unconscious experiences and expectations onto the therapist, hence forming a

transference—a transfer of earlier and current significant relationships—onto the current therapeutic one. As a result: 'the client perceives the helping professional in a distorted way and brings his or her past relationships into the present relationship with the counsellor' (Corey & Corey 2007, p. 67).

By developing insight over time into the transference, change can occur as these needs and desires come under more conscious control. Transference is a part of every relationship in which we engage. In this context, however, it is analysed for what it tells us about ourselves and our ways of relating to ourselves, significant others and the world around us.

Countertransference is a similar process that occurs for the worker, as Corey and Corey (2007, p. 67) note: 'Broadly speaking, helpers may have unconscious emotional responses to a client that result in a distorted perception of a client's behaviour.' Corey and Corey (2007) note that countertransference can block the neutrality of the worker. It is based on the assumption that the worker is in an objective, neutral position of sounding post with the client, an assumption increasingly challenged. In Julia and Karen's situation, focusing on the countertransference would involve Karen's constant reflections on how she feels, and what she is reacting to in the client's story. Supervision is a critical space then for these issues to be discussed and addressed if needed.

This relationship dynamic was symbolised by Jung as a series of links, highlighting what we might understand now to be about a complex web of relationships, as shown in Figure 12.1.

■ Remember that connections with a sense of collective unconscious and other ways of knowing were described in Chapter 2.

Figure 12.1 Conscious and unconscious levels of communication within relationships

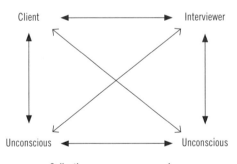

Collective or common unconscious

Source: Jacoby (1984, p. 25).

The aim of engagement throughout your work with your client, therefore, is to foster a positive transference relationship with them so that trust and insight can be achieved.

Unlike other client–worker relationships, contracting around the work does not always happen initially within a psychodynamic approach (Howard 2006). Instead, the emphasis is on experiencing the relationship first, and seeing what emerges in that interaction. The relationship in this sense is as much a focus of the work as other issues raised in the conversation.

The early psychodynamic view of the worker was as a 'blank screen': an objective and neutral listener onto whom the client would 'project' their earlier relationships that had influenced their **psychosexual development**. Over time, the impossibility of maintaining such an unnatural relationship position has been questioned, and the term 'intersubjectivity' is now used to denote the complex, reciprocal relationship between the worker and client (Gibney 2003). Close boundaries are still prescribed around work and the relationship, however, unlike some of the Indigenous practice approaches.

Psychodynamic processes are thought about in many different and even contradictory ways. This has a major impact on the types of skills that you might use. Two major schools of thought are the object relations and ego psychology approaches. The object relations approach proposes that we relate to people in the present on the basis of expectations formed by early experiences within significant relationships. During infancy, we develop internal working models of relationships based on our relationships with those around us, and it becomes necessary in adult life to explore and repair faulty unconscious object relationships internalised since infancy. How the external world is taken in and how the resultant internalisations influence psychic structure and later personality functioning are the focus of this approach (Goldstein 1995).

Many psychodynamic theories also maintain theories of attachment at their core; that is, the infant's primary need for attachment to a caring person (Bowlby 1984), seen to realise itself in the good object (Klein 1962) or the holding environment (Winnicott 1987), respectively. A mature ego develops into seeing ambivalence and complexity rather than the dichotomised 'good' or 'bad'.

Ego psychology argues that we learn a coping repertoire across the life span that has various strengths and deficits, and later difficulties are associated with this lifelong coping repertoire. The focus of intervention is on building **ego strengths**, where the ego is seen as 'a mental structure of the personality that is responsible for negotiating between the internal needs of the individual and the outside world' (Goldstein 1995, p. xi; Walsh 2006, p. 32).

Specific interventions

In light of the above, assessment typically involves taking a detailed history and examining the following dimensions of a person's life:

- drives as related to pleasure, aggression and mastery/competence (Walsh 2006, p. 31)
- management of anxiety
- personality

- experiences across the life span
- defence mechanisms.

Some of the specific psychodynamic skills or techniques you might use include (Gibney 2003; Nelson-Jones 2006; Walsh 2006, pp. 40–3):

1 *Promoting a corrective emotional experience*—As outlined in the previous section, the development and maintenance of the relationship over time is seen to be one of the most critical skills within psychodynamic approaches. This enables the experience of a positive transference to emerge and for insight-oriented work to be done in a supportive yet challenging environment.

2 *Offering containment*—In the previous chapter, containment was mentioned as an important skill within crisis-intervention approaches. Containment refers to 'an exquisite empathy and thoughtfulness with which the [worker] responds to the client throughout the session' (Gibney 2003, p. 46). Containment enables a sense of psychological safety to be experienced, and is therefore crucial in situations of crisis. It is also crucial in Julia's situation, where she does not experience herself normally as psychologically centred and strong. Containment can be offered:

   (a) Within the conversation—At the core, Gibney (2003, p. 51) describes this as relating to the fact that the client feels absolutely understood: accurately and genuinely. This, he and others argue, leads to the client being able to get in touch with their feelings, irrespective of their nature. Thus, there is a containment and affirmation of inner-world experiences.

   (b) In relation to external threats—Through the giving of advice and direction in decision making, the worker in many ways models adult decision-making processes and does not hesitate to advise on particular situations, particularly those of risk. In this sense, the role of 'good' parent is often enacted.

   (c) In context—Unlike other approaches, a psychodynamic approach is typically employed in a structured setting, with clear boundaries around your meeting times and space. This regularity is seen to provide 'containment' for the anxiety of uncertainty. The certainties of this contract are seen to provide some safety and boundary, and therefore provide an opportunity for the client to experience safety and boundary in their inner world as well. In crisis situations, it is important to contain the emotional chaos through clear structuring and planning of actions.

   This notion of containment links with Winnicott's notion of a therapeutic 'holding environment' (Winnicott 1987)—a safe, consistent environment, which is expectable in terms of time and event and surrounds.

3 *Providing interpretations, particularly through exploring internalised relationships across the life span*—In Julia's case, using imagery or analogy (Macnab 1989, p. 101) to explore her inner objects, where she is seemingly quite articulate about her circumstances, might include reflecting to her that it is as if

she has a passenger in the backseat of her car (a backseat driver) who is directing her, and what part of her self this process relates to: 'Every time you're wanting to make a turn it's as if someone else is directing you.' To regain a sense of ego strength, she can begin to listen to herself as the front seat driver and trust her own feelings and sense of knowing.

In conducting what Walsh (2006, p. 43) terms a 'developmental reflection', specific skills outlined in the earlier chapters are emphasised. The tendency within psychodynamic approaches is to emphasise non-directive, 'uncovering' techniques to listen and elicit the history, thoughts, ideas, feelings and perceptions of a person about their circumstances. The relationship is typically high in empathy, although a participant–observer role is strongly encouraged. Skills of interpretation, using summaries, making observations or invitations and 'why' questions are often amplified, for example: 'Earlier you were telling me about your difficulties in finishing a project and just now you're telling me about how you're finding it difficult to leave this relationship.' Or: 'Notice when you talk about that person, each time you become quite choked up and you stop talking so freely about them as you do others.'

The timing of interpretations, however, is critical. Interpretations are usually made in the context of well-established, trusting relationships, where they can be discussed fully in insight-oriented work.

4 *Encouraging the management of anxiety and insight into defence mechanisms*— Anxiety experiences are understood to lead to a distorting of reality, a loss of control and inner conflict. Major anxiety in the form of trauma can lead to dissociation as a defence against such severe stress. Dissociation is the separation of thinking and feeling, leading to alterations in memory, identity and consciousness, where there can be a separating out of various aspects of the self. According to the theory, in the face of anxiety, we unconsciously use these sorts of defence mechanisms, which enable us to channel impulses 'into acceptable behaviors' (Walsh 2006, p. 31).

Returning to Karen's discussion of her work with Julia: a number of areas of ego 'damage' might be assessed, including Julia's high level of disorganisation both in practical terms and in emotional terms, and her high level of self-sabotage and her high level of vulnerability to the needs of others. On the other hand, in talking with Karen it seemed she identified ego strengths that she had underestimated or not developed and was able to begin to focus on these to influence her future functioning.

A key term used in understanding change is resistance. This term is originally from the **defence mechanism** of resistance, or the 'opposition to making what is unconscious conscious' (Reber 1985, p. 642). It explains the unconscious process of pushing back against change in the face of potentially overwhelming anxiety.

Overall, then, some of the goals of intervention in psychodynamic approaches are to:

- free individuals and family members from unconscious restrictions and therefore establish less neurotic patterns of relationship and communication
- work towards eliminating unhelpful patterns of relating
- delineate roles clearly, through establishing the fantasy compared with the reality of expectations
- find a balance of autonomy and mutuality
- develop affect tolerance and impulse control
- restore or develop an integrated self-identity.

These goals are about expanding the person's inner capacities and their capacities to function in daily life.

Core skills of cognitive behavioural practice

Cognitive behaviour approaches are incorporated in many models of counselling, both implicitly and explicitly. In its traditional form, cognitive behavioural practice works on a model of change that sees an inextricable link between feeling, thinking and behaving.

This model was evolved into an 'equation' or theory of change by Ellis (1995):

$$A + B = C \rightarrow D \rightarrow E$$

Where A denotes an 'activating event' or circumstance; B denotes beliefs, which Ellis described initially as irrational or rational; and C denotes the consequences in terms of thoughts, feelings and behaviours. In this equation, Ellis located B as the mediating process on any event or circumstance, and the main area of focus in any intervention. D then denotes the disputation of beliefs and emotions and the attempts to establish more rational beliefs in lieu of irrational ones. Finally, E denotes the evaluation or reappraisal of both the event and beliefs about it and therefore the consequences should vary and change has occurred.

The basis of cognitive behavioural therapy (CBT) is that in changing one dimension of a problem situation—for example, how a particular situation is thought about—change is inevitably influenced in dimensions, as Melissa's description of her work with Craig later in this chapter demonstrates.

Establishing and sustaining the relationship

Engagement in CBT work is usually about a short-term, time-limited client–worker relationship. The relationship is understood primarily as a means to critically reflect on habits, patterns and self-defeating behaviours. The relationship is not reflected on as a particularly significant component of the change agenda in the way that it is with psychodynamic approaches described in the previous chapter.

The key focus in engaging with someone is to develop an empathic relationship in which emotions, behaviours and thoughts can be reviewed and challenged as necessary, and realistic goals can be set.

Specific interventions

Assessment focuses on a number of themes in relation to patterns of thinking, feeling and behaving. Traditionally, the emphasis was on identifying **rational and irrational thoughts** or beliefs. Ellis and others argued that our counterproductive behaviours are sustained by the beliefs we hold onto in our everyday lives. Thus, unhelpful or unhealthy behaviours and feelings are the target of interventions.

Some of the specific skills originating from a cognitive behaviour approach include challenging self-defeating or unhelpful beliefs, controlling thoughts and monitoring thoughts.

Challenging self-defeating or unhelpful beliefs

In earlier chapters where we have looked at the processes of assessment and goal setting, an assumption of rational **decision making** has been at the fore. CBT approaches have been fundamental in highlighting the need to challenge beliefs, behaviours and feelings in order to bring about change. Ellis and others encouraged identification of the following self-defeating messages:

I should …

I must …

I always …

In other words, these messages reflect the ways in which we believe things are compulsory, or are absolute, and therefore are without room to move. We distort beliefs about ourselves and others through catastrophising and awfulising (amplifying the negative consequences), or generalising, for example. The reason for **challenging** these unhelpful beliefs is that more of a 'middle ground' or reality check can be reached. We may not even be aware of many of these taken-for-granted ways of thinking about the world and our behaviour. An outsider (in this case, you as the worker) may be able to hear the ways in which patterns of thinking are unhelpful cognitive patterns.

Ellis identified a number of core beliefs that he saw as the irrational beliefs and illogical deductions that were responsible for creating human experiences of panic, self-blame and self-doubt, as listed below. These have been used extensively to explore the extent to which irrational beliefs create unrealistic expectations of both ourselves and those around us.

Focus on practice: irrational beliefs

Ellis's 'irrational beliefs' include the following:

- It is a dire necessity for an adult to be loved or approved by virtually every significant person in [their] community.
- One should be thoroughly competent, adequate and achieving in all possible respects if one is to consider oneself worthwhile.
- Human unhappiness is externally caused and that people have little or no ability to control their sorrows and disturbances.
- One's past history is an all-important determinant of one's present behaviour and that because something once strongly affected one's life, it should indefinitely have a similar effect.
- There is invariably a right, precise and perfect solution to human problems and that it is catastrophic if this perfect solution is not found.
- If something is or may be dangerous or fearsome, one should be terribly concerned about it and should keep dwelling on the possibility of its occurring.

Source: Ellis (1974, pp. 152–3).

These beliefs that Ellis considered irrational, or unhelpful, could be challenged or neutralised by more rational or helpful beliefs. Fook (1993, p. 86) also identifies resolving or tolerating conflicting beliefs and challenging false beliefs as critical strategies. These are all skills of reframing—of learning to think about something differently because of:

- challenging its helpful or unhelpful characteristics
- including more information into the picture of understanding
- hearing another point of view.

Controlling thoughts: thought stopping

Another central tenet of CBT approaches, therefore, is that thoughts are controllable. Through habit or a lack of conscious attention, the argument is that we are unaware of the thoughts, feelings and behaviours that govern our behaviour. Strategies that combine behavioural and cognitive strategies, such as thought stopping, are used. In thought stopping, the worker can interrupt the client's unhelpful thoughts by literally saying 'stop' and the client is then encouraged to similarly stop their own thoughts when they become aware that they are thinking them. Strategies such as wearing an elastic band around a wrist are encouraged (to be flicked when a negative thought is experienced) so that these automatic, unhelpful thoughts gradually come under more conscious control.

Monitoring thoughts

Other strategies focus more on tracking unhelpful behaviours, through the use of a journal (either around specific behaviours or thoughts), for example. Below, Melissa elaborates on how she worked with Craig to address this interconnection.

Focus on practice: using CBT techniques

Craig is a forty-seven-year-old man who came to see me for psychotherapy, and follow-up, due to suicidal behaviour and an underlying anxiety disorder. He is the recipient of a Disability Support Pension (DSP). Craig's mother died of leukaemia when Craig was thirty-nine years old. Craig's sister Joanne was murdered thirteen years ago. He has one brother with an intellectual disability and another brother who Craig alleges tried to molest him when he was eight or nine years of age and Craig was three. Craig lives alone and has a number of entrenched OCD [obsessive compulsive disorder] rituals to manage his anxiety around checking that taps are off, never having the gas turned on in the house, and washing and rewashing his hands.

Craig does not use alcohol or other substances. He does smoke cigarettes, however. He says: 'I don't drink tea or coffee or coke because it makes my heart go too quickly.' Craig does not utilise public transport because he generally feels uncomfortable around people, he says:

> I can't get on transport: people stare at me. I ride the bike everywhere. I haven't got on transport for at least ten years.

Craig is also self-conscious of his appearance. He is typically dressed in some-what worn tradesman's clothing and he wears woollen gloves on his hands, even on very warm days, noting this is 'because I've got tattoos'. These tattoos are from the time Craig spent in prison.

Of his OCD Craig notes that it takes him sixty to ninety minutes to leave the house. He has a lot of rituals to complete prior to departing. He is meticulous in tidying and cleaning behaviours—with regard to the back garden, the house and his own body. He checks and rechecks the taps:

> I turn 'em off with a spanner because I think they're dripping. But they're not. I wreck the washers, I turn it so tight.

Of his self-harming behaviour Craig says:

The voices tell me what to do. The other day I remember the voices telling me what to do: to take 5 and another 5.

And:

I keep looking at the stay-sharp knife on the stove. I think I'll cut my throat.

After four weeks of talking to me, at his third outpatient appointment, Craig describes his anxiety and suicidal thought as 'like a toothache in me heart'.

1 What would you see as some of the possibilities for intervention with Craig?

Melissa saw that two interventions significantly impacted on Craig's perceived level of coping, the regularity and severity of his presentations to the Emergency Department, and his optimism.

The first was his increased role in his church community. He approached the minister about helping out with the church community as we had discussed. He began to visit an elderly churchgoer and another with a physical disability on a weekly basis. He would help with odd jobs, often in the garden, and in return join them for a cup of tea in their home. Craig felt useful and the structured activity seemed to help by keeping him occupied and his thoughts for the most part off anxious preoccupations.

This intervention is about changing the outer world, through focusing on behaviours and structures that promote well-being.

The second intervention, which used more traditional CBT approaches, was the introduction of a mood journal. Craig and I converted an exercise book to a journal. Each day Craig would write down, as I suggested, any good thing that happened that day, and any upsetting thing that happened that day, and he would give himself a score out of ten. He would then bring the diary with him to sessions and we would discuss his week, and later his fortnight (as we were able to reduce sessions), the journal enabling him to self-monitor between appointments.

Interestingly to me, I did not recommend the daily score keeping at all. I once asked him—when trying to gauge the extent of his depressed mood—what he would give himself out of ten, when 'nought' was terrible and 'ten' was fantastic. He seemed to select this himself as a useful device to include as part of the journal. Of course, since we were more than three months into treatment by then, he had undergone three formal assessments with me as part of the research element of the Suicide Prevention Strategy. The depression measure, BDI-II, uses 0–3 ratings, as does the quality of life tool, the MANSA, which uses a seven-point Likert scale for twenty-five questions. It could be that Craig found the numbering helpful to self-monitor, or it could be, I hypothesise, that Craig interpreted assigning numbers to things as giving them extra legitimacy.

Interesting, too, was that Craig's use of the numbers was highly subjective, so it was important to gain an understanding of his coding over time. While I would myself

continues

hope for a seven- or eight-out-of-ten day as a baseline for myself, when discussing what would be the score for a 'good' day Craig informed me that he was happy when he had a 'five' day. On those days he did not suffer high anxiety or feel a desire to self-harm. On a 'three' or 'four' day he would try to carry out some task in the garden or around the house, phone or visit a friend, or engage in positive self-talk. We worked out a safety plan from there whereby if he was having a 'one' or 'two' day he would call me during business hours or CATT triage after hours to talk instead of engaging in self-harm. He liked this and felt in charge of the process and that he was knowledgeable about his thought processes after all. Always, though, he required validation through my making time in the next outpatient session to read over his entries since we last met and ask him about them.

All of these strategies actively address the ways in which thoughts, feelings and behaviours interconnect and potentially create restrictions on the ways in which we live.

Strengths and limitations of these skills

CBT is often cited as the most successful form of psychological intervention. It has been found to be useful in addressing problems in a short–term, contracted way. However, the reported success of CBT, in part, is due to its relative ease of measuring its inputs and outputs compared with some of the more process- or insight–oriented approaches.

A major criticism of CBT approaches is that the problem is seen to be located at the level of people's inner worlds. The major interventions are around individual behaviour, thought or feeling change, when many human service workers are aware that the very issues clients are grappling with are located, or are sources, in the outer worlds in which they live. For example, poverty can be thought about differently and behaviours can be changed in relation to it, but the real agenda should be to alleviate poverty, not blame the individual for feeling stressed because of their poverty. The lack of attention to structural concerns, so often at the heart of individual experiences of stress and depression, is the major criticism of these approaches.

Psychodynamic approaches have held, therefore, controversial positions in various professions such as social work and psychology. There are three major criticisms made of the approaches. The first is that psychodynamic approaches are inherently intrapsychic and therefore fail to address the social, structural and cultural causes of human distress and oppression. CBT's inherently apolitical stance means that it is not a useful approach for social change; rather, it locates both the causation and responsibility for change at the level of the individual. Human service workers are constantly working at this interface, and thus psychodynamic approaches have been seen to have major limitations in this regard. This critique is noted by Walsh (2006, p. 45) and others; Walsh notes that: 'There is nothing that prohibits a social worker who practices ego psychology from helping clients engage in larger system change activities, but nothing within the theory itself encourages these interventions.'

The second criticism is that many of the key theories of psychodynamic approaches lack an available evidence base to draw conclusions about efficacy. Related to this criticism is that the theories are unfalsifiable.

The third criticism is that psychodynamic approaches can disempower clients—through the lack of explanation to the client of the theories that are being used to understand their inner worlds and thus the assumed authority of the therapist. Healy (2005, p. 57) also raises the question as to the relevance of what she terms the 'psy' (as in psychologically oriented) theories where the relationship is mandated. The basis of the relationship with involuntary clients may not be trust, for example (Healy citing Smith 2001, p. 289), but a formal agreement. Yet the assumptions about engagement in a therapeutic relationship are based on notions of trust and a positive attachment. Healy also notes that psychologised approaches generally may 'limit workers' capacities to undertake responsibilities associated with decision-making in high-risk situations' (Healy 2005, p. 57).

However, psychodynamic approaches are, as Healy (2005) notes, so embedded within many ways of working in the twenty-first century that their usefulness continues despite these criticisms. Their strength is in providing theories of human behaviour as well as a way of understanding the client–worker relationship dynamics. They link individual agency, motivation and coping with their functioning in the outer world. Psychodynamic approaches not only provide a way of understanding individual behaviour in the context of a client–worker relationship, but also behaviour and processes within organisations, groups and families.

Chapter summary

In this chapter, some key skills associated with psychodynamic and cognitive behavioural approaches have been explored. Psychodynamic skills focus on bringing to conscious awareness patterns of relating both to the self and others, and beliefs from the past to understand their impact on present functioning and even future expectations. Cognitive behavioural skills similarly focus on building insight into the present, and establishing more conscious control over thinking, feeling and behaving. A major limitation of these skills is that they seek to bring about inner-world change primarily for the client. They have been criticised for failing to address the social, structural and cultural contexts of people's lives.

Reflective practice questions

1 What dimensions of these skills appeal to you? Why?
2 When would you use these skills and when would you not?
3 What are some of the cultural assumptions embedded in each of the approaches?

Key references

Beck, A., Freeman, A. & Davis, D. (2004). *Cognitive therapy of personality disorders*. New York: Guilford Press.

Brandell, J. (2004). *Psychodynamic social work*. New York: Columbia University Press.

Dean, R. (2002). Teaching contemporary psychodynamic theory for contemporary social work practice. *Smith College Studies in Social Work, 73*(1), 11–27.

Gibney, P. (2003). *The pragmatics of therapeutic practice*. Melbourne: Psychoz.

Howard, S. (2006). *Psychodynamic counselling in a nutshell*. London: Sage Publications.

Additional resources

Beck Institute for Cognitive Therapy and Research: www.beckinstitute.org.

Institute for the Study of Therapeutic Change (ISTC): www.talkingcure.com.

International Association for Cognitive Psychotherapy: www.cognitivetherapyassociation.org.

Tavistock Society of Psychotherapists: www.tavistocksociety.org.

Narrative and Solution-focused Skills

13

LEARNING GOALS

- Identify the core skills of narrative and solution-focused approaches, particularly in relation to the establishment of the relationship between a worker and client and specific interventions.
- Understand the strengths and limitations of these skills.

Core skills of narrative practice

Narrative practice aims to understand and transform the stories people live by—individual stories as well as stories held by communities and even nations. Dowrick (2006, p. 57), talking about the power of story and storytelling, reminds us that,

> Storytelling is one of humankind's most basic arts and the drive to listen to and tell stories is deep in almost everyone. It's the telling of stories that allows us to explore a situation or interaction that matters to us, to make sense of it or to relive it.

Narrative approaches, however, understand both the client–worker relationship and how to listen to stories in particular ways. The stories are seen as both important reflections of us as individuals and/or communities but also as narratives that profoundly influence and maintain our lives.

Establishing and sustaining the relationship

As a result of emerging from postmodern understandings of subjectivity and truths, narrative approaches have adopted a strong focus on the ways in which problem stories are co-created (de Shazer 1994, p. xvi). Thus, the client–worker relationship provides a safe, supportive engagement in which a person's stories can be heard, witnessed and validated. In bearing witness to a person's stories and helping to co-create stories of strength and healing, change can occur. This has proven to be particularly important in coping in the aftermath of trauma experiences (White 2004).

Specific interventions

Change as an agenda within narrative approaches focuses on understanding and re-authoring the stories we live by. Changing people's stories about their lives:

> … can help to change their actual lives. Furthermore, changing these stories often involves challenging larger social stories within people's problem-saturated stories about themselves and their lives. All individual stories are social stories (Brown & Augusta-Scott 2007, p. xvii).

Thus, specific skills in narrative approaches have emerged in relation to what is attended to in stories, and how they are explored. Like the other approaches, skills in validation and exploration are vital—probes, reflections and summaries all assist to establish the dominant narratives of a person's life, both their own narratives and those that others impose on them. Narrative therapy then aims to transform the unhelpful stories, or the inhibiting and self-defeating stories, restoring (or re-storying) them with stories that are strengths-based.

Exploring the dominant stories

For many people, not only are their circumstances difficult, but their circumstances also are not heard by anyone. Experiences of oppression, trauma and grief are often disenfranchised from the dominant social stories. Listening to someone's stories can be in and of itself a transforming experience. As Moore 2004, p. 58) notes: 'The repeated telling of a story gradually allows the pieces of life experiences to find their relation to each other.'

Some of the major skills involved in narrative work, therefore, are good listening skills: listening actively and empathically to what is being told, asking questions and summarising along the way, and enabling the person to tell all they need to tell, no matter how complex, ambiguous or awful their story.

Narrative approaches emphasise that we each carry multiple identities and roles that change and are reconstructed often. Listening for what is told and how it is told is the first skill in narrative practice.

Deconstructing and re-authoring through externalising the problem

Unlike the approaches explored in Chapter 12, narrative approaches understand the problem as residing externally to the person. While the person has a narrative about the problem, its causation and its consequences, for example, the person is not the problem. This skill, in **externalising** the problem, means the person is invited to speak around and about the problem, but not of it as them. Specific questions are then asked of the problem in understanding it as an external issue to the person.

Focus on practice: questions that aim to externalise the problem/s

- Tell me about a time that you stood up to, said 'no' to, or resisted the problem. How was that situation handled differently?
- Have there been times recently when the problem has not played a role in your life?
- Can you think of any time in the past when the problem could have played a role in your life and it did not?
- Do you remember other times in the past when you have stood up to the problem?
- How did it feel when you stood up to the problem?
- How have you been able to keep the problem from getting worse?

Source: Brown & Augusta-Scott (2007, p. xxxv).

Listening for strengths and coping capacities

In Heather's work with a client in a drug and alcohol service, she sets out to explore what has happened in the early days of someone's recovery, when they have experienced difficulties, as illustrated below.

Focus on practice: a conversation with a client who has relapsed

Heather is talking with a client who has attended one session then missed two appointments and has then attended for a second time and reported a relapse in use.

continues

> Heather: Hi Tony, why don't you tell me how the last few weeks have been going for you?
>
> Client: Not so great.
>
> Heather: What hasn't been so great for you?
>
> Client: I relapsed …
>
> Heather: I can see that you aren't very happy about this relapse; was it a shock for you?
>
> Client: Nah, I always relapse.
>
> Heather: It sounds like this is something that happens often for you?
>
> Client: Yeah, like thousands of times, I give up …
>
> Heather: What has happened in the past when you have relapsed?

Notice that rather than pathologising the recurrence of a relapse, Heather moves on to explore this client's narrative of relapse. She invites him to explore this more fully rather than explore what he has 'failed' to do, and it opens up the way to new coping strategies, by becoming aware of some particular patterns of risky behaviour. This is a process of normalising and validating rather than challenging and pathologising the person's story.

Re-authoring stories through listening for unique outcomes

As shown by Heather's questions above, another major skill of narrative approaches is to emphasise when the problem has not been a problem, or there have been ways of managing it differently. This way of thinking again emphasises strengths in a person's coping and that, in some situations, a problem or coping with it varies. This links with challenging some of the ways of thinking about an experience, described in Chapter 12. The challenging to think about **unique outcomes** challenges the client to think again about how a problem dominates their life. This involves the deconstruction of the dominant stories of a person's life and a re-authoring of new, positive and life-affirming stories.

Re-authoring social stories

Unlike the skills in the earlier chapters, narrative approaches seek to challenge the dominant social stories. Through deconstructing and re-authoring individual or group stories, the representations of these at broader social, structural and cultural levels can be changed too.

Core skills of solution-focused practice

Narrative and solution-focused approaches share many common skills—the use of extensive open-ended questioning around a problem, and the strategy of externalising the problem from the person in order to establish a new perspective on a person's circumstances. In this sense, they are both stepping out of the assumptions of other perspectives that assume that 'there is a necessary connection between a problem and its solution' (O'Connell 1998, p. 14). A number of differences, however, are evident in the two approaches. Narrative approaches are based on a very fluid understanding of the story a person lives by. Solution-focused approaches work more within a systems perspective and continuous notions of self.

Establishing and sustaining the relationship

As with narrative approaches, solution-focused approaches emphasise that your relationship with your clients is a short-term, co-creating relationship. The emphasis in listening is to hear both exceptions and solutions to problems in daily life. The goal is 'to identify and amplify client strengths and resources' (Walsh 2006, p. 208), with much of the 'work' being done by clients outside of any counselling or conversational time with you as the worker. In that sense, your role as worker is to stimulate a new way of thinking about problem situations, alongside your client. A positive and rapid engagement is encouraged so that work can occur quickly and not within the context of a lengthy therapeutic relationship. A high emphasis is placed on client expertise and empowerment in finding the solutions they need. The emphasis in client–worker contact is on translating that expertise and empowerment into everyday life (O'Connell 1998, p. 85).

Specific interventions

Many of the interventions are similar to those described in the previous narrative approaches discussion. Questions are asked to explore fully the ways in which the client views their situation, with an emphasis on focusing on exceptions and solutions, as well as the future.

Focusing on exceptions and solutions

The questions that reflect a solution-focused approach relate to the exceptions to problems and their solutions, rather than lengthy exploration of the nature of the problems themselves. This is one of the major differences with the skills and emphases of the approaches described in the previous chapter. The approach presumes that people have strengths and resources that enable them to overcome difficulties and problems at times, and these strengths and resources are what should be amplified, rather than the overwhelming nature of the problem situations themselves. The emphasis is less on insight into current behaviours, thoughts, feelings and events, and more on foresight about the future and a capacity to influence that future.

Focusing on the future

Solution-focused skills are designed to focus the client on the future, not on the past or even the present in great detail. It is about asking questions about the maintenance of problem situations, and in that sense emphasises the consequences of not changing. This encourages the motivation to change— the realisation that unless something happens, problems could remain or be exacerbated rather than diminishing.

At the heart of solution-focused skills is the skill of the 'miracle question' (de Shazer 1985), an open-ended question that is designed to 'enable people to pretend, to transcend the present and imagine a better state of affairs' (Manthei 1997, p. 100). The miracle question was proposed by de Shazer (1994, p. 95): 'Suppose that tonight after you go to sleep a miracle happens and the problems that brought you to therapy are solved immediately. But since you were sleeping at the time you cannot know that this miracle has happened.'

This first part of the miracle question invites the client to think that their difficulties could be different. The next step is to think about how they could be different: 'Once you wake up tomorrow morning, how will you discover that a miracle has happened? Without your telling them, how will other people know that a miracle has happened?'

This question can be adapted in many ways to invite people to think how differently their circumstances could or should look, and thus help set the goals for what needs to shift, even if only in the story someone lives by. Thus, the language of the questions you ask is driven by this focus on the future, and by an emphasis on possibility and change. It is an essentially positive, strengths-oriented approach to practice.

Strengths and limitations of these skills

Narrative skills enable the client to develop a coherent but constantly evolving story about who they are and what the problems are that they face. Solution-focused skills enable clients to think and talk about who they would like to be and how they would like to live. These skills enable the often-disenfranchised stories of people to be told and validated. They are also underpinned by a strengths perspective so that the focus is on positive change rather than inescapable negativity and oppression. Unlike the other approaches, these skills have the potential to transform well beyond individual lives; to cause change and re-authoring of dominant social and cultural narratives.

Some of the limitations, however, are that these approaches may not provide clients the opportunity, both in relation to time and to emphasis, to explore their past and present circumstances in depth. In this sense, some critics are concerned about the lack of depth, and even the lack of understanding of or insight into the nature of personal difficulties. Particularly with solution-focused approaches, critics suggest that there is an emphasis on the positive at the expense of understanding the despair and distress.

Others question the underlying assumption around a shared strengths-oriented discourse, which translates into the assumption that clients are telling socially desirable stories. Many stories are around not-so-desirable actions and perpetrations against others, and it is unclear where these fit within the overtly positive view of human behaviour, given the lack of a political positioning. This criticism is open to questioning, though, as narrative approaches have been profoundly influential in community organising and social action strategies.

Other cautions are raised in relation to the extent that a worker imposes their own views and dominant stories on their clients (Walsh 2006, p. 268), a caution that is pertinent to all approaches. Caution is also raised in relation to the absence of underpinning theories of human development and change. To what extent can stories be so subjectively located that a worker needs no basis in biopsychosocial assessments and understandings of a person's life?

> ■ In the next chapter, we will explore how feminist and critical approaches adopt a strong structural and political critique, which overcomes this criticism of the more subjectively located approaches.

Chapter summary

In this chapter, the skills associated with narrative approaches have been explored, including exploring dominant stories, deconstructing and challenging these stories and re-authoring them using a strengths base. The future- and strengths-focused skills of solution-focused strategies have also been examined, particularly through the use of the miracle question.

Reflective practice questions

1   What have you learnt from this chapter about:
    * exploring the narratives?
    * externalising problems?
    * unique outcomes?
    * asking a miracle question?
    * focusing on personal or community strengths and resources?
2   What do you see as the key strengths of these skills?
3   When do you think you would use these skills? Why?

Key references

Brown, C. & Augusta-Scott, T. (2007). *Narrative therapy: Making meaning, making lives*. Thousand Oaks: Sage Publications.

de Shazer, S. (1994). *Words were originally magic*. New York: W. W. Norton & Co.

O'Connell, B. (1998). *Solution-focused therapy*. London: Sage Publications.

Russell, S. & Carey, M. (2003). Feminism, therapy and narrative ideas: Exploring some not so commonly asked questions. *International Journal of Narrative Therapy and Community Work, 3*(1).

White, M. (2004). Working with people who are suffering the consequences of multiple trauma: A narrative perspective. *The International Journal of Narrative Therapy and Community Work, 1*, 45–76.

Additional resources

Brief Family Therapy Centre: www.brief-therapy.org.

Brief Therapy Institute of Sydney: www.brieftherapysydney.com.au.

Dulwich Centre: www.dulwichcentre.com.au.

Feminist and Critical Theory Skills

14

LEARNING GOALS

- Identify the core skills of feminist and critical approaches, particularly in relation to the establishment of the relationship between a worker and client and specific interventions.
- Understand the strengths and limitations of these skills.

Core skills of feminist practice

Unlike the approaches discussed in the previous chapters, feminist and critical theory approaches have an explicit lens on outer-world dimensions as the focus of the work. Many texts relating to communication and counselling skills exclude discussion of these approaches for this reason. This is because change is not understood to be occurring so much at the microskill or client-worker level of individual communication and interviewing. Rather, the focus of intervention is on social, structural and cultural change. That said, however, a number of key skills emerging from feminist and critical theory perspectives are readily transferable to communication at the client–worker interface. For the purposes of this discussion, unique skills to feminist and critical theory approaches are focused on within the same discussion rather than under separate headings.

Establishing and sustaining the relationship

Within feminist and other critical approaches, the emphasis within your relationship with people is on establishing equality, and, working in partnership, recognising the inherent human rights each has as citizens (Healy 2005, p. 186). Another way of thinking about working with your clients is about 'becoming an ally' (Bishop 2002). In becoming an ally or working in more egalitarian ways, your task is to emphasise the reciprocity of skills within the relationship. As Ife suggests:

> … the critical paradigm requires that skills be shared between the worker and the 'client', that the 'client' be seen as possessing skills that are just as valid and important as those of the worker, and that each should share their skills with the other in a process of mutual empowerment and mutual education (Ife 1997, p. 150).

Within this relationship context, you remain aware that the wider social context—and its issues of sexual, racial and class oppression and **discrimination**—are likely to be reflected. Individual client–worker relationships become the microcosm in which these power relations can be replicated. The client–worker relationship itself provides an opportunity to address power imbalances, and to name and ultimately challenge these sources of oppression. In relation to the assessment of the 'presenting problem', therefore, the personal is understood as inherently connected to the political. Thus, critical and careful attention to these dynamics is required and openly discussed throughout the client–worker contact. This is based on the belief that change occurs through the 'integration of personal and sociocultural transformational processes' (Bricker-Jenkins, Hooyman & Gottlieb 1991, pp. 291–2).

Most feminist and critical approaches see the relationship as a short-term resourcing role or a longer-term collaboration, rather than a 'therapeutic' relationship. This is in recognition that individuals are dealing with the private pains of public problems and therefore the solutions should be structural and political.

There are, however, many models of feminist therapy that embrace the opportunity for both personal insight and political change.

Specific interventions

Underpinning all of the skills of any critical approach is an analysis of individual problems through a wider structural and power analysis, whether in relation to gender, class, culture or ethnicity. Within feminist approaches, this lens is on understanding gender and power, and women's oppression by men specifically. You are not, therefore, using different communication skills as such, but using them in a particular way to focus on a particular understanding of people and their circumstances.

This is affirmed by Mullaly, who states of anti-oppressive practice that intrapsychic approaches are required such as: 'Introspective counselling or behavioural therapy or any other type of individual work that will help

■ Remember in Chapter 2, we looked at the decoding process. As a worker, you are decoding the message within a feminist approach through a gender–power filter or analysis.

to stabilize a victim of oppression, relieve some pain and torment, change symptoms and behaviours, and build some strengths' (Mullaly 2002, p. 172).

Thus, practice within critical approaches draws on many of the skills that we have already explored in the previous few chapters—the skills of questioning, of developing a story or multiple stories of the self, of understanding thoughts, feelings and behaviours, and challenging these where necessary. Feminist and critical approaches also incorporate goal-setting processes into the work. This chapter now explores three skills in addition to these that are more unique to feminist and critical approaches.

Three core practice skills (Bricker-Jenkins, Hooyman & Gottlieb 1991, pp. 292–5) are **validation**, **consciousness-raising** and **transformative action**, which lead to interventions that focus on mobilising of resources to meet basic human needs through relationships that nurture and sustain uniqueness, and the creation of validating environments.

Using validation

To validate someone or something is to 'lend force or validity to; confirm; ratify; substantiate' (Brown 1993, p. 3541). Validation, in an interpersonal sense, is about affirming the 'truth' of a person's subjective experience. Thus, reflecting skills are used to affirm someone's telling of their story and their perceptions of what has occurred. This has emerged as an important skill in recognition that so many people's stories, and particularly women's, are invalidated, disbelieved or rendered invisible. Naming what has occurred is a first step in this process of work together, particularly in relation to experiences of violence, assault and disempowerment.

Some validating statements you might make in your conversation with someone like Mrs B from Chapter 6 could relate to being a mother in a large, patriarchal medical setting and having to negotiate the various disempowerments within that context, or empathising with the care demands falling to her as a mother despite her other work pressures, for example.

Your questioning, reflecting and statement skills would focus on the wider structural and cultural dimensions of her experience, not only the personal dimensions. The focus, like narrative and solution-focused approaches, is on externalising the problem.

Encouraging a process of consciousness-raising

Through validation and dialogue, your skills help your client to engage in a process of consciousness-raising, not only with your client but also the wider social context. This consciousness-raising process leads to a process of liberation, which is sometimes described as spiral in nature (Bishop 2002, p. 100). The process of liberation involves 'breaking the silence, ending the shame, and sharing our concerns and feelings'. The skills we use are story-telling, analysis, strategy and action:

> Story-telling leads to analysis, where we figure out together what is happening to us and why, and who benefits. Analysis leads to strategy, when we decide what to do about it. Strategy leads to action, together, to change the injustices we suffer (Bishop 2002, p. 100).

Action leads to another round of reflection, analysis, strategy and action. This is the process of liberation. Like narrative approaches, story-telling becomes an important process, and thus listening and reflecting are critical skills. Feminist and critical theories, however, in politicising problems, also consider the naming of these issues in their wider social context as critical steps in working together.

Talking with someone about their difficult relationship circumstances may lead to a wider discussion of power and gender, or power and age, so that the person comes to understand their circumstances as emerging from wider social, structural and cultural influences, not from their own particular circumstances. This may mean that the intervention focuses more on forming connections with others in similar circumstances, moving beyond an individual client–worker relationship and participating in transformative action, as described below.

Engaging in transformative action

Through the individual experience of validation and consciousness-raising, liberation from oppression comes about through transformative action. While individual counselling work might be an important step in building insight and strengths for a person, connecting in group or community work is seen as the ultimate step to recovery or adaptation (Herman 1992; Mullaly 2002, p. 173), as the problem no longer resides 'with' the person but is addressed in its wider social context.

Within this perspective, your focus as a worker is not only on the work you undertake with your clients, but also a desire to bring about change with others in the immediate and wider context. Some examples of transformative action include 'bringing people together in order to present a petition or submission about a policy issue, or to advocate for change' (Ife 1997, p. 168). Other actions include the development of groups and community activities. For example, The Women's Circus (Liebman, Jordan, Lewis, Radcliffe-Smith, Sykes & Taylor 1997) was established in 1991, originally as a group for survivors of sexual assault but now it includes all interested women. The circus continues to raise awareness of women's experiences of sexual assault through reaching the wider community through this general outreach and publicity.

The communication skills required for these interventions are still all of those outlined earlier—both verbal and non-verbal—enabling you to explore the story of the individual or the community that is dealing with a particular issue, to challenge where necessary particular ways of thinking and acting, to externalise the problems, and to validate and affirm people and their strengths. The skills may also include working towards linkage with, and referral to, other transformative action opportunities.

Ultimately, your focus is on collective action, however, rather than individual responsibility as the way of bringing about these resources. For example, women's groups have actively lobbied governments for the provision of refuges for women escaping domestic violence. This action requires clear communication and argument with key stakeholders. Your engagement and rapport-building skills are fundamental to these processes, as well as to your direct practice with clients.

Focus on practice: using feminist skills

In Chapter 1, the following scenario was introduced:

A duty worker on a telephone crisis line receives a call from a young distressed woman who has been assaulted by her partner. She doesn't know what to do— whether to leave or stay—and asks the worker to tell her what she should do.

1 How would you go about assessing this situation with this woman?
2 What else would you want to know about her situation?
3 What validation skills might you use?
4 What consciousness-raising strategies would you consider?
5 Would you encourage her engagement in transformative action at all and how?

Strengths and limitations of these skills

The strengths of these skills are that they shift the focus of personal problems to the outer world, where so often the cause lies. They emphasise that people are both victims and survivors of these wider influences, and that through political and communal strategies, change can be achieved. Like narrative and solution-focused approaches, the emphasis is on changing the social and cultural discourses rather than regarding individuals as responsible and pathologising their coping capacities. Radical change has been possible as a result in the lived experience of women, in particular, because of the understanding and validation that a feminist critique has offered of relationships, workplaces and family life.

The major criticism of feminist and other critical theory approaches is that you are potentially imposing a particular worldview on clients. That is, the lens of the worker becomes the lens of the client. The dominance of Western, middle-class views in the development of many of these theoretical understandings has led to the criticism that they are further colonising and disempowering theories, rather than achieving what they fundamentally set out to achieve—equality and empowerment. Thus, as Healy (2005, p. 190) notes: 'A contradiction exists between anti-oppressive theorists' claim to promote dialogue in practice and their assumptions that they hold a true and correct analysis of the world.' Within the multicultural context of Australian services, for example, significant challenges emerge for feminist workers in maintaining a particular critique of gender, power and culture, while at the same time respecting difference and diversity.

Chapter summary

In this chapter, the skills privileged within feminist and critical theory approaches have been explored, including validation, consciousness-raising and transformative action. Understanding your clients' experiences from a feminist and therefore critical theory perspective enables the focus to be shifted from an emphasis on individual responsibility for coping to structural solutions and strategies. The personal is political instead, leading to different solutions and expectations of the client–worker relationship. Some of the challenges inherent in these skills, however, were explored in relation to the potential to replicate the very situation the perspective seeks to eradicate—disempowerment and the imposition of a particular worldview and way of being.

Reflective practice questions

1   What have you learnt from this chapter about:
    • how listening is influenced by feminist or critical theory approaches?
    • the nature of questions and the focus of intervention within these approaches?
    • the six specific skills primarily used within feminist and critical theory approaches?
2   What do you see as the key strengths of these skills?
3   When do you think you would use these skills? Why?

Key references

Bishop, A. (2002). *Becoming an ally: Breaking the cycle of oppression.* Crows Nest: Allen & Unwin.

Bricker-Jenkins, M., Hooyman, N. & Gottlieb, N. (Eds) (1991). *Feminist social work practice in clinical settings.* London: Sage Publications.

Chaplin, J. (1999). *Feminist counselling in action* (2nd edn). London: Sage Publications.

Fook, J. (2000). Critical perspectives on social work practice. In I. O'Connor, P. Smyth & J. Warburton (Eds), *Contemporary perspectives on social work & the human services: Challenges and change*. Frenchs Forest: Addison Wesley Longman Australia.

Kondrat, E. (1999). Who is the 'self' in self aware: Professional self-awareness from a critical theory perspective. *Social Service Review, 73*(4), 451–77.

Stoppard, J. (2000). *Understanding depression: Feminist social constructionist approaches*. London: Routledge.

Additional resources

CASA Forum: www.casa.org.au.

Feminist Majority Foundation: www.feminist.org/research/.

Help Index via Domestic Violence and Incest Resource Centre: www.dvirc.org.au/HelpHub/HelpIndex.htm.

PART 5

Finishing
the Work

In this final part of the book, we explore the tasks of finishing the work with clients, along with the tasks of evaluation. This brings together a way of thinking about practice that is multidimensional and focused on a number of different tasks within the client–worker relationship. The final dimension is added to the framework—finishing the work.

Part 1—Framing the relationship:

- the purpose of human service work
- your value base
- your theoretical and factual knowledge.

Part 2—Forming the relationship:

- your use of self
- your organisational context
- your ongoing support and professional development needs

continues

- meeting the people involved
- opening the communication
- actively listening
- listening empathically
- using self-disclosure.

Part 3—Focusing the communication:

- establishing the story
- forming an assessment
- goal setting.

Part 4—Focusing the intervention:

- drawing on theoretical perspectives
- doing the work.

Part 5—Finishing the work:

- ending well
- evaluating the work.

Finishing the Work 15

- Understand how finishing the work is conceptualised.
- Describe the tasks of finishing the work with your clients.
- Analyse the challenges in finishing the work.
- Consider the ways of evaluating your work.
- Understand how an effective evaluation is conducted.

Thinking about finishing the work

In contrast to all the attention paid to *establishing* a good client–worker relationship, in many texts surprisingly little is paid to the process of ending it well.

Your relationships with your clients will end for many reasons and in many ways, as they do in your other personal relationships. Ideally, a client–worker relationship ends when the work is done; that is, the goals that were agreed upon have been met and change has been able to occur or begin to occur. In some settings, the work ends because the contracted time period ends or the mandate to attend an agency is fulfilled. These endings can be anticipated and planned for as part of the overall contact.

Other endings occur in much more unplanned ways. The circumstances of the client or worker may change, such that the client relocates or the worker changes jobs. The relationship may end because of a poor engagement or rapport within a client–worker relationship. The client may drift away because they are dissatisfied. In some extreme situations, the worker or client dies, through illness or suicide (Shulman 1999, p. 221).

In other circumstances, your relationships with clients in fact do not end as they are expected to. Some relationships continue over long periods of time, across different organisational contexts, particularly if you continue to work across a number of organisations within a particular field of practice. Some continue by virtue of living together in a small rural or remote community (Green 2003; Taylor 2004). In some instances, perhaps more controversially, client–worker relationships have become lifelong ones and are characterised more by friendship than any particular professional stance (Crossley & McDonald 1984; Stansfield 2006). Organisational contact may not be the only context for contact, breaking down the often artificial boundary between the world of a client and their worker.

Different endings are typified in the stories we have explored throughout this book. Remember Karen and Mark from Chapter 4?

Focus on practice

Mark was in his thirties with suicidal concerns when he met with Karen for a first interview. His story related to the recent traumatic event of having watched as his small daughter ran across the road, was hit by a car and dragged a long distance. His daughter had suffered multiple injuries including some brain damage, and he was wracked with guilt as well as the trauma of witnessing the terrible event. He had left his family and the state feeling bereft and hopeless.

And Nicole and Mrs B from Chapter 6?

Mrs B is the mother of an eight-year-old son diagnosed with a treatable but life-threatening condition. She talked with Nicole about the impact of the diagnosis on her, her son and their family. Issues arose about subsequent contact over the following two-month period, until Nicole and Mrs B were able to talk through their issues and expectations of each other. Mrs B decided to continue seeing Nicole for assistance.

And David, and the client who became aggressive towards him, from Chapter 10?

David was working in a prison mental health unit, as a case manager for a client with an acquired brain injury and English as a second language. His client was charged with a serious offence and was distressed about a discussion he had with his solicitor regarding whether he should plead guilty or not guilty at court. Throughout their discussions, he became highly agitated, believing David was now accusing him of being 'guilty'. David's client started to become aggressive and threatening before storming off.

Each of these three circumstances led to very different endings of relationships. In Karen's situation, through regular, supportive counselling, it is anticipated that a strong engagement and working alliance would be established over time. Karen's organisation may have limits on the number of sessions she can work with Mark or she may be able to engage indefinitely with him. This presents specific challenges as to how clearly an ending is contracted in their work together both at the beginning and along the way. The finishing process is likely to be a discussed, planned process in their work together.

In Nicole's situation, she will continue to see Mrs B throughout her child's treatment and possibly through her child's dying and death, if the treatment is not successful. The relationship could be long term or relatively short term. Given the unpredictable illness trajectory, any sense of when this client–worker relationship may end is difficult to establish.

In David's situation, the relationship did not end in this one scenario. The client returned and continued to be aggressive and threatening. David continued to be seen as the case manager for this client until the client left the agency, but there was little direct involvement with him. The relationship was crisis driven and engagement remained tenuous. Given that a working relationship had been so difficult to establish, it was hard to think about how, why and when it would finish. The relationship ended when the client left the agency. His client's needs and rights were unable to be met.

The tasks of finishing the work

One of the challenges in understanding how to effectively finish the work is of course that there is little evaluation of it, for the very reason that there is no further contact.

Endings, like beginnings, are important influences on the work that is achieved. We often consolidate skills and learning over time, well beyond the time we first acquire them. As Loader (1995, p. 38) states: 'Certainly, we "finish" counselling, we "end" a supervisory or a collegial relationship, but the development is within us, within the other, not confined to time.' Thompson (2002, pp. 225–6) argues endings are important for a number of other reasons. First, he emphasises the importance of working towards empowerment rather than dependency, arguing that 'an unfocused, open-ended approach that loses track of ending can have the effect of undermining empowerment by increasing the possibilities for dependency developing' (Thompson 2002, p. 225). Second, workload management can become an issue, with the resources of any organisation and worker being limited. Third, he emphasises the need to end the potential labelling of someone as a client, so as to end the possible stigma of being a client. Fourth, he emphasises job satisfaction, because unfocused, uncontracted work can lead to feelings of frustration and little efficacy in working with someone. Fifth, he identifies the transfer of workers, in particular, but this can equally relate to clients moving on to other services or workers.

What are the important tasks then in ending a client–worker relationship? The following is a fictional conversation at the finishing stage of a group (Yalom 2005, pp. 335–6), highlighting many of the key tasks. A group member asks how the group facilitator is feeling, and he replies that he is tired but ready for the last group meeting that is to take place the following week. The group member asks:

'Okay to bring a ceremonial cake for our last meeting?'

'Absolutely, bring any kind of carrot cake you wish.'

But there was to be no formal farewell meeting. The following day, Julius was stricken by searing headaches. Within a few hours he passed into a coma and died three days later.

While this conversation is about a fictional therapeutic group and its ending, it captures four key tasks in terminating a professional client–worker relationship:

- working towards a planned ending of an intervention
- managing an unplanned interruption to that ending
- participating in a ritual to mark the end of their work together
- managing the evolving familiarity in the client–worker relationship, with the shift from a worker-directed concern to a client-directed concern of the worker, questioning them directly about their well-being.

Making a **referral**, providing follow-up, and **critically reflecting** are three other vital tasks of **termination**. Termination tasks differ depending on the nature and the context of the relationship: whether they are in relation to a short-term or long-term relationship; a mandated or voluntary human service involvement; or a strong or a weak **attachment** bond. Each of these seven tasks will now be considered, taking some of these dimensions into account.

1. Working towards a planned ending

At the early stage of establishing a client–worker relationship, it is important to be thinking about how the work may be ending. Will it end as a result of agency-imposed time limits, workload issues, the end of a mandate or through the attainment of agreed-upon goals? Planned endings can occur when the work is clearly contracted around any of these dimensions. It raises the question of timing of this discussion.

In some situations, you can talk with your client from the beginning of your contact as to how and when the work will end. The process of disengagement is a focus of your work, along with the process of engagement. From a rights and empowerment perspective, the client should always know when and how an ending will occur. Not knowing about how and when a relationship may end creates an unnecessary vulnerability and disempowerment, particularly when difficult or poor relationships are sometimes such a feature of people's personal histories. In other situations, an ending may become planned as the goals are more clearly established through mutual agreement. Thus, some initial time continues relatively unstructured around time frames, until the extent of work both parties wish to engage in becomes more evident. In other situations again, mentioning ending too early may jeopardise engaging in the client–worker relationship. The early phases of much work and contact may need to focus more on building a strong engagement and rapport.

Understanding endings involves reflecting on what the intended outcomes of the work together were; for example:

- What kind of change was being worked towards and how would you know if it had been achieved?
- What are the assumptions about recovery, adaptation or efficacy that both you and your clients have being working with?

Christine Simpson, who described her relationship with her worker earlier in Chapter 4 (Stansfield 2006, p. 16), saw the end of the work as relating to this outcome: 'I still have my pain, and my anger, but I am also very happy with my life as it is.' Working towards finishing the work, therefore, involves both processes of thinking about it and talking about it, ideally well before it happens. Endings mean different things for different people, depending on their age and stage, their past experiences of ending relationships, and what the significance of the work has been for them. Given that bad endings in human relationships are such a major contributor to human distress and suffering, ending a good working relationship well is one way of positively modelling the good relationship experience, even if the relationship has been a mandated one.

With planned endings, you can talk over time about what that will involve and what it might mean for both the client and you. Future contact and referral options can also be discussed, as described later in this chapter.

'Theorising' endings

How we think about endings influences what can and should happen at this point in the worker–client relationship. Each of the theoretical perspectives considered earlier has a different emphasis on the process of ending the work and whether the tasks discussed above are important.

Psychodynamic approaches have dominated understandings of the termination process, because of the centrality of the relationship to the goals of the work. In many discussions of the ending of a client–worker relationship or a therapeutic group, grief and sadness are identified as the dominant emotions in the finishing process. Perhaps in the intensity of therapeutic work, this is anticipated. The goal of psychodynamic work is often the establishment or reparation of secure attachments or good inner objects, thus the focus is on ending well, having worked through both past and present feelings of loss and abandonment. Termination is a very planned and discussed stage of work (Walsh 2006, pp. 43–4).

Consistent with this psychodynamic approach, authors such as Shulman argue that **denial** is the first stage of the ending process. He proposes that there is an inevitable change in the engagement in the relationship prior to it ending, and that there may be both direct and indirect anger. Using grief theory, ending is seen as a process of mourning, 'acknowledging the client's ending feelings and sharing the worker's ending feelings' (Shulman 1999, p. 209).

This is not always the case, however, as it can be a time of realising that change has been achieved and that a new phase is beginning. For many other people, the end of a client–worker relationship can be an incentive to achieve goals. The attainment of goals may mean that the relationship can therefore end because conditions of a court order, for example, have been met. Ending can be about a client regaining a sense of control over their own lives, free from the scrutiny of a worker (Trotter 2006).

Task-centred approaches are based on this premise that ending work together is positive in that it is about empowerment and achievement. As Marsh and Doel (2005, p. 118) state: '[T]here is the effect which we all experience as we move towards a deadline … in which our mind concentrates on the coming event with increasing strength. A time limit is, therefore, motivating.'

Endings signify the achievement of clearly contracted work, and the empowerment of the client to resume independent functioning. Short-term work is seen to be all that is required so that people can resume connections or establish new connections with informal social networks and their own internal resources.

Providing feedback and reviewing goals

Planned endings provide an opportunity for 'systematically adding up the experience' (Shulman 1999, p. 213) and identifying areas for future work if needed (Shulman 1999, p. 215). Whereas engaging in the client–worker relationship is about opening up the story, ending is about closing off and summing up the story, identifying what has been addressed.

Clearly, direct conversations with people about what has been helpful and unhelpful will provide very useful feedback about how circumstances have changed and what has been effective in bringing that about. Marsh and Doel (2005, p. 80) suggest a series of questions to ask in a final session as part of this review. They suggest that questions should focus on: the beginning; the problem, whether it was the right one and whether it has changed; the agreement or the goals; how things have changed in general; and the expectations for the future.

This review could include the following types of questions (adapting and expanding Marsh and Doel 2005):

- Why do you think I got involved with you?
- Do you think we have worked on the right issue?
- How has the situation changed for you?
- How has the situation changed others?
- Do you think we achieved what we set out to achieve?
- What strengths can you now rely upon?
- Do you think we could have done things differently?
- How near to your goals are you now?
- What do you think will happen in the future in relation to these issues?

This review provides an important opportunity to look at the ways in which the client will sustain the gains beyond the contact period. Reviewing what they will now do differently emphasises the strengths and capacities they have acquired. In being aware of the stages of change model, you can also talk through the possibilities of encountering future difficulties and how they may be managed. Identifying your availability for future contact is also critical if this is a possibility. This is discussed further later in this chapter.

In any feedback and review process, social desirability tendencies influence a lot of the feedback we give. That is, we often give positive feedback to maintain relationships rather than provide more accurate and potentially hurtful feedback. Below, Yalom provides another fictional account of feedback from a client to his worker. The client was asked to provide feedback as to whether his worker had been effective.

> ■ Remember the stages of change model presented earlier, which described the pre-contemplation, contemplation, action, maintenance and relapse phases of change management.

Focus on practice: consumer feedback

[E]ventually I realized you didn't know how to help me and I lost faith in our work together. I recall that you spent inordinate amounts of time exploring my relationships—with others and especially with you. That never made sense to me. It didn't then. It still doesn't (Yalom 2005, p. 28).

1 What would you feel and do if your client provided this feedback to you?
2 What would you do in your interactions with your clients to try to ensure that they could possibly talk these issues through earlier?

In asking for feedback, we need to be prepared to hear both positive and negative feedback. If we are serious about a consumer perspective, we need to take all feedback on board and talk it through with the people concerned. We need to talk about these issues in supervision and critically reflect on what

■ Remember the process of giving and receiving feedback, outlined in Chapter 10.

has occurred in specific situations. Other ways of receiving feedback include client satisfaction surveys, used in many organisations, or feedback interviews with other staff members such as managers or supervisors. An anonymous survey gives clients the option of providing critical feedback without fear of any consequences in terms of access to the agency in the future or other outcomes. An opportunity to talk with a supervisor can enable clients to talk about concerns they may have about their experiences with you as a worker.

2. Managing an unplanned ending

Yalom's example is of an interruption to a planned group ending. This can occur in practice, equally, with circumstances for the client or worker interfering with a planned ending. In many other instances, however, the work does not finish in a planned way at all. It ends because the client departs, because of a change in their circumstances and/or transient circumstances, or because there is no other way to address worker ineffectiveness.

Unplanned endings can be disconcerting, in that you can be left wondering what happened. Some strategies you can use at these times include:

- critically reflecting on your work with them and what issues may have been influencing their decision to not return
- trying to follow up with your client to discuss what has happened through telephone contact
- sending a letter that leaves the door open for future contact if this is possible
- fulfilling your reporting requirements in terms of the organisation and duty of care to the client.

In some organisations, clients are not informed when a worker departs. Even if contact is intermittent—for example, a client only comes to the hospital twice a year for an appointment—you may want to consider whether informing them of your departure is desirable and possible.

Unplanned endings can leave people feeling unsettled, angry or distressed, or unclear about what has occurred. In some situations, this outcome is preventable and worth working towards preventing.

3. Participating in ending rituals

Yalom's fictional group ends with the discussion of the making of the ceremonial cake. This sharing of food is not an uncommon gesture in the finishing of work together. Rituals in one-to-one work are similarly important. Rituals provide an opportunity beyond words to acknowledge what is taking place.

An ending ritual may be as simple as the review discussion outlined above, in which the ritual of closing is undertaken. Other rituals that can emerge in the ending of work together include:

- developing creative reminders of the work such as photos, scrapbooks, memory cards, journals or a summary document of what has been achieved. This ensures the recognition of **continuing bonds**; that is, that a relationship can continue beyond your direct contact of your work in other forms such as good memories.
- sharing food—particularly cross-culturally, this is an important way of symbolically shifting the power imbalance to a shared power balance
- expressing gratitude through letters or cards
- attending funerals, or other significant milestones, of someone's experience
- the giving of gifts.

Each one of these gestures is a way of expressing sharing and gratitude, and symbols can remain lifelong reminders of important work that has been done together. Workers and organisations approach these gestures differently, and important choices are to be made about whether they are appropriate and empowering gestures to be supported.

4. Managing the evolving familiarity

In Yalom's group, concern is expressed by a group member towards the worker and the worker responds. In some ways, this depicts a different direction of concern and attention within the client–worker relationship. Surprisingly little is written about the shifts that occur in client–worker relationships over time. Rural workers acknowledge the ongoing basis of relationship (Green 2003; Green, Gregory & Mason 2006) and connection, but within the urban context it is rarely noted. It is important to note the inevitable familiarity that emerges in the context of a client–worker relationship. In many instances, this can lead to a curiosity and concern with someone's well-being to the point where ending the work does not occur when it perhaps should. That workers become attached to clients (and vice versa) for a variety of different needs is inevitable, but it remains one of the less discussed issues in practice.

The literature relating to self-disclosure that we explored earlier in some ways addresses the issues of trust and vulnerability within relationships. The psychodynamic literature talks about it in terms of transference and counter-transference. Accounts of relationships in fiction or in movies depict relationships that would be seen as a gross enmeshment and violation of professional boundaries. They demonstrate, however, that relationships are complex and cannot be neatly compartmentalised into professional or personal.

Indigenous and cross-cultural models have increasingly challenged Western models of practice for their emphasis on the false boundaries between the personal and the professional. Western models have been based on a concern about the power differential and the potential disempowerment and exploitation that can emerge within the client–worker relationship, and thus authenticity and a growing trust and familiarity over time have tended to be minimised as key agents of change. Using supervision to address these issues of boundaries and appropriateness is vital so that work ends when and how it should.

5. Making a referral

In many situations, a referral for ongoing or different services may be required. For example, the work may not be complete but circumstances for the worker or client may have changed. Alternatively, the worker and/or the client may realise that goals cannot be achieved within this setting and that working with someone else may be more appropriate. Ending one client–worker relationship may be about making transitions to 'new experiences and support systems' (Shulman 1999, p. 218). In all of these situations, a process of referral is needed.

Referral processes have been found to be most successful when the following dimensions are attended to:

- discussion of the reason for the referral
- discussion of the process of referral
- a joint meeting with the current and new worker if appropriate to enable the goals to be established for continuing work
- consent of the client to speak with another worker
- the writing of reports as required.

6. Providing follow-up and keeping the door open

As many of the examples in this chapter have highlighted, not all human service work occurs in the context of neat, structured sessions, nor as one-off occasions. Talking about the possibility of future contact is an important step, if this contact is possible within the resource context. This involves being clear about whether the work has definitely ended, that no more contact is possible for whatever reason, or whether work can be recontracted at a later date should other issues arise, for example.

Some of the key reflections within this process include:

- Is the client empowered to access services when and how they need? For example, can they see someone else if they would prefer? Can they continue talking with you within the context of a new 'episode of care' as many organisations term it?
- How does the client reinitiate contact?
- Are there other ways in which the client can stay connected with the organisation, if that is their wish? Many organisations have extensive volunteer networks that enable clients of the service to contribute to the organisation and to others experiencing similar issues. This is often an important marker of recovery and adaptation (Herman 1992).

In some situations, a formal follow-up after a period of time is part of the practice of the organisation. For example, where a death has occurred, some hospital workers will follow up at the time of the anniversary of the death, or invite people back to a memorial service. In some other instances, follow-up is more complex. For example, many clients will not inform other family members that they have been in contact with services, so any contact may breach confidentiality for that person.

Follow-up can be beneficial for clients in that it provides an opportunity for them to reflect upon their own experiences and possible changes, and give feedback about the process. Clients can evaluate the longer-term effects of the work, as they reappraise what they have experienced and the efficacy of the intervention. For the worker, it provides some insight into the ongoing changes people have made and satisfies a curiosity as to how things have progressed for someone. Below, a worker describes their experience of meeting a client a decade after their contact.

Focus on practice: connecting again

I did not expect to bump into my client again. It was in another setting, where neither of us was in a work role. I was really surprised that after ten years, I still remembered so much of her situation and of the work we did together. For me, it was overwhelming to see how well she was doing and all that she had dealt with. I saw that she had survived so much. I am not sure what it was like for her to talk with me again. I think I gave her a fright, but I think she was also pleased to reconnect and to tell me about what she was now doing. We so rarely connect with people down the track and find out how they are doing.

1   What would you do in this situation?
2   What would you be curious about?

The important question is: Who is the follow-up for? Follow-up must first and foremost be for the benefit of the client.

7. Critically reflecting upon and evaluating your work

Evaluating your work occurs in this final phase of contact in two important ways. The first is evaluating the work with the client themselves, to review their perceptions of the work that has occurred and the efficacy of that work, as discussed above. The second is your own **evaluation** of your work in the context of all your practice. This occurs, as Chapter 5 explored extensively, through your own critical self-reflection and your supervision.

Some key dimensions in your evaluation include, first, client perspectives, as discussed above. Second, other workers' perspectives and key stakeholders' perspectives are important. Supervision, peer discussions and annual performance appraisals provide opportunities for you to receive feedback about your practice.

Reviewing the evidence base of your practice (Lewis 2002) is also critical. Supervision and your own professional development opportunities provide the opportunity to constantly review the various sources of information you rely upon. As Morris (2006, p. xxxiii) states in relation to social workers, they:

> ... need to know what interventions and services improve a client's functioning, a community worker needs to know how her or his community can work together to solve its problems and prevent other community problems, and the administrator/policy maker often just needs to know who her or his client community is.

A commitment to learning and self-reflection is essential for effective human service work.

A final word on strengths, optimism and communication

While we continue to know more about experiences of change and adaptation, and the role of intervention in these experiences, much remains unknown and open to question. Throughout this text, we have explored many of those issues, and hopefully you are left with many more questions as you begin your practice. Working with people is itself a life-changing experience—whether that work occurs in the classroom, in the counselling room, in the corridors of a hospital, in people's homes or in our communities.

People's lives and opportunities can change for the better as a result of interventions and resources. Oppression and adversity can be alleviated by the concerted efforts of individuals, groups and communities. Human strength, resilience and optimism are not only traits we encourage in the people with whom we work. They are traits we need to foster and keep alive within ourselves as workers (Mancini & Bonanno 2006). Throughout this book, we have explored some of the ways in which those efforts can be enhanced by effective communication skills. The hope is that you have been encouraged to try these skills out and critically reflect on how they may be useful tools for your practice.

Chapter summary

In this final chapter, we have explored how your work with people can end in planned and unplanned ways. Some of the meanings of endings have been explored, as have the skills required in managing the transition through to the end of the work together. Evaluating your work, both with the client directly and indirectly in your own supervision and reflection, has been emphasised as a critical dimension of your practice.

Reflective practice questions

1   What have you learnt from this chapter about:
    - planned endings to client–worker relationships?
    - unplanned endings to these relationships?
    - the tasks of termination?
    - evaluating your practice?
2   What has been your experience of ending relationships, both professional and personal?
3   How have you felt about these various endings?
4   What do you think are the most important dimensions of finishing the work?

Key references

Klass, D., Silverman, P. & Nickman, S. (1996). *Continuing bonds: New understandings of grief.* Washington: Taylor and Francis.

O'Hara, A. & Weber, Z. (Eds) (2006). *Skills for human service practice: Working with individuals, groups and communities.* South Melbourne: Oxford University Press.

Additional resources

InfoXchange: Technology for Social Justice: www.infoxchange.net.au.

Psychotherapy and Counselling Federation of Australia (PACFA): www.pacfa.org.au.

Glossary

active listening

Refers to all the verbal and **non-verbal skills** that affirm another person's conversation and provides them with a clear message that you are listening to them and understanding them. The **skills** of active listening include the **verbal skills** of questioning, responding, **reflecting** and **summarising**, and the non-verbal skills of physically and psychologically attending to that person.

adversity

Events or conditions of personal, family or community difficulty or distress.

anomie

Refers to the absence of established social norms or standards in a relationship or group of people. It often leads to a sense of anxiety and disorientation as people are unsure as to how to behave.

assertiveness

To put forward a particular point of view with the conviction that it will at least be heard, if not acted upon.

assessment

A very broad term that means different things to different professions. Assessment focuses on exploring how people are functioning and how optimal functioning and well-being can be enhanced through the provision of specific resources for their inner and outer worlds. The type of assessment required varies according to your agency context.

attachment

The relational bond established with primary care-givers in infancy, which enables a sense of a secure base to be established within an individual's inner world. A secure attachment relationship is different from other relationships in that it provides a secure base for the infant and enables the development of a sense of basic trust; an infant seeks this relationship particularly in times of high stress.

authenticity

The quality of being real or genuine in relating to another person.

biopsychosocial-spiritual dimensions

A term referring to all the significant dimensions of an individual that may be taken into account in a multidimensional approach, referring to the biological, psychological, social and spiritual dimensions.

challenging

In counselling work, the process of calling into question a particular view, behaviour or feeling; for example, challenging a self-defeating belief that someone may hold about themselves.

client

In the human services context, a client is a person who is using services in some way. This may be in a voluntary or involuntary capacity.

closed questions

A closed question seeks confirmation or disconfirmation of information by asking a question that requires a simple response of 'yes', 'no', 'maybe' or other singular word response such as 'never'.

cognitive behavioural therapy (CBT)

CBT is based on the understanding that a person's difficulties emerge as a result of the interaction of thoughts, feelings and behaviours. CBT focuses on creating change in any of these domains, particularly cognitions, so that change in the other domains will follow.

compassion fatigue

Refers to the experience of 'a sense of helplessness and confusion, and a sense of isolation from supporters' (Figley 1995, p. 12). It is understood as a trauma reaction **human service workers** may develop in response to their work with **clients** who experience grief, stress or trauma. Unlike burnout, however, compassion fatigue can happen following a single incident.

consciousness-raising

The process of bringing to people's awareness an understanding of experiences of **oppression** and/or **discrimination**. This is the first step in liberation or emancipatory processes.

constructivist perspective

This **paradigm**, in contrast to the **positivist** paradigm, does not consider that there is one objective truth or reality, but subjective positions only. The construction of the individual, family or community is what shapes and informs 'reality'. At the extreme end of the paradigm is the view that there is no such thing as 'reality' outside of these subjective perceptions.

consumer

Another term frequently used to describe a user of a service. As it emphasises the notion that the **client** is making choices about services they use, this term is more frequently used self-referentially and is seen to be more empowering as a term.

containment

Refers to 'an exquisite **empathy** and thoughtfulness with which the [worker] responds to the **client** throughout the session' (Gibney 2003, p. 46). Containment enables a sense of psychological safety to be experienced, and is therefore crucial in situations of **crisis**. Containment can be offered within a particular conversation; in relation to external threats; or in a particular ongoing relationship through offering a structured setting, with clear boundaries around meeting times and space.

continuing bonds

A term coined by grief theorists to refer to the ways in which biopsychosocial-spiritual bonds can be maintained with a person who has died. This is in contrast to other grief theories which saw the work of grief counselling to be about breaking any sense of connection with a person who had died.

conversational style

Refers to the unique verbal and non-verbal communication **skills** that we use in very particular ways, under the influence of, for example, familial, peer, gender, ethnic and regional expectations.

countertransference

Generally speaking, this is the reaction (conscious and unconscious) provoked in the **human service worker** by the **client's** story and presence. Some theorists argue that this may then 'result in a distorted perception of a client's behaviour' (Corey & Corey 2007, p. 67).

crisis

An upset to a steady state of being.

critical incident

An unexpected, stressful incident in which a person experiences unusually strong emotional reactions that have the potential to interfere with their ability to function.

Critical Incident Stress Management (CISM)

A range of specific interventions offered in the aftermath of a **critical incident**, which includes **debriefing**, incident management, psycho-education and counselling support.

critical perspective

A **paradigm** that is based on an explicit ideological or value base and which has change located centrally in its agenda. It is critical of the status quo, seeing **power**, conflict and **oppression** as dominant concerns to be addressed.

cross-cultural communication

The communication that takes place among people of different cultural groups, referring to communication that is sensitive to other peoples' ways of living and norms as much as language differences. In some situations, this involves working with an interpreter where there are language barriers. In other situations, it involves working with a cultural consultant, who can advise on social norms and expectations.

debriefing

A strategy that aims to reduce distress, educate and provide support around reactions to **critical incidents**, and, if appropriate, to review workforce strategies. Debriefing provides an opportunity to emotionally **ventilate** and psychologically process what has occurred. It can occur in dyads or in larger groups.

decision making

A process of coming to a decision about a particular course of action. In counselling work, this involves a series of steps, starting with brainstorming all the options, of considering the pros and cons of each course of action, and deciding on the most manageable, realistic and achievable option.

decoding

The process of translating, analysing or interpreting a message.

defence mechanisms

According to psychoanalytic thought, these are the unconscious patterns of response adopted when a person experiences anxiety.

denial

According to psychoanalytic thought, denial is a **defence mechanism** that enables the refusal to believe a particular thought or observation.

differential use of self

The ways in which you vary your **engagement** with, responses to and focuses of your work according to the particular situation in which you are working.

discrimination

The process of recognising differences between people or things, which then can lead to differential treatment based on these observations.

ego strengths

Refer to the strengths within a person's mental structure. The ego is seen as 'a mental structure of the personality that is responsible for negotiating between the internal needs of the individual and the outside world' (Goldstein 1995, p. xi; Walsh 2006, p. 32). Thus, ego strengths enable a person to cope with demands and stressors by mediating the inner and outer worlds successfully.

emotional intelligence

Distinguished from academic intelligence, emotional intelligence is about the conscious and careful self-management of feelings in social relationships.

empathic highlights

The verbal **skill** of **reflecting** back to the **client** what you have heard in terms of how they feel and in relation to what, to convey that they have been understood.

empathy

Refers to the 'power of mentally identifying oneself with (and so fully comprehending) a person or object of contemplation' (Brown 1993, p. 808). Empathy is an active **skill**, and is about 'entering imaginatively into the inner life of someone else' (Kadushin 1972, p. 52). Many argue that empathy must be expressed verbally as well as non-verbally, to demonstrate to the **client** that they have been heard and understood.

encoding

The process of converting information into another form. In relation to communication, it is the conversion of a thought into words and feelings into non-verbal messages.

engagement

When you as a **human service worker** enter into a positive, trusting relationship with your **client** so that your work together can occur.

evaluation

The action of assessing the process and the outcome of a client–worker relationship.

externalising [the problem]

A strategy within narrative approaches that understands the 'problem' as residing externally to the person. That is, the person is not the problem. The person is invited to explore the problem as they relate to it and as it influences their life.

feminist theory

Feminism as a movement aims to create structural change, redressing the continuing **oppression** of women within male-dominated **power** structures. Feminism locates the focus of its attention beyond the inner world of an individual, arguing that these inner worlds are influenced profoundly by the wider social and political context (Dominelli 2002; Trevithick 1998).

goal setting

Setting particular actions as aims to achieve, such as changing behaviours or actions.

human service worker

Someone who provides targeted services, typically within a government or non-government agency, to alleviate human **adversity** and bring about constructive social and individual change.

invitation

A statement or a question that invites someone to talk more about their situation.

Examples include the question 'Can you tell me about that?' and the statement 'Go on … '.

method

A 'way of doing a thing' (Brown 1993, p. 1759). In the human service context, methods include individual and/or family casework or counselling, group work, community work, program and policy development, education and research.

microskills

The building blocks of human communication in that they are all of the non-verbal (nodding, smiling etc) and verbal (questions, reflections etc) **skills** that we use to influence a communication process.

minimal encouragers

The verbal and non-verbal cues we use to encourage the person to continue in their talking. They are minimal in the sense of not being major statements or questions or reactions—they include smiling or nodding as non-verbal minimal encouragers, or 'aha', 'oh', 'hmmm' as verbal cues.

mutual clarity

When a **human service worker** and **client** have established a shared under-standing and clarity regarding a situation or issue.

narrative theory

A **theory** that places a major emphasis on the way in which an individual constructs and relates the stories, and particularly the problem stories, of their life. This approach is grounded in the belief that meaning making, through the formulation of narrative, is integral to well-being because it leads to an integrated inner state.

non-verbal skills

The cues or **skills** that emanate from our physical reactions and presence, rather than through our use of **verbal skills**. Non-verbal skills include facial expressions, body **posture** and movements, and the use of touch, for example.

normalising

A **skill** of affirmation; typically, it draws upon a wider pool of knowledge or experience to place a person's experience in context. Normalising provides a useful reflection and reminder that people are not alone in their distress and difficulty.

open-ended questions

Questions that are open in the sense that they invite the **client** to provide further elaboration of the details of their story. Questions beginning with the words 'how', 'what', 'why', 'when', 'who' and 'where' are all typically open-ended in that they invite some kind of descriptive, expansive response, not merely confirmation of information that has been provided by the person asking the question.

oppression

Refers to the negative and often overwhelming experience of being weighed down by circumstances or being overpowered by the influence and control of other people.

organisational context

The agency in which you are located and its wider context of operation (influenced by considerations of size, staff composition, management structures, auspice, policy, geography and agency interconnections, for example).

paradigm

A worldview, or way of viewing the world, often dominant among a group of people at a particular period of time.

paraphrasing

A term that describes the process of relating back in your own words what you think you have heard the other person say. Paraphrasing is seen by some to reflect 'cognitive aspects of messages rather than feelings' (Hepworth, Rooney & Larsen 2002, p. 141).

positivist

A worldview that understands social reality as based on 'stable, pre-existing patterns' (Neuman 2006, p. 105). A positivist **paradigm** is based, therefore, on assumptions of cause and effect (Morris 2006, p. 3), whereby it is possible through the identification of various factors to identify the cause of problems or difficulties, and intervene to alter them.

posture

The positioning of your body as a whole, which can indicate to another person varying degrees of interest and attentiveness.

power

Refers to 'the possession of control or authority over others' (Brown 1993, p. 2315), dominance or influence.

practice wisdom

Practice wisdom has been defined as 'the accumulation of information, assumptions, ideologies and judgements that have seemed practically useful in fulfilling the expectations of the job' (De Roos 1990, p. 282 cited in Osmond 2005, p. 891).

probes

The verb 'to probe' means to 'examine or look into closely, especially in order to discover something; investigate; interrogate closely' (Brown 1993, p. 2362). Probes include questions, prompts, statements and even single words (Egan 2002, p. 120).

psychodynamic theory

A **theory** that is primarily concerned with the inner worlds of individuals, and how difficulties arise in functioning because of these past and present inner-world preoccupations. Thus, psychodynamic theories are concerned with human drives or motivations in relation to pleasure, **power**, conflict and anxiety. These experiences are thought to develop across the lifespan, through various psychosocial or **psychosexual** phases.

psycho-education

Education related to psychological process; for example, in the aftermath of a **crisis**, people affected are often provided with psycho-education about what to expect by way of psychological responses in the aftermath experience.

psychosexual development

An approach that understands human development to involve an interconnected series of psychological and sexual development across the lifespan.

purpose

An intention or aim of doing something. In the context of human service work, purpose relates to the overall aim of an intervention or the reason for your professional involvement with a particular person at a particular time.

rational and irrational thoughts

The focus of **cognitive behavioural therapy**, rational thoughts are considered to be thoughts that are helpful in that they are reality based and enable appropriate behaviour and feelings to follow. Irrational thoughts are considered to be unhealthy or unhelpful thoughts in that they distort reality or focus on irrelevant dimensions of experience.

referral

The process of identifying another person who can be of assistance to the person and ensuring that this linkage occurs.

reflecting

A distinction that is sometimes made between the two types of responses—reflecting and **paraphrasing**—'while paraphrases are restricted to what is actually said, reflections concentrate upon less obvious information frequently revealed in more subtle ways' (Dickson 2006, p. 171).

reflexivity or critical reflection

A process of reflection that involves a further step of turning back on oneself in a reflective process to see how your own actions perpetuate or contribute to a particular situation, and to attempt to therefore critically appraise and influence your own positioning within a client–worker relationship. Through a process of reflexive awareness, one of the questions we begin to ask is: 'What do I (we) do in the agency on a day-to-day basis that might contribute to the structuring of unequal outcomes?' (Kondrat 1999, p. 468).

repetition

A psychoanalytic term referring to a person's tendency to remain stuck, repeating particular ways of behaving, thinking or feeling, because they have not been understood and resolved.

resistance

In psychoanalytic terms, the opposition to the emergence of particular insights, memories or repressed desires. In narrative terms, it is the process of withstanding particular stories being perpetuated about a person that maintain their **oppression** or particular status.

respect

Respect is about 'assuming the intrinsic worth of individuals regardless of their attributes or achievements' (Dowrick 1983, p. 14). It involves demonstrating a positive and sometimes deferential attitude to another person's point of view and/or circumstances.

risk assessment

An **assessment** of the likelihood that certain things will or may happen, based on the currently available evidence.

self-care

Strategies that are about taking care of yourself, in relation to all your **biopsychosocial–spiritual dimensions** and in relation to the impact of your work.

self-disclosure

A term that is 'loosely defined as what individuals verbally reveal about themselves to others (including thoughts, feelings and experiences)' and is seen to play 'a major part in close relationships' (Derlega, Metts, Petronio & Margulis 1993, p. 1). While we are always revealing things about ourselves through both our verbal and non-verbal interactions, we mediate these decisions and provide some boundary around some information. Self-disclosure can also be thought of as your explicit use of your own circumstances, either past or present, within your conversations with your **clients**.

skill

An ability to do something well. In the context of practice, this means having the ability to communicate or intervene successfully.

smoothing skill

A communication **skill** that is designed to smooth over difficulties and conflict, rather than escalate the disagreement that is currently being expressed.

social intelligence

Distinguished from academic and **emotional intelligence**, social intelligence refers to the conscious self-management of relationships and social interactions.

social justice

The maintenance of social rights, integrity and fairness for individuals, families and communities within the wider social order.

stages of change

A model that understands the change process as occurring in a series of stages, within which someone can 'relapse' at any point. Developed from research in relation to addictions, the model proposes people move from a pre-contemplation to a contemplation stage, then to preparation and on to action. When change is achieved, a maintenance phase begins.

structural context

The wider context of systems that influence our daily lives, such as legal, political, educational, health and welfare systems.

summarising

Skills used in a conversation to draw together the various issues that have been discussed.

supervision

For **human service workers**, a supervisor is someone who takes responsibility, typically within the context of your agency, for you, your learning and your practice. A supervisor assists you in developing your practice and **practice wisdom** through direct modelling, support and intervention as an experienced worker. Supervision is the time focused on this discussion of your work, your learning and your support needs.

survival

Continuing to live after some event.

task-centred

A practice that has emerged from a pragmatic approach to human service delivery. It is a time-limited, contracted and highly structured approach. Interventions focus on 'doing'—on activities either within the context of the contact itself or outside as homework (Marsh & Doel 2005, p. 38).

termination

The process of finishing the work and the relationship with a **client**.

theory

A system of ideas that provides an explanation of a phenomenon.

therapeutic

A healing influence.

transference

A part of every relationship in which we engage, referring to the unconscious motivations and desires, conflicts and anxieties that we experience in our relationships. These patterns of relationship are thought to have emerged in infancy in the context of parent–infant relationships. In **therapeutic** work, the intention is to understand these conscious and unconscious experiences and expectations in the context of the client–worker relationship, enabling the working through of earlier and current significant relationships. By developing insight into the transference, change can occur as these needs and desires come under more conscious control.

transformative action

Action that creates change, often more at broader social, structural and cultural levels than just the individual level of experience.

unique outcomes

In narrative approaches, the situations when the problem under analysis has not been a problem. Exploring unique outcomes enables a focus on what helps to understand what changes the problem's influence in a person's life.

validation

In counselling work, the process of confirming the story or emotions of another person, so that they feel affirmed and understood in their subjective experience.

values

The 'generally accepted or personally held judgement of what is valuable and important in life' (Brown 1993, p. 3542). Professions will often define a set of values that they regard as core to the practice of their work.

ventilation

The expression and, therefore, the release of feelings, often referred to as a process of catharsis.

verbal skills

Verbal communication processes include everything that is spoken or uttered in a conversation and refer primarily to the content or message that is exchanged. Verbal **skills** are therefore specific verbal communication processes that influence a communication in a positive and/or directed way.

vicarious traumatisation

Similar to **compassion fatigue**, vicarious traumatisation refers to a **human service worker's** reaction in response to hearing or witnessing the traumatic experiences of **clients**. It is also referred to as secondary traumatisation.

violence

The use of force to cause injury or harm to another person. Violence is usually thought about in its physical, sexual and emotional forms, but others such as Mullaly (2002) have suggested that the wider social context can be responsible for structural violence; that is, the abuse of people through the failure to eliminate poverty and **oppression**.

Bibliography

AASW. See Australian Association of Social Workers.

Adams, R., Dominelli, L. & Payne, M. (Eds) (2005). *Social work futures: Crossing boundaries, transforming practice*. Basingstoke: Palgrave Macmillan.

Adolescent Forensic Health Service. (2007). *Male Adolescent Program for Positive Sexuality (MAPPS)*. 2007, from www.rch.org.au/afhs/mapps/index.cfm?doc_id=1150.

American Board of Examiners in Clinical Social Work. (2004). *The practice of psychoanalysis: A specialty of clinical social work*. American Board of Examiners in Clinical Social Work.

American Psychiatric Association. (2000). *The diagnostic and statistical manual of mental disorders—Text revised*. Washington: American Psychiatric Association.

Anderson, H. (1997). *Conversation, language and possibilities: A postmodern approach to therapy*. New York: Basic Books.

Andrews, D., Keissling, J., Russell, R. & Grant, B. (1979). *Volunteers and the one-to-one supervision of adult probationers*. Toronto: Ontario Ministry of Correctional Services.

Anglem, J. & Maidment, J. (2004). Introduction to assessment. In J. Maidment & R. Egan (Eds), *Practice skills in social work and welfare: More than just common sense*. Crows Nest: Allen & Unwin (chap. 8, pp. 112–26).

Antonovsky, A. (1979). *Health, stress and coping*. San Francisco: Jossey-Bass.

Antonovsky, A. (1987). *Unraveling the mystery of health: How people manage stress and stay well*. San Francisco: Jossey-Bass.

APA. See American Psychiatric Association.

Arendt, M. & Elklit, A. (2001). Effectiveness of Psychological Debriefing. *Acta Psychiatrica Scandinavica, 104*(6), 423–37.

Armstrong, J. (2006). *Love, life, Goethe: How to be happy in an imperfect world*. London: Allan Lane.

Atkinson, J. (2002). *Trauma trails: Recreating song lines. The transgenerational effects of trauma in Indigenous Australia*. North Melbourne: Spinifex.

Australian Association of Social Workers. (2002). *Code of ethics* (2nd edn). Kingston: Australian Association of Social Workers.

Australian Association of Social Workers. (2003). *Practice standards for social workers: Achieving outcomes*. ACT: Australian Association of Social Workers.

BACP. See British Association for Counselling and Psychotherapy.

Bandura, A., Caprara, G., Barbaranelli, C., Gerbino, M. & Pastorelli, C. (2003). Role of affective self-regulatory efficacy in diverse spheres of psychosocial functioning. *Child Development, 74*(3), 769–82.

Banks, S. (2006). *Ethics and values in social work* (3rd edn). Basingstoke: Palgrave Macmillan.

Beck, A., Freeman, A. & Davis, D. (2004). *Cognitive therapy of personality disorders.* New York: Guilford Press.

Bird, A. (2006). *We need to talk: The case for psychological therapy on the NHS.* London: Mental Health Foundation.

Bishop, A. (2002). *Becoming an ally: Breaking the cycle of oppression.* Crows Nest: Allen & Unwin.

Black, D. & Trickey, D. (2005). *Children bereaved by murder and manslaughter.* Seventh International Conference on Grief and Bereavement in Contemporary Society, 12 July, London.

Blagg, H. (1997). A just measure of shame? Aboriginal youth and conferencing in Australia. *The British Journal of Criminology, 37*(4), 481–501.

Blankenship, K. (1998). A race, class and gender analysis of thriving. *Journal of Social Issues, 54*(2), 393–404.

Bloch, S. & Singh, B. (Eds) (2007). *Foundations of clinical psychiatry.* Carlton: Melbourne University Press.

Bluebond-Langner, M. (1978). *The private worlds of dying children.* Princeton: Princeton University Press.

Bond, T. (2000). *Standards and ethics for therapy in action* (2nd edn). London: Sage Publications.

Bowlby, J. (1984). *Attachment.* London: Penguin.

Bramwell, M. (2005). *Living with HIV/AIDS.* Paper presented at the Human Risk and Vulnerable Populations Lecture, University of Melbourne.

Brandell, J. (2004). *Psychodynamic social work.* New York: Columbia University Press.

Bricker-Jenkins, M., Hooyman, N. & Gottlieb, N. (Eds) (1991). *Feminist social work practice in clinical settings.* London: Sage Publications.

Briggs, H. & Cocoran, K. (Eds) (2001). *Social work practice: Treating common client problems.* Chicago: Lyceum Books Inc.

Brink, D. (1987). The issues of equality and control in the client- or person-centered approach. *Journal of Humanistic Psychology, 27*(1), 27–37.

British Association for Counselling and Psychotherapy. (2002). *Ethical framework for good practice in counselling and psychotherapy.* Rugby.

Bronfenbrenner, U. (1979). *The ecology of human development: Experiments by nature and design.* Cambridge, MA: Harvard University Press.

Brown, C. & Augusta-Scott, T. (2007). *Narrative therapy: Making meaning, making lives.* Thousand Oaks: Sage Publications.

Brown, F. & Rainer, J. (2006). Too much to bear: An introduction to crisis intervention and therapy. *Journal of Clinical Psychology, 62*(8), 953–7.

Brown, G. (2006). Explaining. In O. Hargie (Ed.), *The handbook of communication skills.* Hove: Routledge (3rd edn, chap. 7, pp. 195–228).

Brown, L. (Ed.) (1993). *The new shorter Oxford English dictionary.* Oxford: Clarendon Press.

Brun, C. & Rapp, R. (2001). Strengths-based case management: Individuals' perspectives on strengths and the case manager relationship. *Social Work, 46*(3), 278–88.

Bucknell, D. (2006). Outcome focused supervision. In H. Reid & J. Westergaard (Eds),

Providing support and supervision: An introduction for professionals working with young people. London: Routledge (chap. 44, pp. 41–56).

Bull, P. (2002). *Communication under the microscope: The theory and practice of microanalysis.* New York: Routledge.

Burstow, B. (1987). Humanistic psychotherapy and the issue of equality. *Journal of Humanistic Psychology, 27*(1), 9–25.

Butchart, A. & Kahane, T. (2006). *Preventing child maltreatment: A guide to taking action and generating evidence.* Geneva: World Health Organization and International Society for Prevention of Child Abuse and Neglect.

Campfield, K. & Hills, A. (2001). Effect of timing of Critical Incident Stress Debriefing (CISD) on posttraumatic symptoms. *Journal of Traumatic Stress, 14*(2), 327–40.

Canda, E. & Furman, L. (1999). *Spiritual diversity in social work practice: The heart of helping.* New York: The Free Press.

Caplan, G. (1990). Loss, stress and mental health. *Community Mental Health Journal, 26*(1), 27–48.

Carroll, M. (1996). *Counselling supervision: Theory, skills and practice.* London: Cassell.

Carroll, M. & Gilbert, M. (2006). *On being a supervisee: Creating learning partnerships.* Kew: Psychoz.

Cartney, P. (2006). Using video interviewing in the assessment of social work communication skills. *British Journal of Social Work, 36*, 827–44.

Catty, J. (2005). 'The vehicle of success': Theoretical and empirical perspectives on the therapeutic alliance in psychotherapy and psychiatry. *Psychology and Psychotherapy: Theory, Research and Practice, 77*(2), 255–72.

Chaplin, J. (1999). *Feminist counselling in action* (2nd edn). London: Sage Publications.

Chenowith, L. & McAuliffe, D. (2005). *The road to social work and human service practice: An introductory text.* Southbank: Thomson.

Chodorow, N. (1999). The anxieties of uncertainty: Reflections on the role of the past in psychoanalytic thinking. In N. Chodorow (Ed.), *The power of feelings: Personal meaning in psychoanalysis, gender and culture.* New Haven: Yale University Press (pp. 34–65).

Chui, W. H. & Wilson, J. (Eds) (2006). *Social work and human services best practice.* Leichhardt: The Federation Press.

Clarke, A., Andrews, S. & Austin, N. (1999). *Lookin' after our own: Supporting Aboriginal families through the hospital experience.* Melbourne: Aboriginal Family Support Unit—Royal Children's Hospital.

Cleak, H. & Wilson, J. (2004). *Making the most of field placement.* Southbank: Thomson.

Cnaan, R. (1999). *The newer deal: Social work and religion in partnership.* New York: Columbia University Press.

Connolly, M. (Ed.) (2001). *New Zealand social work: Contexts and practice.* South Melbourne: Oxford University Press.

Connolly, M. (2004). *Child and family welfare: Statutory responses to children at risk.* Christchurch: Te Awatea Press.

Cooper, M. & Lesser, J. (2002). *Clinical social work practice: An integrated approach.* Boston: Allyn and Bacon.

Corey, M. & Corey, G. (2007). *Becoming a helper* (5th edn). Belmont: Thomson.

Coulehan, J. & Block, M. (2006). *The medical interview: Mastering skills for clinical practice.* Philadelphia: F. A. Davis Co.

Coulton, C. (2004, January 17). *The place of community in social work practice research: Conceptual and methodological developments.* Paper presented at the Aaron Rosen Lecture, Society for Social Work Research, New Orleans.

Cournoyer, B. (2004). *The evidence-based social work skills book.* Boston: Pearson Education.

Cournoyer, B. (2005). *The social work skills workbook.* Belmont: Thomson Brooks/Cole.

Cox, D. (1982). *Religion and welfare: A study of the role of religion in the provision of welfare services to selected groups of immigrants in Melbourne.* Parkville: Department of Social Studies, University of Melbourne.

Coyne, J., Aldwin, C. & Lazarus, R. (1981). Depression and coping in stressful episodes. *Journal of Abnormal Psychology, 90*(5), 439–47.

Coyne, J. & Downey, G. (1991). Social factors and psychopathology: Stress, social support and coping processes. *Annual Review of Psychology, 42*, 401–25.

Cramer, P. (1998). Defensiveness and defense mechanisms. *Journal of Personality, 66*(6).

Crawford, K. (2006). *Reflective reader: Social work and human development.* Exeter: Learning Matters.

Crossley, R. & McDonald, A. (1984). *Annie's coming out.* Ringwood: Penguin Books.

Crumpton-Cook, R. (1996). But we have the expertise. *Psychotherapy in Australia, 3*(1), 16–17.

Cunningham, M. (2003). Impact of trauma work on social work clinicians: Empirical findings. *Social Work, 48*(4), 451–9.

D'Cruz, H., Gillingham, P. & Melendez, S. (2007). Reflexivity, its meanings and relevance for social work: A critical review of the literature. *British Journal of Social Work, 37*(1), 73–90.

Daines, B., Gask, L. & Usherwood, T. (1997). *Medical and psychiatric issues for therapists.* London: Sage Publications.

Dalton, D. (1993). *Mahatma Gandhi: Nonviolent power in action.* New York: Columbia University Press.

de Boer, C. & Coady, N. (2007). Good helping relationships in child welfare: Learning from stories of success. *Child and Family Social Work, 12*, 32–42.

de Shazer, S. (1994). *Words were originally magic.* New York: W. W. Norton & Co.

Deahl, M., Srinivasan, M., Jones, N., Neblett, C. & Jolly, A. (2001). Evaluating psychological debriefing: Are we measuring the right outcomes? *Journal of Traumatic Stress, 14*(3), 527–9.

Dean, R. (2001). The myth of cross-cultural competence. *Families in Society: The Journal of Contemporary Human Services, 82*(6), 623–30.

Dean, R. (2002). Teaching contemporary psychodynamic theory for contemporary social work practice. *Smith College Studies in Social Work, 73*(1), 11–27.

Derlega, V., Metts, S., Petronio, S. & Margulis, S. (1993). *Self-disclosure.* Newbury Park: Sage Publications.

Deveson, A. (1991). *Tell me I'm here.* Ringwood: Penguin.

Dickson, D. (2006). Reflecting. In O. Hargie (Ed.), *The handbook of communication skills.* New York: Routledge (3rd edn, chap. 6, pp. 165–94).

Dickson, D. & Hargie, O. (2006). Questioning. In O. Hargie (Ed.), *The handbook of communication skills.* Hove: Routledge (chap. 4, pp. 121–45).

Diller, J. (2004). *Cultural diversity: A primer for the human services.* Belmont: Brooks/Cole.

Division for the Advancement of Women. (2003). Women, nationality and citizenship. *Women2000 and Beyond.* Geneva: World Health Organization.

Doka, K. (1989). *Disenfranchised grief: Recognizing hidden sorrow.* New York: Lexington Books.

Dominelli, L. (2002). *Feminist social work theory and practice.* Basingstoke: Palgrave.

Dow, B. & McDonald, J. (2003). Social support or structural change? Social work theory and research on care-giving. *Australian Social Work, 56*(3), 197–208.

Dowrick, C. (1983). Strange meeting: Marxism, psychoanalysis and social work. *British Journal of Social Work, 13*, 1–18.

Dowrick, S. (2006, June 10). The heart of the story. *The Age*, p. 57.

Dryden, W. & Mytton, J. (1999). *Four approaches to counselling and psychotherapy.* London: Routledge.

Duffy, S., Jackson, F., Schim, S., Ronis, D. & Fowler, K. (2006). Cultural concepts at the end of life: How do culture, race, gender and ethnicity influence nursing interventions in end-of-life care? *Nursing Older People, 18*(8), pp. 10–15.

Duncan, B. & Miller, S. (2005). The manual is not the territory: Treatment manuals do not improve outcomes. In J. Norcross, R. Levant & L. Beutler (Eds), *Evidence-based practices in mental health: Debate and dialogue on the fundamental questions.* Washington, DC: American Psychological Association Press.

Dwairy, M. (2006). *Counselling and psychotherapy with Arabs and Muslims.* New York: Teachers College Press.

Dyregrov, A. (1997). The process in psychological debriefings. *Journal of Traumatic Stress, 10*(4), 589–605.

Edward, J. (1998). Psychodynamic psychotherapy after managed care. In G. Schamess & A. Lightburn (Eds), *Humane managed care?* Washington: NASW Press.

Egan, G. (2002). *The skilled helper: A problem-management and opportunity-development approach to helping* (7th edn). Pacific Grove: Brooks/Cole.

Egan, G. (2007). *The skilled helper: A problem-management and opportunity-development approach to helping* (8th edn). Pacific Grove: Brooks/Cole.

Elkhuizen, K., Kelleher, R., Gibson, L. & Attoe, R. (2006). 'Sitting on the mourning bench': Mental health workers and an elderly client. *Australian Social Work, 59*(3), 281–7.

Ellis, A. (1974). *Humanistic psychotherapy: The rational emotive approach.* San Francisco: McGraw-Hill.

Ellis, A. (1995). *Better, deeper, and more enduring brief therapy: The Rational Emotive Behavior Therapy approach.* Bristol, PA: Brunner/Mazel.

Ellis, A. (2004). Post-September 11th perspectives on religion, spirituality, and philosophy in the personal and professional lives of selected REBT cognoscenti: A response to my colleagues. *Journal of Counseling and Development, 82*, 439–42.

Epstein, L. (1994). The therapeutic idea in contemporary society. In A. Chambon & A. Irving (Eds), *Essays on postmodernism and social work.* Toronto: Canadian Scholar's Press Inc. (pp. 3–15).

Esteva, G. & Prakash, M. (1998). Human rights: The Trojan horse of recolonization? In G. Esteva & M. Prakash (Eds), *Grassroots post-modernism: Remaking the soil of cultures.* London: Zed Books.

Evans, J. & Benefield, P. (2001). Systematic reviews of educational research: does the medical model fit? *British Educational Research Journal* 27(5), 527–41.

Evans, W., Tulsky, J., Back, A. & Arnold, R. (2006). Communication at times of transitions: How to help patients cope with loss and re-define hope. *Cancer Journal, 12*, 417–24.

Everly, G. (2000). Five principles of crisis intervention: Reducing the risk of premature crisis intervention. *International Journal of Emergency Mental Health, 2*(1), 1–4.

Everly, G., Flannery, R. & Mitchell, J. (2000). Critical Incident Stress Management (CISM): A review of the literature. *Aggression and Violent Behavior, 5*(1), 23–40.

Figley, C. (Ed.) (1995). *Compassion fatigue: Coping with secondary traumatic stress disorder in those who treat the traumatized*. New York: Brunner/Mazel.

Flannery, R. & Everly, G. (2000). Crisis intervention: A review. *International Journal of Emergency Mental Health, 2*(2), 119–25.

Floyd, K. & Morman, M. (Eds) (2006). *Widening the family circle: New research on family communication*. Thousand Oaks: Sage.

Folstein, M., Folstein, S. & McHugh, P. (1975). Mini-mental state: A practical method for grading the cognitive state of patients for the clinician. *Journal of Psychiatric Research, 12*, 189–98.

Fonagy, P. (1999). Process and outcome in mental health care delivery: A model approach to treatment evaluation. *Bulletin of the Menninger Clinic, 63*(3), 288–304.

Fonagy, P. (2002). *Attachment theory and psychoanalysis*. New York: Other Press.

Fonagy, P., Moran, G. & Target, M. (1993). Aggression and the psychological self. *International Journal of Psychoanalysis, 74*, 471–85.

Fook, J. (1993). *Radical casework: A theory of practice*. St Leonards: Allen & Unwin.

Fook, J. (1999). Critical reflectivity in education and practice. In B. Pease & J. Fook (Eds), *Transforming social work practice: Postmodern critical perspectives*. St Leonards: Allen & Unwin (chap. 13, pp. 195–208).

Fook, J. (2000). Critical perspectives on social work practice. In I. O'Connor, P. Smyth & J. Warburton (Eds), *Contemporary perspectives on social work & the human services: Challenges and change*. Frenchs Forest: Addison Wesley Longman Australia.

Fook, J. (2002). *Social work: Critical theory and practice*. Thousand Oaks: Sage.

Freire, P. (1996). *Pedagogy of the oppressed*. Camberwell: Penguin Books.

Froggett, L. (2002). *Love, hate and welfare: Psychosocial approaches to policy and practice*. Bristol: Policy Press.

Furlong, M. & Ata, A. (2006). Observing different faiths, learning about ourselves: Practice with inter-married Muslims and Christians. *Australian Social Work, 59*(3), 250–64.

Gaita, R. (1999). *A common humanity: Thinking about love and truth and justice*. Melbourne: Text Publishing.

Gaita, R. (2004). *Good and evil: An absolute conception* (2nd edn). Abingdon: Routledge.

Gallagher, E., Wadsworth, A. & Stratton, T. (2002). Religion, spirituality and mental health. *The Journal of Nervous and Mental Disease, 190*(10), 697–704.

Gambrill, E. (1999). Evidence-based practice: An alternative to authority-based practice. *Families in Society, 80*(4), 341–50.

Ganzer, C. & Ornstein, E. (1999). Beyond parallel process: Relational perspectives on field instruction. *Clinical Social Work Journal, 27*(3), 231–46.

Garland, C. (1998). *Understanding trauma: A psychoanalytic approach*. New York: Routledge.

Geldard, D. & Geldard, K. (2005). *Basic personal counselling: A training manual for counsellors* (5th edn). Frenchs Forest: Pearson Education Australia.

Gelman, C. R. & Mirabito, D. (2005). Practicing what we teach: Using case studies from 9/11 to teach crisis intervention from a generalist perspective. *Journal of Social Work Education, 41*(3), 479–94.

George, L., Larson, D., Koenig, H. & McCulloch, M. (2000). Spirituality and health: What we know, what we need to know. *Journal of Social and Clinical Psychology, 19*(1), 102–16.

Germain, C. (1991). *Human behavior in the social environment: An ecological view* (2nd edn). New York: Columbia University Press.

Germain, C. & Bloom, M. (1999). *Human behavior in the social environment: An ecological view*. New York: Columbia University Press.

Gibney, P. (2003). *The pragmatics of therapeutic practice*. Melbourne: Psychoz.

Giddens, A. (1991). *Modernity and self-identity: Self and society in the late modern age*. California: Stanford University Press.

Giddens, A. (2002). *Runaway world: How globalisation is reshaping our lives* (2nd edn). London: Profile Books.

Ginzburg, K., Solomon, Z. & Bleich, A. (2002). Repressive coping style, acute stress disorder, and posttraumatic stress disorder after myocardial infarction. *Psychosomatic Medicine, 64*(5), 748–57.

Gist, R. & Woodall, S. (1999). There are no simple solutions to complex problems: The rise and fall of Critical Incident Stress Debriefing as a response to occupational stress in the fire service. In R. Gist & B. Lubin (Eds), *Response to disaster: Psychosocial, community and ecological approaches*. Philadelphia: Brunner/Mazel (chap. 9, pp. 211–35).

Glintborg, B., Andersen, S. E. & Dalhoff, K. (2007). Insufficient communication about medication use at the interface between hospital and primary care. *Quality and Safety in Health Care, 16*(1), 34–9.

Goldberg, D. (1978). *Manual of the General Health Questionnaire*. Windsor: NFER Publishing.

Goldstein, E. (1995). *Ego psychology and social work practice*. New York: Free Press.

Goleman, D. (2005). *Emotional intelligence*. New York: Bantam Books.

Goleman, D. (2006). *Social intelligence: The new science of human relationships*. London: Hutchinson.

Goodman, D. (2001). *Promoting diversity and social justice: Educating people from privileged groups*. Thousand Oaks: Sage.

Gordon, C. (Ed.) (1980). *Power/knowledge: Selected interviews and other writings by Michel Foucault*. New York: Pantheon Books.

Gordon, R. (1995a). *Contrasting trauma and Critical Incident Stress: Theory and intervention strategies*. Paper presented at the ACISA–ASTSS Conference, Hobart.

Gordon, R. (1995b). *Psychological effects of work related stress*. Paper presented at the ACISA–ASTSS Conference, Hobart.

Gordon, R., Druckman, D., Rozelle, R. & Baxter, J. (2006). Non-verbal behaviour as communication: Approaches, issues and research. In O. Hargie (Ed.), *The handbook of communication skills*. New York: Routledge (3rd edn, chap. 3, pp. 73–120).

Gotlib, I. & Wheaton, B. (Eds) (1997). *Stress and adversity over the life course: Trajectories and turning points*. Melbourne: Cambridge University Press.

Gottlieb, B. (Ed.) (1997). *Coping with chronic stress*. New York: Plenum.

Granot, H. (1996). The impact of disaster on mental health. *Counselling, May*, 140–3.

Green, R. (2003). Social work in rural areas: A personal and professional challenge. *Australian Social Work, 56*(3), 209–19.

Green, R., Gregory, R. & Mason, R. (2006). Professional distance and social work: Stretching the elastic? *Australian Social Work, 59*(4), 449–61.

Gunzberg, J. (1996). Healing through meeting: Martin Buber's conversational approach to psychotherapy. *Psychotherapy in Practice, 3*(1), 33–8.

Haebich, A. (2006). *Broken circles: Fragmenting Indigenous families 1800–2000*. Fremantle: Fremantle Arts Centre Press.

Happell, B., Pinikahana, J. & Roper, C. (2003). Changing attitudes: The role of a consumer academic in the education of postgraduate psychiatric nursing students. *Archives of Psychiatric Nursing, 17*(2), 67–76.

Hargie, O. (2006a). Training in communication skills. In O. Hargie (Ed.), *The handbook of communication skills*. New York: Routledge (3rd edn, chap. 20, pp. 553–65).

Hargie, O. (Ed.) (2006b). *The handbook of communication skills* (3rd edn). New York: Routledge.

Harms, L. (2005). *Understanding human development: A multidimensional approach*. South Melbourne: Oxford University Press.

Harms, L. & McDermott, F. (2003). Trauma: A concept and a practice across borders. *Psychotherapy in Australia, 10*(1), 32–7.

Harms, L., Rowe, C. & Suss, S. (2006). *Family adaptation following trauma*. Paper presented at the Fifth International Conference on Social Work in Health and Mental Health, Hong Kong.

Harris, J. (1995). Where is the child's environment? A group socialization theory of development. *Psychological Review, 102*(3), 458–89.

Harris, J. (1998). *The nurture assumption: Why children turn out the way they do*. Sydney: Free Press.

Hart, M. (2002). *Seeking Mino-Pimatisiwin: An Aboriginal approach to helping*. Halifax: Fernwood Publishing.

Healy, K. (2005). *Social work theories in context: Creating frameworks for practice*. Basingstoke: Palgrave Macmillan.

Heath, R. & Bryant, J. (2000). *Human communication theory and research: Concepts, contexts and challenges*. New Jersey: Lawrence Erlbaum.

Hepworth, D., Rooney, R. & Larsen, J. A. (2002). *Direct social work practice: Theory and skills* (6th edn). Pacific Grove: Brooks/Cole.

Herman, J. (1992). *Trauma and recovery*. New York: Basic Books.

Hobfoll, S., Ennis, N. & Kay, J. (2000). Loss, resources and resiliency in close inter-personal relationships. In J. Harvey & E. Miller (Eds), *Loss and trauma: General and close relationship perspectives*. Philadelphia: Brunner-Routledge (pp. 17, 267–85).

Hollis, F. & Woods, M. (1981). *Casework: A psychosocial therapy* (3rd edn). New York: Random House.

Holloway, E. & Neufeldt, S. (1995). Supervision: Its contributions to treatment efficacy. *Journal of Consulting and Clinical Psychology, 63*(2), 207–13.

Holloway, R. (2006). Looking in the distance: Spirituality in God's absence. In J. Moore & C. Purton (Eds), *Spirituality and counselling: Experiential and theoretical perspectives*. Ross-on-Wye (chap. 1, pp. 15–25).

Holman, E. & Silver, R. (1996). Is it the abuse or the aftermath? A stress and coping approach to understanding responses to adversity. *Journal of Social and Clinical Psychology, 15*(3), 318–39.

Howard, S. (2006). *Psychodynamic counselling in a nutshell*. London: Sage Publications.

Howe, D. (1987). *An introduction to social work theory*. Aldershot: Gower.

Howe, D. (1994). Modernity, post-modernity and social work. *British Journal of Social Work, 24*(5), 513–32.

Howe, D. (1998). Relationship-based thinking and practice in social work: The use of relationship. *Journal of Social Work Practice, 16*(2), 45–56.

Howe, D. (2002). Relating theory to practice. In M. Davies (Ed.), *The Blackwell companion to social work* (2nd edn). Oxford: Blackwell Publishing (chap. 2.1, pp. 81–7).

Hubble, M., Duncan, B. & Miller, S. (1999). *The heart and soul of change: What works in therapy*. Washington DC: American Psychological Association Press.

Hudson, C. (2000). At the edge of chaos: A new paradigm for social work? *Journal of Social Work Education, 36*(2), 215–30.

Hutchison, E. (2003). *Dimensions of human behavior: The changing life course*. Thousand Oaks: Sage Publications.

Ife, J. (1997). *Rethinking social work: Towards critical practice*. South Melbourne: Longman.

Ife, J. (2001). *Human rights and social work: Towards rights-based practice*. Melbourne: Cambridge University Press.

Ife, J. & Tesoriero, F. (2006). *Community development: Community-based alternatives in an age of globalisation*. Frenchs Forest: Pearson Education.

Ignatieff, M. (2001). The attack on human rights. *Foreign Affairs, November/December*, pp. 102–16.

Jacoby, M. (1984). *The analytic encounter—transference and human relationship*. Toronto: Inner City Books.

Janoff-Bulman, R. (1992). *Shattered assumptions: Towards a new psychology of trauma*. New York: Free Press.

Jenaro, C., Flores, N. & Arias, B. (2007). Burnout and coping in human service practitioners. *Professional Psychology: Research and Practice, 38*(1), 80–7.

Jenkins, R. (2002). *Legal issues in therapy and psychotherapy*. London: Sage Publications.

Jessup, H. & Rogerson, S. (1999). Postmodernism and the teaching and practice of interpersonal skills. In B. Pease & J. Fook (Eds), *Transforming social work practice: Postmodern critical perspectives*. St Leonards: Allen & Unwin (chap. 11, pp. 161–78).

Jung, C. (1963). *Memories, dreams, reflections*. Glasgow: Collins Fount.

Kadushin, A. (1972). *The social work interview*. New York: Columbia University Press.

Kadushin, A. & Kadushin, G. (1997). *The social work interview: A guide for human service professionals*. New York: Columbia University Press.

Kessler, M., Gira, E. & Poertner, J. (2005). Moving best practice to evidence-based practice in child welfare. *Families in Society, 86*(2), 244–50.

Kirst-Ashman, K. & Hull, G. (2001). *Generalist practice with organizations and communities.* Belmont, CA: Brooks/Cole.

Klass, D., Silverman, P. & Nickman, S. (1996). *Continuing bonds: New understandings of grief.* Washington: Taylor and Francis.

Klein, M. (1962). *Love, hate and reparation.* London: The Hogarth Press and the Institute of Psychoanalysis.

Kleinman, A., Das, V. & Lock, M. (Eds) (1997). *Social suffering.* Berkeley: University of California Press.

Kobasa, S. (1979). Stressful life events and health: An inquiry into hardiness. *Journal of Personality and Social Psychology, 37,* 1–11.

Koltko-Rivera, M. (2006). Rediscovering the later version of Maslow's hierarchy of needs: Self-transcendence and opportunities for theory, research, and unification. *Review of General Psychology, 10*(4), 302–17.

Kondrat, M. E. (1999). Who is the 'self' in self aware: Professional self-awareness from a critical theory perspective. *Social Service Review, 73*(4), 451–77.

Kondrat, M. E. (2002). Actor-centered social work: Re-visioning 'person-in-environment' through a critical theory lens. *Social Work, 47*(4), 435–48.

Koprowska, J. (2005). *Communication and interpersonal skills in social work.* Exeter: Learning Matters.

Kotzman, A. (1995). *Listen to me, listen to you.* Camberwell: ACER.

Lambert, M. (2005). Early response in psychotherapy: Further evidence for the importance of common factors rather than 'placebo effects'. *Journal of Clinical Psychology, 61*(7), 855–69.

Laming, C. (2006). *A constructivist approach to challenging men's violence against women.* The University of Melbourne, Melbourne.

Laub, D. & Auerhahn, N. (1993). Knowing and not knowing massive psychic trauma: Forms of traumatic memory. *International Journal of Psycho-Analysis, 74,* 287–302.

Lazarus, R. & Folkman, S. (1984). *Stress, appraisal, and coping.* New York: Springer Publishing Company.

Leeds-Hurwitz, W. (Ed.) (1995). *Social approaches to communication.* New York: Guilford Press.

Lepore, S. & Smyth, J. (Eds) (2003). *The writing cure: How expressive writing promotes health and emotional well-being.* Washington DC: American Psychological Association.

Levesque, D., Cummins, C., Prochaska, J. & Prochaska, J. (2006). Stage of change for making an informed decision about Medicare health plans. *Health Services Research, 41*(4), 1372–92.

Lewis, J. (2002). The contribution of research findings to practice change. *MCC: Building knowledge for integrated care, 10*(1), 9–12.

Liebman, A., Jordan, J., Lewis, D., Radcliffe-Smith, L., Sykes, P. & Taylor, J. (Eds) (1997). *Women's Circus: Leaping off the edge.* North Melbourne: Spinifex Press.

Lindemann, E. (1944). Symptomatology and management of acute grief. *American Journal of Psychiatry, 101,* 141–9.

Lindsay, R. (2002). *Recognizing spirituality: The interface between faith and social work.* Crawley: University of Western Australia Press.

Lloyd, M. & Taylor, C. (1995). From Hollis to the Orange Book: Developing a holistic model of assessment in the 1990s. *British Journal of Social Work, 25,* 691–710.

Loader, R. (1995). A personal statement about counselling and an exploration of the person as counsellor. *Australian Social Work, 48*(2), 35–8.

Lohrey, A. (2006). Voting for Jesus: Christianity and politics in Australia. *Quarterly Essay, 22.*

Lupton, D. (1999). *Risk.* London: Routledge.

Lynn, E. (1999). Value bases in social work education. *British Journal of Social Work, 29,* 939–53.

Lynn, R. (2001). Learning from a 'Murri Way'. *British Journal of Social Work, 31,* 903–16.

Macnab, F. (1989). *Life after loss.* Newtown: Millennium Books.

Macnab, F. (2000). *Traumas of life and their treatment.* Melbourne: Spectrum Publications.

Maidment, J. & Egan, R. (Eds) (2004). *Practice skills in social work and welfare: More than just common sense.* Crows Nest: Allen & Unwin.

Mancini, A. & Bonanno, G. (2006). Resilience in the face of potential trauma: Clinical practices and illustrations. *Journal of Clinical Psychology, 62*(8), 971–85.

Mander, A. & Rush, A. (1977). *Feminism as therapy* (2nd edn). New York: Random House.

Manthei, R. (1997). *Counselling: The skills of finding solutions to problems.* New York: Routledge.

Marris, P. (1986). *Loss and change* (2nd edn). London: Routledge.

Marris, P. (1993). The social construction of uncertainty. In C. Parkes, J. Stevenson-Hinde & P. Marris (Eds), *Attachment across the lifecycle.* London: Tavistock/Routledge (pp. 77–90).

Marris, P. (1996). *The politics of uncertainty: Attachment in private and public life.* London: Routledge.

Marsh, P. & Doel, M. (2005). *The task-centred book.* London: Routledge.

Martin, P. (1997). *The sickening mind: Brain, behaviour, immunity and disease.* London: HarperCollins.

Martyn, H. (2000). *Developing reflective practice: Making sense of social work in a world of change.* Bristol: The Policy Press.

Mayhew, C. (2000). *Preventing client-initiated violence: A practical handbook.* Canberra: Australian Institute of Criminology.

McCluskey, U. (2002). The dynamics of attachment and systems-centred group psychotherapy. *Group Dynamics, 6*(2), 131–42.

McCubbin, H., Thompson, E., Thompson, A. & Fromer, J. (Eds) (1998). *Stress, coping and health in families: Sense of coherence and resiliency.* Thousand Oaks: Sage.

McNally, R., Bryant, R. & Ehlers, A. (2003). Does early psychological intervention promote recovery from posttraumatic stress? *Psychological Sciences in the Public Interest, 4*(2), 45–80.

McNamara, M. (2006, 1 July). Protectors need protecting too. *The Age,* p. 9.

Merrett, L. (2004). Closure with clients. In J. Maidment & R. Egan (Eds), *Practice skills in social work and welfare: More than just common sense.* Crows Nest: Allen & Unwin (chap. 17, pp. 273–86).

Miller, J., Donner, S. & Fraser, E. (2004). Talking when talking is tough: Taking on conversations about race, sexual orientation, gender, class and other aspects of social identity. *Smith College Studies in Social Work, 74*(2), 377–93.

Miller, S. (2004). Losing faith: Arguing for a new way to think about therapy. *Psychotherapy in Australia, 10*(2), 44–51.

Miller, S., Duncan, B. & Hubble, M. (2004). Beyond integration: The triumph of outcome over process in clinical practice. *Psychotherapy in Australia, 10*(2), 2–19.

Mitchell, J. (1983). When disaster strikes: The Critical Incident Stress Debriefing process. *Journal of Emergency Medical Services, 8*, 36–9.

Mitchell, J. (1984). High tension: Keeping stress under control. *Firehouse* (September).

Mitchell, J. (2004). *Crisis intervention and Critical Incident Stress Management: A defense of the field.* Maryland: International Critical Incident Stress Foundation Inc.

Moon, J. (2004). *A handbook of reflective and experiential learning: Theory and practice.* London: Routledge/Farmer.

Moore, J. & Purton, C. (Eds) (2006). *Spirituality and counselling: Experiential and theoretical perspectives.* Ross-on-Wye: PCCS Books.

Moore, T. (2004). *Dark nights of the soul: A guide to finding your way through life's ordeals.* London: Piatkus Books.

Moran, C. & Massam, M. (1997). An evaluation of humour in emergency work. *The Australasian Journal of Disaster and Trauma Studies, 3*, 1–11.

Morley, C. (2004). Conducting risk assessments. In J. Maidment & R. Egan (Eds), *Practice skills in social work and welfare: More than just common sense.* Crows Nest: Allen & Unwin (chap. 9, pp. 127–45).

Morley, L. & Ife, J. (2002). Social work and love of humanity. *Australian Social Work, 55*(1), 69–77.

Morris, T. (2006). *Social work research methods: Four alternative paradigms.* Thousand Oaks: Sage Publications.

Mullaly, B. (2002). *Challenging oppression: A critical social work approach.* Toronto: Oxford University Press.

Myer, R. & Conte, C. (2006). Assessment for crisis intervention. *Journal of Clinical Psychology, 62*(8), 959–70.

National Drug and Alcohol Research Centre. (2007). Links 2007, from http://ndarc.med.unsw.edu.au/NDARCWeb.nsf/page/Links.

Nelson, D. & Burke, R. (2002). *Gender, work stress, and health.* Washington, DC: American Psychological Association.

Nelson-Jones, R. (2002). *Basic counselling skills: A helpers manual.* Thousand Oaks: Sage.

Nelson-Jones, R. (2006). *Theory and practice of counselling and therapy* (4th edn). Thousand Oaks: Sage Publications.

Neuman, W. (1999). *Social research methods: Qualitative and quantitative approaches.* Needham Heights: Pearson Education Co.

Neuman, W. (2006). *Social research methods: Qualitative and quantitative approaches* (6th edn). Needham Heights: Pearson Education Co.

O'Connell, B. (1998). *Solution-focused therapy.* London: Sage Publications.

O'Donoghue, K. (2003). *Restorying social work supervision.* Annandale: Federation Press.

O'Hagan, K. (2001). *Cultural competence in the caring profession.* London: Jessica Kingsley Publishers.

O'Hara, A. (2006). The practitioner's use of self in the professional relationship. In A. O'Hara & Z. Weber (Eds), *Skills for human service practice: Working with individuals, groups and communities*. South Melbourne: Oxford University Press (chap. 4, pp. 46–57).

O'Hara, A. & Weber, Z. (Eds) (2006). *Skills for human service practice: Working with individuals, groups and communities*. South Melbourne: Oxford University Press.

Ogloff, J. (2006). Advances in violence risk assessment. *InPsych, 28*(5), 12–16.

Okun, B. (2002). *Effective helping: interviewing and counseling techniques*. Pacific Grove, CA: Brooks/Cole-Thomson Learning.

Ornstein, E. & Ganzer, C. (2003). Dialectical constructivism in clinical social work: An exploration of Irwin Hoffman's approach to treatment. *Clinical Social Work Journal, 31*(4), 355–69.

Osmond, J. (2005). The knowledge spectrum: A framework for teaching knowledge and its use in social work practice. *British Journal of Social Work, 35*, 881–900.

Parker, S. (2006). Measuring faith development. *Journal of Psychology and Theology, 34*(4), 337–48.

Payne, M. (2006). *What is professional social work?* (2nd edn). Bristol: The Policy Press.

Pearlman, L. & Saakvitne, K. (1995). *Trauma and the therapist: Countertransference and vicarious traumatisation in psychotherapy with incest survivors*. New York: W. W. Norton.

Pearlman, L. A. & Macian, I. S. (1995). Vicarious traumatization: An empirical study of the effects of trauma work on trauma therapists. *Professional Psychology: Research and Practice, 26*(6), 558–65.

Pease, B. & Fook, J. (Eds) (1999). *Transforming social work practice: Postmodern critical perspectives*. St Leonards: Allen & Unwin.

Pelling, N., Bowers, R. & Armstrong, P. (2006). *The practice of counselling*. South Melbourne: Thomson.

Pennebaker, J. (Ed.) (1995). *Emotion, disclosure and health*. Washington: American Psychological Association.

Pennebaker, J. & O'Heeran, R. (1984). Confiding in others and illness rates among spouses of suicide and accidental-death victims. *Journal of Abnormal Psychology, 93*, 473–6.

Perlman, H. H. (1979). *Relationship: The heart of helping people*. Chicago: The University of Chicago Press.

Petrakis, M. (2004). *Keeping the client safe: Complexities and clinician risk in working with the suicidal client*. Paper presented at the RISK (Faculty of Arts Research Student Colloquium: antiTHESIS Forum), University of Melbourne.

Pilkington, C. & Woods, S. (1999). Risk in intimacy as a chronically accessible schema. *Journal of Social and Personal Relationships, 16*(2), 249–63.

Poindexter, C. (1997). In the aftermath: Serial crisis intervention for people with HIV. *Health and Social Work, 22*(2), 125–32.

Pope, S. (2000). *Postnatal depression: A systematic review of published scientific literature to 1999*. Canberra: National Health and Medical Research Council.

Prochaska, J. & DiClemente, C. (1983). Stages and processes of self change of smoking: Toward an integrative model of change. *Journal of Consulting and Clinical Psychology, 51*, 390–5.

Rakos, R. (2006). Asserting and confronting. In O. Hargie (Ed.), *The handbook of communication skills*. Hove: Routledge (chap. 12, pp. 345–81).

Ramsay, R. (2003). Transforming the 'Working Definition of Social Work' into the 21st century. *Research and Social Work Practice, 13*(3), 324–38.

Raphael, B. (1983). *The anatomy of bereavement.* New York: Basic Books.

Rasmussen, B. (2005). An intersubjective perspective on vicarious trauma and its impact on the clinical process. *Journal of Social Work Practice, 19*(1), 19–30.

Reamer, F. (2001). *Ethics education in social work.* Alexandria: VA Council on Social Work Education.

Reber, A. (1985). *The Penguin dictionary of psychology.* Ringwood: Penguin Books.

Reeves, A. & Seber, P. (2004). Working with the suicidal client. *Counselling and Psychotherapy, 15*(4), 45–50.

Reid, H. & Westergaard, J. (2006). *Providing support and supervision: An introduction for professionals working with young people.* London: Routledge.

Reiter, A. (2000). *Narrating the Holocaust.* London: Continuum.

Renzenbrink, I. (2005). Staff support: Whose responsibility? *Grief Matters, 8*(1).

Resick, P. (2001). *Stress and trauma.* Philadelphia: Taylor and Francis Inc.

Ribner, D. & Knei-Paz, C. (2002). Client's view of a successful helping relationship. *Social Work, 47*(4), 379–87.

Rice, S. (2002). Magic happens: Revisiting the spirituality and social work debate. *Australian Social Work, 55*(4), 303–12.

Rider, E. & Keefer, C. (2006). Communication skills competencies: Definitions and a teaching toolbox. *Medical Education, 40*, 624–9.

Rigney, D. & Cooper, L. (2004). Preparing for practice. In J. Maidment & R. Egan (Eds), *Practice skills in social work and welfare.* Crows Nest: Allen & Unwin (chap. 4, pp. 51–68).

Robbins, S., Chatterjee, P. & Canda, E. (1999). Ideology, scientific theory and social work practice. *Families in Society, 80*(4), 374–84.

Robinson, M. (2004). Therapeutic collaboration: Bridging the gap between statutory and therapeutic work. *Australian Social Work, 57*(4), 374–80.

Robinson, R. (2003). Psychological debriefing: A closer look at the facts. *Critical Incident Stress Management Foundation Australia Newsletter: Special Edition, 5*(3), 1–15.

Robinson, R. & Mitchell, J. (1995). Getting some balance back into the debriefing debate. *The Bulletin of the Australian Psychological Society, October*, 5–10.

Rogers, C. (1967). *On becoming a person: A therapist's view of psychotherapy.* London: Constable.

Rogers, C. (1980). *A way of being.* Boston: Houghton Mifflin.

Rogers, C. (1987). Comments on the issue of equality in psychotherapy. *Journal of Humanistic Psychology, 27*(1), 38–9.

Rogers, C., Ellis, A. & Perls, F. [Writer] (1977). *Three approaches to psychotherapy.* United States: P. F. Inc. [Producer].

Room, G. & Britton, N. (2006). The dynamics of social exclusion. *International Journal of Social Welfare, 15*, 280–9.

Rose, S. & Bisson, J. (1998). Brief early psychological interventions following trauma: A systematic review of the literature. *Journal of Traumatic Stress, 11*(4), 697–710.

Rose, S., Bisson, J. & Wessely, S. (2003). Counselling and psychotherapy: Media distortion. *British Journal of Psychiatry, 183*, 263–4.

Roth, A. & Fonagy, P. (2005). *What works for whom?: A critical review of psychotherapy research.* New York: Guilford Press.

Russell, S. & Carey, M. (2003). Feminism, therapy and narrative ideas: Exploring some not so commonly asked questions. *International Journal of Narrative Therapy and Community Work, 3*(1).

Rutter, M. & English and Romanian Adoptees Study Team. (1998). Developmental catch-up and deficit following adoption after severe global early privation. *Journal of Child Psychology and Psychiatry, 39*(4), 465–76.

Saggese, M. (2005). Maximising treatment effectiveness in clinical practice: An outcome-informed collaborative approach. *Families in Society, 86*(4), 558–64.

Saleebey, D. (1996). The strengths perspective in social work practice: Extensions and cautions. *Social Work, 41*(3), 296–305.

Saleebey, D. (1997). *The strengths perspective in social work practice* (2nd edn). New York: Longman.

Saleebey, D. (2001). Practicing the strengths perspective: Everyday tools and resources. *Families in Society—the Journal of Contemporary Human Services, 82*(3), 221–2.

Salzberger-Wittenberger, I. (1970). *Psychoanalytic insight and relationships: A Kleinian approach.* London: Routledge and Kegan Paul.

Schacter, D. (1996). *Searching for memory: The brain, the mind and the past.* New York: Basic Books.

Schon, D. (1987). *Educating the reflective practitioner.* San Francisco: Jossey-Bass.

Schore, A. (1994). *Affect regulation and the origin of the self: The neurobiology of emotional development.* Hillsdale: Lawrence Erlbaum Associates.

Schore, A. N. (2005). Attachment, affect regulation, and the developing right brain: Linking developmental neuroscience to pediatrics. *Pediatrics in Review, 26*(6), 204–17.

Schubert, M. (1991). *Interviewing in social work practice: An introduction.* Alexandria, Virginia: Council on Social Work Education.

Sciarra, D. (1999). *Multiculturalism in counselling.* Itasca: F. E. Peacock Publishers Inc.

Scott, D. (1990). Practice wisdom: The neglected source of practice research. *Social Work, 35*(6), 564–8.

Seden, J. (2005). *Counselling skills in social work practice* (2nd edn). Maidenhead: Open University Press.

Seligman, M. (1992). *Learned optimism.* Milsons Point: Random House.

Seligman, M., Reivich, K., Jaycox, L. & Gillham, J. (1995). *The optimistic child.* Milsons Point: Random House Australia.

Selye, H. (1987). *Stress without distress.* London: Corgi.

Sharp, C. (2006). Towards a phenomenology of the divine. In J. Moore & C. Purton (Eds), *Spirituality and counselling: Experiential and theoretical perspectives.* Ross-on-Wye: PCCS Books (pp. 65–80).

Sharry, J., Darmody, M. & Madden, B. (2002). A solution-focused approach to working with clients who are suicidal. *British Journal of Guidance & Counselling, 30*(4).

Shemmings, D. (2004). Researching relationships from an attachment perspective: The use of behavioural, interview, self-respect and projective measures. *Journal of Social Work Practice, 18*(3), 299–314.

Shulman, L. (1999). *The skills of helping individuals, families, groups and communities.* Itasca, IL: F. E. Peacock Inc.

Sinason, V. (1992). *Mental handicap and the human condition.* London: Free Association Books.

Singer, P. (1995). *How are we to live? Ethics in an age of self-interest*. Port Melbourne: Mandarin.

Smith, L. T. (2001). *Decolonizing methodologies: Research and indigenous peoples*. Dunedin: University of Otago Press.

Smith, P. (1998). How do we understand practice? A qualitative approach. *Families in Society, 79*(5), 543–50.

Smith, R., Marshall-Dorsey, A., Osborn, G., Shebroe, V., Lyles, J., Stoffelmayr, B., Van Egeren, L., Mettler, J., Maduschke, K., Stanley, J. & Gardiner, J. (2000). Evidence-based guidelines for teaching patient-centered interviewing. *Patient Education and Counseling, 39*, 27–36.

Smith, S., Thomas, S. & Jackson, A. (2004). An exploration of the therapeutic relationship and counselling outcomes in a problem gambling counselling service. *Journal of Social Work Practice, 18*(1), 99–112.

Sommers-Flanagan, J. & Sommers-Flanagan, R. (2004). *Counseling and psychotherapy theories in context and practice: Skills, strategies and techniques*. New Jersey: John Wiley and Sons.

Specht, H. & Courteney, M. (1994). *Unfaithful angels: How social work has abandoned its mission*. New York: Free Press.

Spooner, C., Hall, W. & Mattick, R. (2001). An overview of diversion strategies for Australian drug-related offenders. *Drug and Alcohol Review, 20*(3), 281–94.

Stack Sullivan, H. (1953). *The interpersonal theory of psychiatry*. New York: Norton.

Stansfield, C. (2006, 23 September). The two of us. *The Age*, p. 16.

Steier, F. (1995). Reflexivity, interpersonal communication and interpersonal communication research. In W. Leeds-Hurwitz (Ed.), *Social approaches to communication*. New York: Guilford Press (chap. 4, pp. 63–87).

Stoppard, J. (2000). *Understanding depression: Feminist social constructionist approaches*. London: Routledge.

Stroebe, M., Schut, H. & Finkenauer, C. (2001). The traumatization of grief? A conceptual framework for understanding the trauma-bereavement interface. *The Israel Journal of Psychiatry and Related Sciences, 38*(3/4), 185–201.

Stroebe, M., Schut, H. & Stroebe, W. (2006). Who benefits from disclosure? Exploration of attachment style differences in the effects of expressing emotions. *Clinical Psychology Review, 26*, 66–85.

Sullivan, H. (1953). *Conceptions of modern psychiatry*. New York: Norton.

Swain, P. (2005). 'No expert should cavil at any questioning': Reports and assessments for courts and tribunals. *Australian Social Work, 58*(1), 44–57.

Swain, P. (Ed.) (2002). *In the shadow of the law: The legal context of social work practice*. Annandale: Federation Press.

Tamasese, K. (2000). Talking about culture and gender. In D. Centre (Ed.), *Working with the stories of women's lives*. Adelaide: Dulwich Centre Publications.

Tannen, D. (1994). *Gender and discourse*. New York: Oxford University Press.

Tannen, D. (2000). 'Don't just sit there—interrupt!': Pacing and pausing in conversational style. *American Speech, 75*(4), 393–5.

Tao, J., Kang, Y. & Li, A. (2006). Prosody conversion from neutral speech to emotional speech. *IEEE Transactions on Audio, Speech and Language Processing, 14*(4), 1145–50.

Taylor, S. (2004). Public secrets/private pain: Difficulties encountered by victims/survivors of sexual abuse in rural communities. *Women against Violence, 15*, 12–21.

Thompson, N. (2002). *People skills* (2nd edn). Basingstoke: Palgrave Macmillan.

Thompson, N. (2003a). *Communication and language: A handbook of theory and practice.* Basingstoke: Palgrave Macmillan.

Thompson, N. (2003b). *Promoting equality: Challenging discrimination and oppression* (2nd edn). Basingstoke: Palgrave.

Thompson, N. (2006). *Anti-discriminatory practice.* Basingstoke: Palgrave Macmillan.

Tobin, M. (2005). *Lost opportunity or lifeline? Women with substance use issues and their perceptions of the barriers to pregnancy care.* Master of Social Work thesis, The University of Melbourne.

Tolson, E., Reid, W. & Garvin, C. (2003). *Generalist practice: A task-centered approach.* New York: Columbia University Press.

Tong, R. (1998). *Feminist thought: A more comprehensive introduction* (2nd edn). St Leonards: Allen & Unwin.

Trainor, B. (2002). Postmodernism, truth and social work. *Australian Social Work, 55*(3), 204–13.

Trevithick, P. (1998). *Feminism and psychotherapy: Reflections on contemporary theories and practices.* London: Sage.

Trevithick, P. (2003). Effective relationship-based practice: A theoretical exploration. *Journal of Social Work Practice, 17*(2), 163–76.

Trevithick, P. (2005). *Social work skills: A practice handbook* (2nd edn). Maidenhead: Open University Press.

Trotter, C. (2006). *Working with involuntary clients: A guide to practice.* Thousand Oaks: Sage Publications.

United Nations General Assembly. (1948). *Universal declaration of human rights.* From www.un.org.

Van der Kolk, B., McFarlane, A. & Weisaerth, L. (Eds) (1996). *Traumatic stress: The effects of overwhelming experience on mind, body and society.* New York: Guilford Press.

Veer, V. (1998). *Counselling therapy with refugees and victims of trauma.* Chichester: John Wiley & Sons.

VFST. See Victorian Foundation for Survivors of Trauma and Torture.

Victorian Foundation for Survivors of Torture Inc. (2000). *Guide to working with young people who are refugees.* Brunswick: The Victorian Foundation for Survivors of Torture Inc.

Victorian Foundation for Survivors of Trauma and Torture. (2004). *Towards a health strategy for refugees and asylum seekers in Victoria.* Brunswick: VFST.

Victorian Government Department of Human Services. (2006). *Building better partnerships: Working with Aboriginal communities and organisations: A communication guide for the Department of Human Services.* Melbourne: Victorian Government Department of Human Services.

Victorian Interpreting and Translating Service. (2006). *We speak your language: A guide to cross-cultural communication.* Melbourne: VITS LanguageLink.

Vogel, D., Wester, S., Heesacker, M., Boysen, G. & Seeman, J. (2006). Gender differences in emotional expression: Do mental health trainees overestimate the magnitude? *Journal of Social and Clinical Psychology, 25*(3), 305–32.

Walsh, J. (2006). *Theories of direct social work practice.* Southbank: Thomson Brooks/Cole.

Warren, L. (2006). Managing the client who threatens violence. *InPsych, 28*(5), 20–1.

Weaver, H. (1999). Indigenous people and the social work profession: Defining culturally competent services. *Social Work, 44*(3), 217–26.

Webb, S. (2006). *Social work in a risk society: Social and political perspectives*. Basingstoke: Palgrave Macmillan.

Weber, Z. (2006). Professional values and ethical practice. In A. O'Hara & Z. Weber (Eds), *Skills for human service practice: Working with individuals, groups and communities*. South Melbourne: Oxford University Press (chap. 2, pp. 17–33).

Weeks, W. (2004). Creating attractive services which citizens want to attend. *Australian Social Work, 57*(4), 319–30.

Weick, A. (1983). Issues in overturning a medical model of social work practice. *Social Work, 28*(6), 467–71.

Weingarten, K. (1991). The discourses of intimacy: Adding a social constructionist and feminist view. *Family Process, 30*, 285–305.

White, M. (2004). Working with people who are suffering the consequences of multiple trauma: A narrative perspective. *The International Journal of Narrative Therapy and Community Work, 1*, 45–76.

Whyte, J. (2005). *Contesting paradigms: Indigenous worldviews, western science and professional social work*. Unpublished Doctoral, The University of Melbourne, Melbourne.

Williams, M., Zinner, E. & Ellis, R. (1998). The connection between grief and trauma: An overview. In E. Zinner & M. Williams (Eds), *When a community weeps: Case studies in group survivorship*. London: Brunner/Mazel.

Wiltshire, J. (1995). Telling a story, writing a narrative: Terminology in health care. *Nursing Inquiry, 2*, 75–82.

Wingard, B. (2001). *Telling our stories in ways that make us stronger*. Adelaide: Dulwich Centre.

Winnicott, D. (1987). *Babies and their mothers*. Reading: Addison-Wesley.

Wolterstorff, N. (1987). *Lament for a son*. Grand Rapids: Eerdsman.

Worden, J. W. (2003). *Grief counselling and grief therapy: A handbook for the mental health practitioner*. Hove, East Sussex: Brunner-Routledge.

World Health Organization. (2003). *Constitution of the World Health Organization*. Geneva: United Nations.

Yalom, I. (2005). *The Schopenhauer cure*. Melbourne: Scribe.

Yedidia, M. J. (2007). Transforming doctor–patient relationships to promote patient-centered care: Lessons from palliative care. *Journal of Pain and Symptom Management, 33*(1), 40–57.

Yip, K.-S. (2006). Self-reflection in reflective practice: A note of caution. *British Journal of Social Work, 36*, 777–88.

Yoo, S., Matsumoto, D. & LeRoux, J. (2006). The influence of emotion recognition and emotion regulation on intercultural adjustment. *International Journal of Intercultural Relations, 30*(3), 345–63.

Young, I. (1990). *Justice and the politics of difference*. Princeton: Princeton University Press.

Youssef, J. & Deane, F. (2006). Barriers to mental health care and opportunities to facilitate utilisation of services in Arabic-speaking communities. *Synergy, 1*, 5–16.

Zon, A., Lindeman, M., Williams, A., Hayes, C., Ross, D. & Furber, M. (2004). Cultural safety in child protection: Application to the workplace environment and casework practice. *Australian Social Work, 57*(3), 288–98.

Index